I0896496

ST. CYPRIAN

Pamphlets on Pandemics

To Demetrian and *The Deadly Pestilence*

Ancient Christian Writers

THE WORKS OF THE FATHERS IN TRANSLATION

ADVISORY BOARD

Brian Dunkel, SJ, *Chair*

Thomas Cattoi

Thomas Clemmons

Dawn Teresa LaValle

J. Boniface Ramsey

Erin Gilgay Walsh

No. 78

ST. CYPRIAN: PAMPHLETS ON PANDEMIC

To Demetrian
and *The Deadly Pestilence*

TRANSLATED AND INTRODUCED
BY GEOFFREY D. DUNN

The Newman Press
New York / Mahwah, NJ

Cover design by Sharyn Banks
Book design by Lynn Else

ENGLISH TRANSLATION AND INTRODUCTION COPYRIGHT © 2024
BY GEOFFREY D. DUNN

All rights reserved. No part of this publication may be reproduced, stored in a retrieval system, or transmitted in any form or by any means, electronic, mechanical, photocopying, recording, scanning, or otherwise, without either the prior written permission of the Publisher, or authorization through payment of the appropriate per-copy fee to the Copyright Clearance Center, Inc., www.copyright.com. Requests to the Publisher for permission should be addressed to the Permissions Department, Paulist Press, permissions@paulistpress.com.

Library of Congress Cataloging-in-Publication Data
Names: Cyprian, Saint, Bishop of Carthage, author. | Dunn, Geoffrey D., 1962– translator, writer of introduction. | Cyprian, Saint, Bishop of Carthage. Ad Demetrianum. English. | Cyprian, Saint, Bishop of Carthage. De mortalitate. English.
Title: St. Cyprian: pamphlets on pandemics: The deadly pestilence and To Demetrian / translated and introduced by Geoffrey D. Dunn.
Description: New York The Newman Press, [2024] | Series: Ancient Christian writers; no. 78 | Includes bibliographical references and index. | Summary: "This ACW volume contains his De mortalitate and Ad Demetrianum, both dealing with a Christian understanding of pandemic, a topic of international interest given the COVID-19 experience of the last few years"—Provided by publisher.
Identifiers: LCCN 2023057096 (print) | LCCN 2023057097 (ebook) | ISBN 9780809104468 (hardcover) | ISBN 9780809188734 (ebook)
Subjects: LCSH: Plague—Rome—History—3rd century. | Consolation—Early works to 1800. | Death—Early works to 1800. | Reward (Theology)—Early works to 1800.
Classification: LCC BR65.C82 E5 2024 (print) | LCC BR65.C82 (ebook) | DDC 270.1—dc23/eng/20240607
LC record available at https://lccn.loc.gov/2023057096
LC ebook record available at https://lccn.loc.gov/2023057097

ISBN 978-0-8091-0446-8 (hardcover)
ISBN 978-0-8091-8873-4 (e-book)

Published by The Newman Press
an imprint of Paulist Press
997 Macarthur Boulevard
Mahwah, New Jersey 07430
www.paulistpress.com

Printed and bound in the
United States of America

In memory of G. W. Clarke, AO FAHA (1934–2023),
whose five volumes in this series continue to inspire

CONTENTS

ABBREVIATIONS

ACW	Ancient Christian Writers
AELIUS ARISTIDES	
Or.	*Oratio*
AESCHYLUS	
PV	*Prometheus vinctus*
AHC	*Annuarium Historiae Conciliorum*
AJP	*American Journal of Philology*
ARISTOTLE	
Rh.	*Rhetorica*
ARNOBIUS	
Adv. nat.	*Adversus nationes*
Aug	*Augustinianum*
AUGUSTINE	
Serm.	*Sermo*
AURELIUS VICTOR	
De Caes.	*De Caesaribus*
CAESAR	
B.Gall.	*Bellum Gallicum*
CASSIUS DIO	
Hist. Rom.	*Historia Romana*
CCL	Corpus Christianorum, series Latina

CEASA	Collection des Études Augustiniennes. Série Antiquité
CH	*Church History*
CICERO	
Att.	*Epistulae ad Atticum*
Div.	*De divinatione*
Fam.	*Epistulae ad familiares*
Har. resp.	*De haruspicum responsis*
Inv. rhet.	*De inventione*
Nat. d.	*De natura deorum*
Senec.	*De senectute*
Tusc.	*Tusculanae disputationes*
Vat.	*In Vatinium*
Verr.	*In Verrem*
CJ	*Classical Journal*
CP	*Corona Patrum*
CQ	*Classical Quarterly*
CRAI	*Comptes rendus de l'Académie des inscriptions et belles-lettres*
CSEL	Corpus Scriptorum Ecclesiasticorum Latinorum
CTP	Collana di Testi Patristici
CUAPS	The Catholic University of America Patristic Studies
CYPRIAN	
Ad Deme.	*Ad Demetrianum*
Ad Dona.	*Ad Donatum*
Ad Fort.	*Ad Fortunatum*
Ad Quir.	*Ad Quirinum*
De bono	*De bono patientiae*

De domi.	*De dominica oratione*
De habi.	*De habitu virginum*
De laps.	*De lapsis*
De mort.	*De mortalitate*
De oper.	*De opera et eleemosynis*
De unit.	*De ecclesiae catholicae unitate*
De zelo	*De zelo et livore*
Ep.	*Epistula*
Quod idola	*Quod idola dii non sunt*
De rebapt.	*De rebaptismate*
ECS	Early Christian Studies
Epit. de Caes.	*Epitome de Caesaribus*
EURIPIDES	
Hyp.	*Hypsipyle*
EUSEBIUS	
Hist. eccl.	*Historia ecclesiastica*
EUTROPIUS	
Brev.	*Breviarium*
FC	Fathers of the Church
FRONTO	
Laud. fumi et pulv.	*Laudes fumi et pulveris*
GRBS	*Greek, Roman, and Byzantine Studies*
Hist. Aug.	*Historia Augusta*
HJ	*Heythrop Journal*
HORACE	
Carm.	*Carmina*
Ep.	*Epistula*
Epod.	*Epodi*
HSCP	*Harvard Studies in Classical Philology*

HTR	*Harvard Theological Review*
IAB	*Institute of Archaeology Bulletin*
JECS	*Journal of Early Christian Studies*
JEH	*Journal of Ecclesiastical History*
JETS	*Journal of the Evangelical Theological Society*
JHS	*Journal of Hellenic Studies*
JRA	*Journal of Roman Archaeology*
JRH	*Journal of Religious History*
JRS	*Journal of Roman Studies*
JSJ	*Journal for the Study of Judaism in the Persian, Hellenistic, and Roman Period*
JTI	*Journal of Theological Interpretation*
JTS	*Journal of Theological Studies*

JUVENAL

Sat.	*Saturae*
LAHR	Late Antique History and Religion
Lat	*Latomus*

LUCRETIUS

Nat.	*De rerum natura*
MAAR	*Memoirs of the American Academy in Rome*

MARTIAL

Epig.	*Epigrammaton*

MINUCIUS FELIX

Oct.	*Octavius*
n.s.	new series
NTS	*New Testament Studies*

OROSIUS

Hist. adv. pag.	*Historia aduersus paganos*

OVID

Met.	*Metamorphoses*
Tr.	*Tristia*
Ph & Rh	*Philosophy & Rhetoric*

PLATO

Alc.	*Alcibiades*
Chrm.	*Charmides*
Leg.	*Leges*
Phdr.	*Phaedrus*
Phlb.	*Philebus*
Prt.	*Protagoras*
Tim.	*Timaeus*

PLINY (THE ELDER)

HN	*Naturalis historia*

PLINY (THE YOUNGER)

Ep.	*Epistula*

PONTIUS

V. Cyp.	*Vita Cypriani*
QJS	*Quarterly Journal of Speech*

QUINTILIAN

Inst.	*Institutio oratoria*
RBPH	*Revue belge de Philologie et d'Histoire*
REAug	*Revue d'Études Augustiniennes (et Patristiques)*
RecAug	*Recherches Augustiniennes*
Rhet. Her.	*Rhetorica ad Herennium*
RHT	*Revue d'Histoire des Textes*

SALLUST

Ad Caes.	*Epistulae ad Caesarem senem de re publica*

Iug.	*Bullum Iugurthinum*
SC	Sources Chrétiennes
Scr	*Scrinium*
SEAug	Studia Ephemeridis Augustinianum
SENECA	
Ben.	*De beneficiis*
Constant.	*De constantia sapientis*
Ep.	*Epistula*
Helv.	*Consolatio ad Helviam*
Ira	*De ira*
Marc.	*Consolatio ad Marciam*
Otio	*De otio*
Phaed.	*Phaedra*
Poly.	*Consolatio ad Polybium*
Prov.	*De providentia*
Vita	*De vita beata*
Sent. episc.	*Sententiae episcoporum LXXXVII*
SP	*Studia Patristica*
SUETONIUS	
Claud.	*Claudius*
TACITUS	
Ann.	*Annales*
Hist.	*Historiae*
TERTULLIAN	
Ad nat.	*Ad nationes*
Adv. Iud.	*Adversus Iudaeos*
Adv. Marc.	*Adversus Marcionem*
Apol.	*Apologeticum*
De cult.	*De cultu feminarum*

De idol.	*De idololatria*
De paen.	*De paenitentia*
De pat.	*De patientia*
De praescr.	*De praescriptione haereticorum*
De res.	*De resurrectione mortuorum*
De spect.	*De spectaculis*
TS	*Theological Studies*
VC	*Vigiliae Christianae*

VIRGIL

Aen.	*Aeneid*
Georg.	*Georgica*
VP	*Vox Patrum*
WUNT	Wissenschaftliche Untersuchungen zum Neuen Testament

XENOPHON

Mem.	*Memorabilia*
ZAC	*Zeitschrift für Antikes Christentum*

ZOSIMUS

Hist. nov.	*Historia nova*

INTRODUCTION

In a world familiar with the miracle of penicillin and other antibiotics as well as antiviral drugs and vaccines, not to mention a sophisticated understanding of germs and micro-organisms and the relationship between hygiene and sickness, it is difficult to imagine, at least in those regions in which the wonders of modern medicine are readily available, the devastating and catastrophic impact that infectious and incurable pandemic disease had in the ancient world. Yet, even with all the advances in modern medicine, health crises do continue with calamitous impact. There is something incredible to the Western, twenty-first-century mind about reports of the myriad deaths from contagion, yet these diseases and fatalities do continue to happen. On top of that, there are other types of natural disasters, such as floods, earthquakes, famine, drought, and fire. They all seem to strike at random, with little that can be done either to predict or to stop them. The debate about the contribution of human-induced climate change to the frequency and seriousness of such disasters is a modern one in the light of carbon pollution. In the ancient world, with its comparatively limited understanding of and ability to control health and environmental disasters, it was little wonder that people turned to claims of divine punishment for human hubris or sin to explain all kinds of natural disease and disasters.

In the past century one can point to the H1N1 (influenza A virus) pandemic of 1918 (the so-called Spanish flu) that infected up to a third of the world's population and resulted in anywhere between 50 and 100 million deaths, the 1931 floods in China that killed somewhere between one and four million people, the 1970 Cyclone Bhola that killed more than half a million people in Bangladesh, the 1976 Tangshan earthquake in China, with some estimating a death toll of over 600,000, the tsunami of Christmas 2004 in the Indian Ocean as the result of the Sumatra-Andaman earthquake, which killed more than a quarter of a million people, the 2009 H1N1 (Swine flu, another influenza A virus) pandemic that killed perhaps as many as half a million people (even though the official laboratory count stands at about 18,000), the earthquake in Haiti in 2010 that killed an estimated 300,000, the Ebola hemorrhagic fever outbreaks that swept West Africa between 2013 and 2016 that killed more than 11,000 people and again in the Congo in 2019 with more than 1,300 deaths, and the 35 million or more people who have died from AIDS since 1981.

It is the random bad luck of health and natural disasters (compounded and complicated where human activity exacerbates the results or even is a factor in the cause) that elicits human sympathy and relief efforts. The scale of disaster and disease is almost too vast for comprehension, but the fact that these outbreaks of disease have been concentrated in Africa and East Asia, where the standard of living is lower than in economically developed countries, had perhaps encouraged a sense of unassailability in the West until recently.

The COVID-19 pandemic that started sweeping the world at the start of 2020, with over 701 million reported infections and 6,969,000 deaths as of January 2024, demonstrates once again human suffering on an all too unbelievable scale. Reactions throughout the world in the early stages were enlightening if not always enlightened, especially regarding the battle between public health directives and personal liberties in some countries and among some people. The initial lack of information about the virus's pathology and epidemiology, its virulence and contagiousness, the lack of a cure, the unavailability of treatment and care when healthcare systems were overwhelmed, especially during 2020 before vaccines started to be rolled out in early 2021, and the patchy responses, including initial lethargy followed by lockdowns with all their social and economic ramifications, saw panic buying and anxiety, complacency and denial, as well as variants, protests, virus fatigue, vaccine hesitancy, and even resilience and inventiveness. The waves of variants dashed the hopes of those who thought that the development of a vaccine would be the end of public health impositions. Mainstream and social media made sure that there was little else on our minds through a constant bombardment of COVID news, some reliable, some much less so, especially regarding wacky solutions and questions of its origins. The lexicon of the average person was expanded with such terms as "contact tracing," "flattened curves," "herd immunity," "double vaxed," and the less-than-precise "social distancing." Familiarity with the letters of the Greek alphabet increased among those previously unfamiliar with this language.

Not only do the vast number of fatalities stagger us, whatever form the natural disaster takes, but so too especially does the feeling of helplessness in the face of an unstoppable onslaught that spreads so rapidly, targets without discrimination, all too often leads to death, and cannot be controlled or treated. Although the most recent pandemic initially seemed confined and not so severe, the world soon learned that this disease is highly contagious and much more severe than first reported (more pneumonia-like than merely flu-like). The fear was not only due to the health crisis itself but also because of the economic uncertainty and social instability that has followed in its wake. Although 2021 became the year of virus variants and of vaccines, with new issues of who gets first access to vaccines and how to balance individual rights to refuse with community needs to be protected, 2020 was the year in which many people felt defenseless and unprotected. Each new variant brings back that feeling of uncertainty and fear, fatigue and fatalism. It is with that feeling in mind that we can best look at reactions to pandemic in the ancient world.

For once, the people of the ancient world are not so foreign and their thinking not that dissimilar to ours today in many ways. In addition to those who have displayed great courage and a community spirit of doing the right thing, we have seen seemingly rational people looking for someone to blame, eager to try any kind of quackery in search of a cure, engaging in denial, and displaying great selfishness and irresponsibility. Perhaps, like never before, some of the writings of Cyprian, bishop of Carthage in Africa Proconsularis from 248 or 249 to 258, written in light of an experience of unstoppable deadly disease, will resonate more with a modern reader than they did before. When the fleetingness of life and the inevitability of death are before us so starkly how do we react, how do we cope, what meaning does life hold?

"PLAGUE" OF CYPRIAN

A pandemic had swept through the Roman empire during the reigns of Marcus Aurelius (161–80) and Lucius Verus (161–69), the latter of whom might have been one of its victims.[1] It has come to be known as the Antonine plague. It seems to have spread throughout the empire via legionaries returning from a campaign against Parthia. Kyle Harper supports the notion that the pathogen was smallpox, a virus transmitted through airborne droplets or contact with contaminated items.[2] Fluid-filled pustules that covered and scarred the skin made this a particularly horrifying disease to behold, particularly with the risk of blindness and a mortality rate approaching 30 percent in its more virulent strain (or even closer to 100 percent with the rarer hemorrhagic smallpox in which, instead of blisters, there was bleeding under the skin, turning it black). Disease was an ever-present threat and all too familiar occurrence in the ancient world,[3] but a pandemic made the specter of death too much to bear. While the Chinese appear to have practiced some form of inoculation from the tenth century, in the West it was not until Edward Jenner, at the end of the eighteenth century, that vaccination against smallpox became common, until in 1980 the World Health Organization could certify its eradication.[4]

Such widespread tragedy in the ancient world is reflected in some of the literature that survives from the period. Lucretius, the Epicurean philosopher, believed that poisonous atoms in the atmosphere (or in the rotting earth after a drenching) brought disease, such as happened with the Athenians in the Peloponnesian War. People who travelled and experienced unfamiliar imbalances in the environment were more susceptible to epidemic.[5] Galen, the Roman world's most famous physician and medical researcher, described the symptoms in *Methodus medendi*.[6] Eutropius reported the widespread nature of this pestilence (*pestilentia*) and the severe impact on the population, particularly among the troops.[7] Aelius Aristides, the Greek orator of the Second Sophistic, contracted the disease in 165 and survived to recount the despair and suffering around him as well as his own survivor guilt.[8] Ammianus Marcellinus noted its spread from Persia to troops along the Rhine.[9] Cassius Dio assessed the second outbreak under Commodus (176–92) in 189 as the greatest disease (*nosos*) he knew, killing two thousand a day in Rome as well as many others throughout the entire empire, with many infected deliberately by those who wished them harm.[10]

Some sixty years later death and disease stalked the empire once again. Our most detailed account, such as it is, comes from Cyprian of Carthage, and so he has the dubious honor of having this outbreak named after him.[11] It was one of the events that made the third century one of crisis for the empire.[12] If we take the political instability of 238, when there were six emperors in the one year, then we have to accept that the later health emergency did not create the crisis, but we could assert that it certainly contributed to it. Indeed, the empire might not have recovered from the impact of the Antonine plague upon the population size and the subsequent reduction in agricultural and industrial capacity, and the earlier pandemic might have contributed to the political instability. Harper identifies climate change as being evident during the middle of the third century, along with the resultant drought and famine.[13] He claims that this Cyprianic plague is a rather forgotten pandemic in scholarship even though there is better evidence for it than for the Antonine plague, and it was more devastating.[14]

The outbreak that concerns us here seems to have started south of Egypt and spread west throughout the empire, reaching Rome itself in the second half of 251 and lasting for some fifteen years. However, in a very recent reassessment, Sabine Huebner argues that it entered the empire from the Gothic incursions over the Danube.[15] She takes the evidence of Zosimus that the pandemic appeared while the Scythians were attacking the empire across the Danube.[16] Eutropius, in a passage in which his knowledge of emperors proves to be deficient, stated that "pestilences, diseases, and afflictions" [*pestilentia et morbis atque aegritudinibus*] were the only things of note to have happened during the reigns of Hostilian and Volusian.[17]

Harper's reading of the evidence, both Christian and non-Christian, suggests that this episode of disease was widespread and significant. From the description of the symptoms ("[t]he pestilence manifested itself as an acute onset disease with burning fever and severe gastrointestinal disorder, and its symptoms included conjunctival bleeding, bloody stool, esophageal lesions, and tissue death in the extremities"), he concludes that it was likely to have been a zoonotic viral hemorrhagic fever, possibly Ebola.[18] Others have argued for another outbreak of smallpox, some for bubonic plague, and others still for measles.[19]

We are familiar today with such viral hemorrhagic fevers as dengue, yellow fever, and Ebola. These viruses, highly infectious and frequently transmitted through mosquitos, other insects, and rodents but also through person-to-person contact, target multiple organs and not only lead to fever, dizziness, weakness, vomiting, and diarrhea, but can result in internal bleeding and kidney, liver, and respiratory failure. There is no cure as yet and the death rate can be extremely high.

If we take plague in its strict sense as referring to the bacterium *Yersinia pestis* (bubonic plague), as evidenced in the later first plague pandemic (the plague of Justinian)[20] and the second plague pandemic (the Black Death)[21] and accept that what occurred in the third century was not bubonic plague, then we can only refer to this episode in the middle of the third century as a plague in the broad, derivate sense (as in "plague of locusts") to mean a large number of something that will cause extensive damage. To avoid confusion, the term *plague* will be avoided in this volume.

Pontius, one of Cyprian's deacons, wrote a biography of the Carthaginian bishop soon after his death in 258. There is an entire section in the modern numbering of it dedicated to the disease. It conveys the sense of the impact of the disease and the helplessness, desperation, panic, resignation, and even the self-absorption and disregard people felt for others:

> Yet, if it seems good, let us review all the other things. A little later the awful scourge [*lues*] and the overwhelming devastation of execrable disease [*morbus*] burst forth, daily snatching innumerable people in their own homes by a sudden attack. It broke into the homes of the quivering public one after another without exception. Everyone was petrified; fleeing from contact and callously abandoning their own, as if someone were able to shut out even death itself along with that person about to die from the fatal illness [*pestis*]. Meanwhile, street by street over the whole city there were lying what were no longer bodies but the corpses of so many and [people], reflecting on the fate they would share, were entreating the mercy of those passing by for themselves. No one considered anything other than their own heartless benefit.[22]

Most startlingly, Pontius conveys the notion that everyone, Christian or not, reacted in this selfish way. This provides the context in which to understand what Cyprian would write for his own community concerning how people, whether Christian or not, were not responding but ought to, given what Pontius later would identify as their shared moral failings.

Nearly a century later, Eusebius, bishop of Caesarea Maritima in modern Israel between about 314 and 340 and the great ecclesiastical historian of the pre-Constantinian church, discussed this mid-third-century pandemic through information he found in a letter of Dionysius, bishop of Alexandria (248–64). Dionysius cast the experience as one of no greater challenge to Christians, who long had faced persecutions, than others they had faced, although it was regarded with fear as a calamity by their non-Christian neighbors. Dionysius wanted to assert that it was just another time of discipline and testing.[23] What Eusebius highlighted from Dionysius's letter was the fact that Christians responded positively to the moral challenge through their selfless care of those in need:

> The most, at all events, of our brethren in their exceeding love and affection for the brotherhood were unsparing of themselves and clave to one another, visiting the sick without a thought as to the danger, assiduously ministering to them, tending them in Christ, and so most gladly departed this life along with them; being infected with the disease from others, drawing upon themselves the sickness from their neighbours, and willingly taking over their pains.[24]

What Harper notes is that instead of having a Galen, as with the Antonine plague, with this pandemic we hear mainly from Christian voices.[25] That is certainly true, but what must equally be borne in mind is that, in the hands of someone like Eusebius, this narrative and the way the evidence from Dionysius was selected and presented was framed within a Greek historiographical tradition that went back to Thucydides' account of the plague in Athens, which he himself had contracted and survived.[26] Yet, as David DeVore has postulated recently, not only was Eusebius commenting on an outbreak in about 250 (although in his narrative he placed it deliberately a decade later), but his use of Dionysius could create contrasts ("ethical bipolarity" in DeVore's words) with Thucydides in that the pandemic had split the Athenian community (and the contemporary non-Christian one in Alexandria) while it united the Christians.[27] From Eusebius's point of view the outbreak of disease was the consequence of the persecution (as a punishment of those persecuting) and not, as was popularly believed, the result of Christian nonparticipation in support of the empire that merited their persecution.

Eusebius's historiographical objectives probably explain what will become apparent to readers of Cyprian's two texts translated here: Cyprian's assessment of Christian performance during the pandemic is less positive than that presented in Dionysius as edited by Eusebius in the text addressed explicitly to Christians; he will be seen to align with what his deacon reported. This is less true of *Ad Demetrianum*, addressed to a non-Christian readership. However, even Dionysius did not extol his own community completely. At the beginning of the extract quoted from his letter he did admit that he was talking about most (*pleistoi*) Christians. In other words, there is a concession here, even if attention was being deflected from it, that not all the Christians of Alexandria performed so admirably. Part of the contrast between the situation in Alexandria and that in Carthage could be in the fact that Dionysius was reporting how Christians eventually responded, after some motivation from their bishop (and perhaps with some exaggeration), while Cyprian's text informs us of what Christians were doing (or not doing) before they were motivated by their bishop through the text he delivered. In Cyprian's text for non-Christians, any flaws in the Christian character were not something to which he wished to draw attention and so could be papered over. When we consider Dionysius's letter, Eusebius's rendition of it, and Cyprian's two works designed for two different audiences, we can appreciate the importance and necessity of analyzing texts critically and to understand them not so much as stating facts as presenting arguments.

The pandemic forced people then, as pandemics continue to do whenever they appear, to confront the most profound existential questions about the meaning of life. That early Christians were no more exempt from the ravages of pandemic and pestilence, earthquakes, volcanoes, floods, and fires than were their non-Christian neighbors, inevitably meant that serious challenges to faith perspectives emerged. This led to a variety of theodicies in response to the age-old question of why bad things happen to good people. The natural world was not the only challenge to Christian confidence; religious discrimination and state-sanctioned violence that resulted in persecution and martyrdom, as well as backsliding and dissent, added to that threat and insecurity.

We know that toward the end of 249, upon becoming emperor, Decius (249–51) issued his decree demanding universal sacrifice.[28] Traditionally, scholarship, following the lead of Cyprian himself, saw this as a targeted anti-Christian measure. Recently, James Rives argued that it was more likely that Decius wanted to promote the revival of traditional religion (and the fact that it trapped those Christians who refused to comply with it was a fortuitous by-product that would have been popular with a public already suspicious of and inimical toward Christians).[29] There is much to recommend this perspective. Although open to the possibility that "an unusual decree can best be explained as a response to an unusual problem," in the end he argues that "we can only speculate on Decius' motivations."[30] He does not consider the possibility that the unusual problem that demanded a return to traditional religion could have been the appearance of another round of pandemic disease. This is something suggested recently by Kyle Harper.[31] The fact that Christian faith prohibited them from participating in cultic sacrifice (and that at least a good number did not, even if many did) could have antagonized their non-Christian neighbors more than usual because it was easy to see a link between a failure to sacrifice if not as a cause of the visitation of pandemic than at least as an explanation for its continuance.

However, if the spreading sickness did not reach Rome until sometime late in 251 or in early 252, this would indicate that Decius's measure preceded the impact of disease across the empire rather than followed it and that Harper's position must be rejected. This is the position taken recently by Huebner, who dates the appearance of this pestilence within the empire to 252 or 253.[32] It also makes sense of something we find in Cyprian's letters, to be discussed later in this introduction, that in 253 there was the fear of another persecution. The excruciating death of so many could be blamed directly on the Christians as convenient scapegoats, since the efforts instigated by Decius had brought them and their intransigence (even allowing for many of them having compromised their faith) into an even clearer focus in the minds of the general populace. That Christians had not supported the religious revival led to the punishing presence of disease that affected everyone. Demands for harsher reprisals would only have been natural. Thus, we should associate this outbreak of disease not with the initial decree from Decius but with the fear of a new decree under Gallus.

The two works composed by Cyprian—*Ad Demetrianum* and *De mortalitate*—are to be understood in that context set by Pontius. In the first, addressed to the non-Christian world, we witness Cyprian's response to accusations of Christian culpability for disaster by turning blame back onto the non-Christians for not worshipping the one, true God and by asserting Christian innocence. In the second, addressed to the Christian community, we learn of a situation of an inadequate response by Christians to the challenge that confronted them. Seeing the texts as responses to the blame apportioned by non-Christians and to the moral failure of Christians outlined by Pontius (as opposed to simply being responses to the presence of disease in the community) is the key to understanding these two works. I have no doubt that Pontius's words reflect the framework in which Cyprian must have expressed himself on many occasions. This perspective is central to the way in which I read these two pamphlets.[33] In other words, they are rather different from what we read in Dionysius's letter. Cyprian was castigating and upbraiding his community to be true to their faith in one, and yet he was defending them against outside accusations of their culpability in the other.

This pandemic seems to have continued for more than a decade. *Historia Augusta*, a series of imperial biographies modeled on Suetonius's *De vita Caesarum* and of dubious quality and reliability,[34] reports in the heavily fictionalized life of Claudius Gothicus (268–70) that the emperor was one of many victims of a pestilence.[35] Previously it had struck the Goths in the Balkans and its severity was sufficient to bring Rome's war against them to an end.[36] Of course, it is impossible to be certain that this was still the same pandemic swirling around the empire, but there is a good chance that it was. For our purposes here it is not of that much significance how long it lasted after Cyprian composed his two pamphlets; what is of concern to us is that when he wrote them it was of significant impact and there was no end to it in sight.

DATE OF *AD DEMETRIANUM* AND *DE MORTALITATE* IN THE CONTEXT OF DECIUS'S EDICT

It has long been understood that both *Ad Demetrianum* and *De mortalitate* were written around the same time as Cyprian wrote *Epistulae* 56, 57, and 58. However, scholars have disagreed about when to date those letters, and most have not considered the question of the relationship between the pamphlets and the letters in any great detail to help resolve the issue. It is important for us to consider those issues here.

The first of these letters responds to a request from several African bishops that Cyprian support their intention to readmit to communion several confessors who, although they had resisted valiantly at first, had succumbed eventually to torture simply through physical weakness and had offered sacrifice and then had been engaged in penance for the next three years. Cyprian was supportive of their plan.[37] This would better equip them if persecution should come again.[38] We must date this letter to after the African synod of 251, in which the decision had been reached to readmit any penitent *lapsus* in danger of death and any penitent (that is, someone who had been performing constant penance since excommunication as opposed to someone who had not shown sufficient contrition since their lapse) *libellaticus* to communion immediately, and to readmit any penitent *sacrificatus* to communion just before death.[39] This synod is mentioned in the letter.[40] Before we say something about the *terminus ante quem* of this letter (and of the other documents of concern to us), we need to consider the controversy that embroiled the church as a result of Decius's decree in a little more detail in order to appreciate these letters and then these two pamphlets of Cyprian that arose out of the experience of pandemic and offer some ideas about their dates of composition.

Decius's edict for the revival of traditional religion through the imposition of universal sacrifice required proof of compliance.[41] Some people, Christians included, appear not to have been targeted to perform the sacrifice, while some, like Cyprian himself, fled and went into hiding to avoid the requirements (an action for which he was criticized and had to offer a justification). Some Christians refused to participate in the required rituals when their turn came, resulting in their imprisonment. They had confessed their faith and were known as confessors. All those in good standing (either through not being targeted or through imprisonment) were known as *stantes*. While imprisoned, some confessors died and were regarded as martyrs. The terms are not always used with such exactitude as they would achieve later in Christian history. The confessors were held in high regard, and even those who had not died were regarded as martyrs since they were prepared for the final step, even though it had been denied them.

However, a significant number of Christians throughout the empire complied with the imperial demand in order to avoid imprisonment and torture. They complied with varying degrees of willingness and with varying degrees of participation. Some offered the sacrifice (*sacrificati*), some offered incense only (*thurificati*), some bribed officials or got someone else to stand in their place or in some other way falsely obtained the certificate of compliance (*libellatici*). All these people were regarded as having sinned to various degrees, although since all of them had lapsed from their faith (and collectively were called *lapsi*), the sin of all of them was serious enough to result in excommunication (that is, a suspension of their membership in the church and their eligibility to receive communion in the eucharistic liturgy and a denial of their possibility of entering heaven should they die). This led to tension and eventually schism in the churches of Africa (and Italy and elsewhere) among the those who remained faithful (*stantes*) over the question of what to do with the *lapsi* who were demanding readmission to the church and to eternal salvation.

As the enforcement of the imperial decree slackened over the course of 250, the *lapsi* wanted to be reconciled as active members of the church. Some of the *stantes* took a hardline approach (the rigorists), saying that the *lapsi* could never be reconciled, while others among the *stantes* took a more liberal approach (the laxists), saying that the *lapsi* could be reconciled with minimal demands placed on them once they had received the recommendation of a confessor. Cyprian himself eventually took a middle position, demanding that the issue be discussed at a synod of bishops when he was able to return to Carthage, that the performance of penance be a prerequisite before any reconciliation could be decided upon, that the speed of reconciliation be determined by the seriousness of the sin and the seriousness of the regret for the sin, and that it was for bishops, not confessors or clergy, to decide on readmissions. The theological issues were intertwined with sociopolitical ones as well, in that Cyprian needed to restore control over his community through his ability to exercise patronage locally over the rigorists and laxists among them, including his own clergy, and also to gain other bishops elsewhere as allies, especially in Italy.[42] The solution he proposed, mentioned above, was endorsed at the synod held after Eater in 251.[43] So this group of three letters must date after this, but before when?

Changed circumstances in subsequent years meant that this synodal policy of 251 had to be revisited at later episcopal synods. We find such change prefigured in *Epistula* 58[44] in a letter to the laity of Thibaris and then delivered in an episcopal synod described in *Epistula* 57. In that letter Cyprian informed Cornelius, bishop of Rome between 251 and 253, of the changes.[45] In light of an expected renewal in demands for sacrifice with resultant persecutions[46]—about which Cyprian seems to have had premonitions[47] and to have seen the writing on the wall in terms of reliable signs and warning, which I take as a reference to the pandemic (among other things)[48]—the African bishops decided that those lapsed still performing penance (the penitent *sacrificati*) should be reconciled into communion, such that only any unrepentant *lapsi* were still denied reconciliation. The question is whether that synod took place in 252 or 253.[49] We should place *Epistula* 56, considered above, prior to this synod and prior to *Epistula* 58, as an even earlier foreshadowing of the policy that would be adopted by the African churches, in that there is no hint within it that renewed persecution was on the horizon.[50]

Although there is debate among scholars (some of which we shall encounter below), I have argued that dating the synod discussed in *Epistula* 57 to 253, as proposed by Graeme Clarke, is most convincing, as opposed to dating the synod to 252.[51] Thus, *Epistulae* 56 and 58 would date to before May 253, and probably only shortly before in the case of *Epistula* 58 and perhaps even at the end of 252 or start of 253 for *Epistula* 56. *Epistula* 57 would be shortly after the May 253 synod had met.

We may turn now to consider how scholars in the past century have seen connections between those letters, where the fear of renewed persecution and the change to the reconciliation policy feature, and the two pamphlets of Cyprian that are our concern here.

Late in the nineteenth century Archbishop Benson considered the letters to have been written in conjunction with the African synod of bishops (which he dated to 252 rather than 253) and a supposed recommencement of persecution under Gallus. Further, he commented that *Epistula* 58 to the Christian community in Thibaris was written before *De mortalitate* and *Ad Demetrianum* because otherwise Cyprian would have sent copies of these treatises with the letter and would have mentioned that he was so doing in the letter. He argued further that *Epistula* 58 was to be dated before the synod of 252 based on what is found in *Epistula* 58.8.[52] That still left open the question of whether the two pamphlets were composed before or after the synod itself, even though he thought that what is in *Epistula* 58 would be developed in the two pamphlets. In other words, he was noncommittal about whether *Epistula* 57 came before or after the two pamphlets.

A generation later Mary Hannan, on the basis of Monceaux's treatment, in her dissertation on *De mortalitate* assigned *Epistulae* 57 and 58 to 252, and since *De mortalitate* 15 refers to the prospect of further persecution (an idea found also in those two letters, as we have noted), dated this pamphlet to that year.[53] She singled out Koch's suggestion that *De mortalitate* was composed before *Ad Demetrianum*, the opposite to the sequence in which they are mentioned in Pontius, based on what each says about contemporary events.[54] She made the point that *Epistula* 59 reveals that toward the middle of 252 the emperor Gallus issued a new order for public sacrifice that resulted in fresh persecution.[55] However, on the specific question of whether the pamphlets pre- or post-dated the synod she was silent.

In his 1958 volume of translations of Cyprian into English, Roy Deferrari, who used Hannan's translation for this pamphlet, also followed Monceaux and his dating of *Epistulae* 57 and 58 to 252 to argue that *Ad Demetrianum* and *De mortalitate* (following the sequence in Pontius) should also be dated to that year. He also accepted that *Epistula* 59.6.1 referred to a universal decree issued by Gallus.[56] He was in no doubt that *Ad Demetrianum* 17 referred to the death of Decius and his sons.[57] On other issues he was silent.

Giuseppina Stramondo accepted 252 as the date for *De mortalitate*.[58] Sage, among others, believes that the sequence of questions in Pontius refers to Cyprian's pamphlets and that they are presented in a relative chronological sequence.[59] Thus, he places *Ad Demetrianum* prior to *De mortalitate*.[60] He states that the latter is connected with the so-called persecution of Gallus, which he dates to 252.[61] He also accepts the reference in *Ad Demetrianum* 17 as referring to the death of Decius.[62] Yet, when he discusses these two pamphlets in some detail, Sage not only presents *De mortalitate* before *Ad Demetrianum* (although, it must be admitted, he nowhere suggests that this reflects their order of composition) but notes that *De mortalitate* seems to focus on the fact that the end of persecution (under Decius) need not be the end of the possibility of Christian perfection, while *Ad Demetrianum* is more concerned with the possibility of a renewal of persecution due to the pestilence.[63] Although Sage has not noticed it, this could suggest that the idea that Pontius presented Cyprian's treatises in a chronological sequence needs to be revisited. Only after the presentation of these two pamphlets does Sage go on to consider *Epistula* 58 to Thibaris and then the synod of forty-two bishops presented in *Epistula* 57, which he dates to spring 252.[64]

Alföldy dated the two pamphlets to 253.[65] Manlio Simonetti's edition for Corpus Christianorum took the year as 252 without question.[66] Ezio Gallicet produced an edition of *Ad Demetrianum* in the same year as Simonetti's. In his discussion about the date he noted that scholars were divided between 251, 252, and 253.[67] His preference was for 253 given that the presence of the pandemic in the second half of 252 led to a bad harvest for 253.[68] He rejected the necessity of interpreting the reference in *Ad Demetrianum* 17 as being to the death of Decius, which was taken by some as a reason to date the pamphlet to the end of 251 or the start of 252.[69] He dated *De mortalitate* before *Ad Demetrianum*.[70]

In more recent years Quacquarelli accepts that Gallus issued an edict in 252, and that was when Cyprian's letter to the Christian community in Thibaris was written.[71] He acknowledges that some prefer to date the letter to 251.[72] Regarding the two pamphlets, all he says is that they were written sometime between 252 and 253[73] but says nothing about the relationship between the two treatises and the letter in terms of sequence of composition.

Graeme Clarke, in his outstanding translation of Cyprian's letters, put forward several things of relevance to our topic. For one thing, he considered *Epistulae* 56, 57, and 58 to refer to 253 rather than 252.[74] He was skeptical of an empire-wide persecution having been ordered by Trebonianus Gallus.[75] He noted that there is nothing in either of the two pamphlets to indicate that the churches of North Africa were actually experiencing a fresh round of persecution, only that they felt one was likely.[76] His comment on the date for the two pamphlets was that it "is at once a vague and a delicate matter."[77] For him, the connection is "a fair surmise (but surmise only) that this epidemic occasioned the *edictum*."[78] In addition, this *edictum* was not a universal one supposedly issued by Trebonianus Gallus, but a more local African one. He placed the two pamphlets before the *edictum* and before the synod of 253.[79]

In his Italian translation of *De mortalitate*, which appeared in 1984, Mario Ruggiero attempted no greater precision than to date the pestilence (and hence the writing of the pamphlets) to between 251 and 254.[80] Antonella Cerretini, in her Italian translation in the same series, only offers the parameters of 252 and 254.[81]

Jean-Claude Fredouille's 2003 edition and French translation in the Sources Chrétiennes series states that a date between 251 and 253 was probable and that further precision would only be illusory.[82] A date between Decius's and Cyprian's own death and the relative date provided by Pontius's sequence of texts are all that he will admit. Accepting Clarke's argument that Gallus did not issue an edict removes one point scholars have used to anchor our pamphlets to a particular date, even though any local renewed push against the Christians would have provided Cyprian with some motive to compose his work. Fredouille does not consider the date of the arrival of the pandemic in North Africa as providing some guide to the date of composition of the two pamphlets. Apart from briefly noting some of the comments about the sequence of our two works found in other scholars, Fredouille does not stop to consider this much himself.[83] He dates the two pamphlets to before *Epistulae* 57, 58, and 59.[84]

It should be noted that nothing in the three letters mentions pestilence explicitly as a reason for further changes to the policy agreed upon in 251. The enemy that needed to be confronted by a relaxation of that policy was renewed persecution. Pandemic as the cause of any renewal in persecution is not explicit in the letters, it is only to be inferred. Of course, the possibility that renewed persecution was a response to non-Christian interpretations of the cause of the pandemic is not denied, but the contribution of the spreading of disease was not presented as a principal reason in itself or in connection with renewed persecution for changing the reconciliation policy in the African churches. The closest we come to a hint of a reference in the letters to an outbreak of disease is in 58.2.1, when Cyprian referred to the dawning day of affliction, a world that is dying (an important theme in *Ad Demetrianum*), and the time of the antichrist (mentioned in *De mortalitate*). What Cyprian seems to have been suggesting was that the appearance of disease (a sign of the end of the world) would bring about the probability of renewed persecution, for which the repentant *sacrificati* needed to be fortified through reconciliation.[85] In *Epistula* 57.4.3, Cyprian observed that soldiers for Christ, who ran the risk of being attacked by robbers or coming down with a fatal fever, could be lost eternally because they had not been reconciled. It would make chronological sense for Cyprian to have discussed the meaning of the pandemic in his two pamphlets, which then prompted him to consider the implications of that for the 251 reconciliation policy in *Epistulae* 58 and 57. It would have been great if Cyprian had mentioned in *Epistula* 58.1.2 (in reference to the day of affliction), the demise of the world and the coming of the antichrist, which he had discussed this in his two pamphlets, but alas he did not.[86] Of course, the 251 policy had allowed for the reconciliation of *sacrificati* in danger of death. It could be argued that, with death harvesting so many victims, sheer numbers alone would have been enough of a reason to extend the reconciliation policy, but that is not canvassed in the letters; it was the possibility or probability of renewed persecution that demanded a change. The connection between the pamphlets and the letters is not based so much on reference in the letters to disease as it is on reference in the pamphlets to the outbreak of renewed persecution, something that we find in *Ad Demetrianum* 11 and *De mortalitate* 4 and 15.

However, a close reading of the two pamphlets reveals little concrete information about a renewal of persecution. The mention of "repeated havoc" (*frequenti strage*) in section 11 of *Ad Demetrianum* could be taken as such a reference. Yet, the way Cyprian discusses it, he seems to be referring to repeated episodes of persecution in the past, not a future one. If this work contains any sense about future persecution, it is only in the most general sense that what has happened before is bound to happen again. Any indication in Cyprian that another bout was imminent is lacking; there is no mention of Cyprian's premonitions. My argument in note 54 of my translation of *De mortalitate* is that the reference in section 4 to persecution is back to the events under Decius, presented in such a way as to suggest this was the usual state of affairs in the relationship between world and church. Similarly, in note 163 the mention of "when the hostile encounter will come" (*cum proelium venerit*) seems to be more about an inevitable rather than an imminent round of persecution. This further suggests to me that the two pamphlets are to be dated before *Epistulae* 58 and 57 if not 56 as well.

On the basis of the evidence and the arguments, I would offer the following working hypothesis about the chronological order of these texts. The pandemic reached the West sometime in the second half of 252. Thus, when the episcopal synod met in Carthage in May 252 (evidenced in *Epistula* 64), it did not warrant any consideration by the assembled bishops. At some point during that year *Epistula* 56 was written, but again without needing to refer to the pestilence. However, as the year progressed, so did the impact of disease. Toward the end of the year, as the full savagery of this health crisis was unfolding, there was popular agitation again against the Christians, whose previous failure to support the empire (through a failure to participate in the renewal of the religious cult demanded by Decius) was held as the cause for the spreading fatalities. Cyprian wrote his two pamphlets, *Ad Demetrianum* and *De mortalitate.* A provincial edict requiring more sacrifice to the gods as a way of addressing the growing unease among the general community was feared by Christians. I would place *Epistula* 58 after the two pamphlets on the basis of the presence in the letter of Cyprian's growing fear of an imminent return of persecution and the need to do something more about the repentant *lapsi* still performing penance. Thus, a date of late 252 or, more probably, early 253 for the two pamphlets seems most likely to me. Not long after *Epistula* 58 came the synod of May 253 (evidenced in *Epistula* 57 written after the synod).

We have to explain why *Epistula* 57 made no reference to the pandemic. The possibility is mentioned of those in penance falling victim to a dangerous illness.[87] Perhaps we can say simply that having addressed that topic for his own community in *De mortalitate*, Cyprian's synod was less concerned with pestilence than he was with persecution. It could be an indication that the sting of the pandemic was weakening (although it would be odd that anti-Christian sentiment was increasing) or that the threat of persecution was felt even more keenly by the still penitent *sacrificati* than was rampant disease. More likely than those two, in my opinion, is the possibility that the synod did not want to seem to be granting reconciliation reactively on the basis of the risks presented by illness but to be acting proactively by equipping the newly reconciled with the strength that comes from belonging to face the trials of persecution once again, this time triumphantly. The synod had agreed that reconciliation was not for the sick and dying but for the strong and living.[88] The 251 synod had decided already that reconciliation was appropriate for the sick and the dying, and this synod was not rescinding that. In our interpretation we must insert the word *primarily*. While the sick and dying could be reconciled, this was a second-best option; better that they were reconciled before falling victim to debilitating illness so that they could demonstrate their newly found or restored resolve through facing the fury of persecution. The less talk there was about the pandemic at the 253 synod, the more Cyprian could continue to appease those rigorist elements within the North African churches.

One further question remains: in what order were the two pamphlets themselves written? We have no real evidence, apart from the supposed chronological order in which Pontius presented Cyprian's pamphlets, to determine which of the two was written first. However, when we look at *Ad Demetrianum*, mentioning the scourge of disease as one of the reasons for non-Christian hostility toward the Christian community, it does so within a much broader context of Christians being blamed for wars, famine, and drought as well.[89] The same is true when Cyprian mentions the divine prophecies for the world's troubles; disease is just one of several.[90] Very quickly any specific cause for this particular outbreak of community loathing and resentment was subsumed into a more general non-Christian prejudice that blamed Christians for many woes; disease is a cause but not so prevalent and virulent as to dominate the pamphlet.

Indeed, as we read through the pamphlet, the urgency of freeing Christians from the blame for this particular disaster is not developed much at all. Cyprian's arguments are generic rather than specific. What he had to say by way of rebutting such hostility was applicable in any number of situations. This is not surprising given his dependency upon the Christian apologetic tradition as exemplified by Tertullian, upon whom Cyprian patently was dependent. In discussing the world growing old (*senectus mundi*), Cyprian left implicit the connection between disease as a sign of the world's approaching collapse. The Christian failure to worship non-Christian gods was true no matter what situation brought that refusal to the attention of the wider community. In turning the tables and blaming non-Christians, Cyprian referred to illness as only one of several situations in which the failures of non-Christians were responsible for divine punishment on the world.[91] In fact, in the second half of the pamphlet, disease and pandemic are hardly mentioned at all.[92] In other words, while disease might have sparked that particular outbreak of anti-Christian sentiment, the fact that Cyprian's comments were largely generic rather than specific suggests that the full impact of the pandemic had yet to be felt.

This contrasts with what we find in *De mortalitate* where the overwhelming impact of disease is at the center of Cyprian's thoughts and is described in lurid detail in section 24. On this basis, I would place *Ad Demetrianum* prior to *De mortalitate*, following the sequence offered by Pontius. The former was composed in the early days of the outbreak in North Africa and the latter sometime later when this pestilence had become a full-blown natural disaster of monumental proportions.

Thus, the order of composition of these texts seems to me to be: *Epistula* 56 (second half of 252), *Ad Demetrianum* (late 252 or early 253), *De mortalitate* (early 253), *Epistula* 58 (early 253), and *Epistula* 57 (after May 253), written over several months between the end of 252 and the middle of 253.

PURPOSE OF THE PAMPHLETS

This leads us to the question of Cyprian's motive for composing these texts. What did he hope to achieve by writing them? In other words, into what literary genre can we classify them? We shall be aided in this by appreciating the impact of classical rhetoric upon these works. Rhetoric was the tertiary education of the Roman empire, and anyone who wished to display themselves as men of polished culture who belonged to the upper echelons of society or who wished to achieve success in public life as either an advocate in trials (where the skills of forensic rhetoric were relevant), a politician in the assembly (where the skills of deliberative rhetoric were relevant), or a Sophistic public speaker (where the skills of epideictic rhetoric were relevant) would have spent time learning its art.[93]

Pontius noted that, before his adult conversion, Cyprian had learned the liberal arts (*bonae artes*) that gave him his secular advantage (*ad utilitatem...saeculi*).[94] He also noted the bountiful fruitfulness of Cyprian's eloquence (*eloquentiae...larga fecunditas*) in his writings.[95] This would indicate that he was well versed in the art of oratory. Indeed, Graeme Clarke reviewed the evidence and concluded that not only could Cyprian have practiced as an orator but could have been a rhetorician, that is, a teacher of rhetoric.[96] As a teacher one would expect that it would have been second nature for Cyprian to construct his pamphlets according to the general tenets of classical rhetoric.

The aim of rhetoric was to persuade or, in the case of epideictic oratory, to entertain and bedazzle. Forensic rhetoric sought to persuade about events in the past (and in the law court setting it would be about guilt or innocence), while deliberative rhetoric sought to persuade about a future course of action (and in the public assembly setting it would be about advantage or disadvantage about pursuing a particular policy). Epideictic rhetoric, despite it having been envisaged by Aristotle as having a practical application, was, especially as employed during the Second Sophistic, all about orators brandishing their talents and abilities through declamations, frequently on quite frivolous topics.[97]

When we come to these two pamphlets, Pontius provides some sense of their purpose when he writes about Cyprian's writings:

> Through whom were the falsely accusing non-believers defeated by turning those things they heap on us back on themselves? By whom were Christians of a cowardly disposition concerning the loss of their fellows or, what is greater, of a more worthless faith consoled by the promise of the future?[98]

Ad Demetrianum may be considered as Cyprian's version of Tertullian's *Apologeticum*, a forensic pamphlet addressed to a non-Christian arguing for the innocence of Christians with regard to charges asserted against them.[99] *De mortalitate* has a deliberative rhetoric construction; it focuses on the future and how Christians need to change their thinking and behavior in order to respond appropriately to the presence of deadly disease.

Interestingly, just as Pontius seems to have commented on each of Cyprian's works, so too did Augustine, in one of his homilies on the anniversary of Cyprian's martyrdom.[100] First, he mentioned a work in which Cyprian confronted those who complained against the teaching of Christ. In eighth place, he mentioned that Cyprian recommended the joys of eternal life and banished the fear in those dying and the grief in those mourning. There is no mention of disease at all.

As to the question of whether these texts were originally sermons, an opinion frequently encountered in comment about the dozen or so texts from Cyprian apart from his letters, I would be inclined to say they were not. I am taking sermon here in the strict sense of the homily delivered during the weekly eucharistic liturgy.[101] We really have little idea about how Cyprian approached this part of his episcopal responsibilities. If he preached liturgically only on Sundays, we would arrive at a minimum figure of about five hundred homilies Cyprian ought to have preached during his ten years as bishop. That no other homily is preserved and that none of the pamphlets has an obvious eucharistic setting should give us pause to identify them as such. This is not to say that most of Cyprian's pamphlets were not delivered orally as an oration or address, that is, a speech in some other setting. Indeed, in *De mortalitate* 1 he referred to his work as a *sermo*, which I understand here simply as speech. Even here I would suspect that Cyprian always intended these works to end up as written compositions. Some (such as *De habitu virginum*, *De dominica oratione*, and *De bono patientiae*) were obviously inspired by Tertullian's literary output and so it would make sense that a piece of writing be matched by another literary composition. Of course, this does not preclude them from having been presented orally as well. It is as pieces of literature that we shall engage *Ad Demetrianum* and *De mortalitate* here, without neglecting this orality.

Certainly, in the case of *Ad Demetrianum*, it would be even more than unlikely that it was ever delivered in a liturgical setting. It has an apologetic form and is addressed to Demetrian and other non-Christians. Even though not intended explicitly for Christians, this would not preclude the work from being made available to Christians to read, so that they could know how their bishop argued or could be armed with arguments for them to use against other non-Christians who blamed them for all the woes that seemed to be befalling the world. Yet, it remains fairly clear that the work was actually intended for non-Christians. Unless Cyprian and Demetrian confronted one another in some face-to-face setting, I would think that this was always a written text.

A. *Ad Demetrianum*

This would suggest some kind of forensic purpose for *Ad Demetrianum.* Unlike Tertullian's *Apologeticum,* which was offered to the leaders of the empire in general, people he had never met in person and never would, Cyprian's pamphlet is addressed to someone he had known personally for quite some time. Even in Tertullian's much later work addressed to the proconsul in Carthage, *Ad Scapulam,*[102] a work that, I believe, has a deliberative rather than forensic purpose,[103] there is no indication that Tertullian had ever met him.

In a forensic work addressed to a non-Christian reader one would not expect to find much appeal to the scriptures. For one thing, as texts that imperial officials and local elites did not take as authoritative, Christians could hardly justify their actions or inaction (depending on the charge they were defending) by such an appeal. Throughout *Ad Demetrianum* we do find Cyprian quoting passages of Scripture in sections 1, 6, 7, 9, 11, 16, 17, 20, 22, 23, and 24. Indeed, one of the arguments Lactantius, another African teacher of rhetoric and convert to Christianity, used against him half a century later was that in confronting Demetrian Cyprian ought to have deployed logic rather than passages of the scriptures, which his opponent would not have regarded as authoritative texts.[104] This was noted another century later by Jerome.[105]

Was the inclusion of Scripture mainly for the benefit of Christian readers of the pamphlet? If so, does this indicate that such early Christian apologies were never really intended for non-Christian readers? Such a conclusion does not follow as a matter of necessity. Regardless of whether a non-Christian would be swayed by what Scripture had to say, a Christian could wish to explain their behavior by reference to their own authoritative texts. This is what Cyprian seems to have done at the start of the pamphlet in the *exordium* when explaining why previously he had not engaged in refuting objectionable views he believed Demetrian held. He was simply justifying what he believed, whether or not the opponent accepted the basis of that justification. However, in some other instances he did introduce scriptural passages as part of the argument, as evidence that ought to prove a point and convince a jury/audience/reader. We find that in section 6, for example. The claim that the God of the Christians (and the Jews) was the only God and that this God promised to punish those who were not followers was not something that would be the least bit persuasive to a non-Christian who, as Lactantius rightly asserted later, would simply regard such writings as fantasy and fiction.

The forensic purpose of the work is clear from an identifiable *partitio* or *propositio* in 3a, although admittedly only in an abbreviated form. Cyprian identified the charges against the Christians but did not indicate that he was going to contest those charges nor offer any indication about how he intended to proceed. He wanted to show that Christians were not to blame for the troubles being experienced and that, as a result, the non-Christians ought to stop blaming and persecuting Christians and ought to believe in the God in whom they believed. It is a forensic piece that ends with a deliberative call.

Gallicet denied the idea that *Ad Demetrianum* was merely an imitation of Tertullian's *Apologeticum.* He considered Cyprian as rooted very much in his own situation.[106] This is not to deny that the work was forensic, but rather to assert that Cyprian's basis for arguing was different to Tertullian's. He saw Cyprian emphasizing the serious nature of the current problems and contrasting, more than Tertullian did, the goodness of Christians with the wickedness of non-Christians.[107] Although he was certainly correct to insist Cyprian was no mere imitator of Tertullian, perhaps Gallicet erred by not showing the extent to which Cyprian did borrow (and then refashion) some of Tertullian's material.

Apology was certainly a feature of pre-Nicene Christianity, so much so that the second century can be described within Christianity as the age of apologetics. We need only mention Quadratus, Aristides, Justin Martyr, Apollinaris of Hierapolis, Melito of Sardis, Athenagoras of Athens, Tatian, Theophilus of Antioch, the author of *Epistula ad Diogentum,* Clement of Alexandria, and Tertullian himself.[108] It was the activity, and the record of that activity, of Christian engagement with the non-Christian world around them. In part, it took inspiration from a scriptural text such as 1 Peter 3:15–16, whereby Christians were told to have an answer (*apologia*) for those who wanted to know the reason for their hope. Thus, it could encompass evangelization and the outreach to non-Christians seeking to convert them to the new faith, seeking ways to explain their faith in ways that nonbelievers could understand and accept. It could also involve exchanges between

Christians and Jews as the distinctions between the two groups became ever sharper.[109] Both sides would seek to defend their faith, much of which was shared, as the only legitimate one by criticizing the other. All this involved using the philosophy, science, literature, language, history, and culture of that wider group to express the essence of Christianity.

However, given that most non-Christians not only were unpersuaded by such efforts but also took an active dislike to Christian exclusivism, sectarianism, and separatism, Christian apologists needed not only to explain their faith but also to justify it in the face of antagonism and hostility. They were not only promoting themselves but defending themselves. As Christianity became a capital crime, apology became forensic defense, a rational plea to be left unmolested if nothing else. It involved a variety of arguments and could be written as much for internal consumption (to provide ammunition for other Christians to use in their own everyday encounters with non-Christians and to reassure those having doubts) as for officials and intellectuals of the empire. Further, such officials were little likely to be interested in what Christians had to say, resulting in apologetic literature being read principally by Christians themselves. Authors could adopt different tones, from accommodating and conciliatory to shrill and defiant. That the aims of those who produced this literature could be so diverse means that apology as a genre is hard to define. The editors of a fine volume on apologetics in the Roman empire raise questions, for example, about the relationship or distinction between apologetics and polemics.[110]

Simon Price offers brief comment about *Ad Demetrianum* in his chapter on Latin Christian apologetics, although without specifying the purpose of the work any further than saying it that it was written in exoteric form, confronting a more imminent threat of persecution due to non-Christians blaming Christians for all kinds of troubles in the world.[111]

With *Ad Demetrianum* we have an apology in the form of a forensic defense, as with Tertullian's *Apologeticum*. Cyprian set out to exonerate and exculpate Christians from the accusations Demetrian had unleashed, that the current pestilence was further evidence that they were responsible for the bad things that were happening in the world because of their failures to participate in the religious customs of the empire. He set about doing this by showing that such woes were to be expected as the world came to an end and that they were caused actually by the non-Christian persecution of Christians and failure to worship the one, true God resulting in divine punishment.

B. *De mortalitate*

Hannan identified *De mortalitate* as an example of consolation literature.[112] More explicitly, she stated:

> To comfort the members of his flock, to strengthen them in the throes of such a calamity, to reconcile them to the will of God, and to recall their minds to the glory of Paradise—this, then was Cyprian's purpose in writing the *De Mortalitate.*[113]

Sage noted:

> Cyprian strove to renew the faith and hope of his community, but this was not sufficient. With the breakdown of all bonds, what was required was a reaffirmation of virtue towards one's fellow man, and a return to God through faith.[114]

This he identified as being fulfilled through *De opera et eleemosynis.* Of *De mortalitate* he had nothing much to say about its purpose, other than that Cyprian was showing his community other ways to remove sin apart from martyrdom. Ruggiero takes the work more as a theological tract in which Cyprian presented a theology of death, about hope for heaven while suffering in this life.[115] He does not consider a rhetorical purpose to the work; for him it is more expository than motivational.

What does it mean to call a work consolatory? We shall examine the question in the context of Greco-Roman culture. Consolation refers to the comfort that words can offer to someone suffering loss and bereavement, such as the death of someone close to them, in the hope of providing emotional and physical support and sympathy, of making that grief bearable or even subside, and of easing their sorrow by putting the experience into a better context.[116] When committed to writing, such works could take many forms: letters, poems, essays, and even philosophical treatises on grief. With such form they could range from being very personal to rather abstract and theoretical. Over time in the classical world, the topics covered in such literature became standardized, particularly under the influence of Stoicism.[117] Death was inevitable and needed to be accepted as such (*memento mori*) as the first step to ultimate happiness. Grief was a response to evil, and since death was natural and not evil, grief was held to be an inappropriate though undeniable response. Of course, how one dealt with grief was only one aspect of how classical philosophers and others dealt more generally with the passions through the cardinal virtues.[118]

Rhetorically, we could try to distinguish works that sought to eulogize the dead from those that sought to comfort the living. The former would be epideictic and the latter would be deliberative, in that they recommended a course of action, even if such a course of action were an intellectual or emotional change of attitude. Yet, things are not always so easily categorized. Thucydides's version of the oration delivered by Perikles for the dead of Athens at the end of the first year of the Peloponnesian War in 431 BCE was to praise the dead.[119] Indeed, the Thucydidean Perikles did that, but he did more besides. He praised the dead by praising the city for which they died[120] before turning to the citizens in front of him. He exhorted them to continue the fighting spirit of the dead warriors, lest their sacrifice were in vain. The comfort he gave to the loved ones of those who had died was the knowledge that they died with honor and that the mourning of those who missed them was appropriate tribute.[121] Thus, Perikles's motive was ultimately deliberative; he wanted to persuade his fellow citizens to continue the war effort and not abandon it because of the loss of life.[122] Even though it only appears at the end, it is clear that Perikles's principal purpose was to use the eulogy to promote a political agenda. However, funeral speeches were just one particular kind of consolatory activity.

Such a powerful emotion as grief was held as intensely inconvenient and disruptive by philosophically educated Romans. Crantor of Soli's *De luctu* from the third century BCE was a work particularly useful for Cicero in his *Tusculanae disputationes.* Generally ignored in scholarship in the nineteenth and twentieth centuries, these five books popularized several Greek philosophical schools in Rome and described what made for a happy life. In his later *De divinatione* he summarized its content:

> For the first volume treats of indifference to death, the second of enduring pain, the third of the alleviation of

> sorrow, the fourth of other spiritual disturbances; and the fifth embraces a topic which sheds the brightest light on the entire field of philosophy since it teaches that virtue is sufficient of itself for the attainment of happiness.[123]

Cicero spent a great deal of the first book of the debate, set at his country villa in the Alban Hills some 20 kilometers (12.5 miles) to the southeast of Rome, discussing the immortality of the soul and a disdain for death since disease cannot touch the soul.[124] When talking about grief Cicero noted that people often felt it because it was expected of them in certain circumstances and that because, in some circumstances, it could be embraced or deferred, it means that it is not necessary.[125] In 3.32 Cicero presented some commonplaces about how to administer consolation: show that what happened was not evil, that it will happen to all, and that it will gain a person nothing.[126] The purpose was to exhort the reader to overcome their grief. This is Cicero offering a theoretical understanding of the purpose of consolation.

Cicero's *Consolatio* on the death of his daughter Tullia in 45 BCE, which survives only in fragments and quotations and was also dependent upon Crantor or simply agreed with him, was written, uniquely, as a self-help remedy after he had reflected on the nature of grief. In it he indicated that he believed his daughter was worthy of deification.[127]

Yet, from his letters, we can see that Cicero had difficulty in adopting such a detached attitude to the death of his daughter. While at times Cicero's consolation of others was bound by social conventions of rivalry where emulation played such an important part,[128] we do find raw and unmitigated grief pouring forth in his letters in the aftermath of his daughter's death, noting "but sometimes I am overwhelmed, and scarcely offer any resistance to grief."[129] The death of his daughter meant that the escape he could find at home from the rough and tumble of the politics surrounding the death throes of the republic, which would shortly consume him, was gone. To Atticus he would write that "my sorrow is stronger than any consolation."[130] Solitude was both a help and a hindrance, for he would find himself bursting into tears.[131] He realized that being with friends helped, as could distracting himself by thinking about something else, even if that were planning a monument in Tullia's honor.[132] Although he did not expect it, Cicero found writing about it therapeutic.

We should not judge Cicero as being unable to live by his own philosophical tenets. In fact, we have considered these texts in a reverse chronological order. The insight of Han Baltussen that we should see in Cicero stages of grief is helpful.[133] By the time he wrote *Tusculanae disputationes* Cicero had had time to process his thoughts and come to terms with his emotions and to offer the wisdom of his considered experience.

Two further Roman authors to consider are the younger Seneca and Plutarch. The first of three pieces by Seneca to be discussed briefly here is *De consolatione ad Marciam*, written to the daughter of the historian and senator Cremutius Cordus three years after the death of her son. Her inordinate grief required stern counsel.[134] He operated on an inductive basis, starting by contrasting Octavia the younger with Livia, one of whom was consumed by grief and the other of whom conquered it.[135] One's grief cannot bring the dead back to life, so what is the point of it?[136] He dismissed Marcia's self-centered reasons for her grief, saying that she ought to be grateful for having raised him rather than being sorrowful at his loss.[137] He also dismissed her concerns for her dead son, saying that nothing could hurt him any longer and that no one lives too short a life but for as long as destined.[138]

Relegated to Corsica in 41 for an alleged affair with Julia Livilla, sister of Caligula, Seneca wrote a letter of consolation to his mother, Helvia, who had suffered much loss in her life (*De consolatione ad Helviam*).[139] It is a masterpiece of Stoicism and more essay-like than letter-like. Unusually, the one who was being mourned was the one who offered comfort to the bereaved. For him grief was to be borne and not interfered with too quickly, but when one does offer consolation, it should be to encourage people to be staunch and resolute and tough and to accept wretchedness. Consolation was to be a remedy or a cure, it was for "repressing and controlling sorrow."[140] Grief needs to be conquered.[141] Seneca assured his mother that nothing could be done to upset his equilibrium and that this should help ensure that nothing upset hers either. But, at the same time, in the very opening of the letter he confesses that his own grief is like a gash that must be covered so that he can bind up his mother's wounds.[142]

To be truly wise is neither to court the things whose pleasures are fleeting nor to fear the things whose pains are terrifying. Seneca offered the fact that he was still alive as a solace to his mother, as well as the fact that happiness can be found in a simple life,[143] and exile means nothing since one place is much the same as another.[144] Even the disgrace of exile can be endured for one's sense of self-worth does not rely upon how others see them.[145]

In *De consolatione ad Polybium*, in which appears a rather unexpected encomium of the emperor Claudius, Seneca consoled one of Claudius's freedmen bureaucrats on the death of his brother.[146] Nothing, living or dead, is everlasting. Grief accomplishes nothing good for either mourned or mourner. Again, we find the paradox of the author's point that grief is pointless alongside such commonplaces that the consoler shared in the mourner's grief.[147] The sense that Polybius ought to distract himself from his feelings by throwing himself into this work is indicated by warning him that it is in idle time that sorrow will visit.[148] He concludes not with a Stoic call to *apatheia* but to the control of the emotions.[149]

The final example with which to consider the classical world's development of a body of consolatory literature is Plutarch. In about 90 the absent Plutarch wrote a consolatory letter to his wife after he heard of the death of their toddler daughter that is at once both deeply personal and yet intended for a wider audience. Han Baltussen argues that, although ancient and modern customs surrounding grief may vary and although it has a public dimension and is full of philosophy, this letter does give some access to the inner workings of Plutarch's mind and ancient psychotherapy.[150] "Strong indications that Plutarch's prime objective is to practice a form of *psychagogia*, occur at important moments in his advisory exhortations and betray a preference for rational argument intended to control emotions."[151]

Deliberative rhetoric is all about bringing change: a change of attitude or a change of behavior as being advantageous or disadvantageous. Consolation was to persuade the person suffering in grief to change their outlook. Such persuasion could be warm and tender, which is more the modern sense of consolation, or it could be stark and confronting, as we may note from the variety of approaches taken by some of the authors discussed above. Perhaps we could classify consolation as a subset of deliberative rhetoric. Abraham Malherbe regarded consolation as a task of *paraenesis*, defined as "moral exhortation in which someone is advised to pursue or abstain from something."[152] He continued, "It contains useful rules for conduct in common situations and adopts styles that range from censure to consolation."[153] For our purposes, it is sufficient to say that consolation falls under the general rhetorical heading of deliberative oratory. We have seen some of the standard arguments produced in order to bring about that change of attitude or feeling: death is not evil, death is an escape from evil, all people are mortal, everything must perish, the dead do not suffer, and time heals.

Christians were no different from non-Christians in pursuing this aim, and scholarship has been interested in establishing a canon of Christian consolatory literature. In the 1930s Charles Favez examined the Christian Latin contribution to this literature (from Cyprian to Ambrose, Jerome, and Paulinus of Nola) and concluded that the influence of the classic tradition on Christian consolation in terms of content rather than style was more limited than one might have imagined.[154]

In light of the Christian faith in sharing in the death and resurrection of Jesus, Christians could be expected to hold a different attitude from their non-Christian neighbors when it came to death. Yet, any kind of separation can cause grief and loss, even if it lasts only for a day or two, so it is not surprising that Christians would share to some extent with initial reactions. Indeed, the fact that Christian writers felt the need to compose consolatory literature is a strong indication that Christians did not always possess and display an acceptably Christian attitude toward death. From a Christian perspective, however, the commonplaces in consolation could or should be different from those offered by others. One would expect to find the idea of being reunited in heaven to the fore in Christian consolation. The template for such a position must be found in 1 Thessalonians 4:13–18, the earliest piece of the New Testament to be written, especially given the presence of the verb *parakaleō* in verse 18, which has the idea both of "comfort" and "appeal" or "entreat."[155] A correct understanding that the dead as well as the living will benefit from the imminent second coming means that the dead will not be mourned or will be mourned, but in a different way. This ambiguity in Paul's text is indicative of a dilemma within Christianity of how to understand and deal with death.[156] George Kennedy sees the Johannine discourse (John 13—17) as consolatory in nature.[157] When he came to the tomb of Lazarus Jesus wept (John 11:35) and in the Sermon on the Mount we are told that those who mourn will be comforted (Matt 5:4). Being led away to crucifixion, Jesus told the daughters of Jerusalem not to weep for him but for themselves and their children (Luke 23:28). Paul himself acknowledged that people mourned, although given the imminence of the parousia he called on them to live as though not mourning, just as the happy should live as though there was nothing to be happy about (1 Cor 7:30). In contrast, Jesus told the widow of Nain (Luke

7:13) and the crowd mourning Jairus's daughter (8:52) not to weep. Mourning could be taken as a sign of doubt in the resurrection. It is little wonder that Stoic *apatheia* could prove to be so appealing to Christians.

Just as there are issues in classical scholarship about considering consolation as a distinct literary genre, so too in early Christian scholarship.[158] Scourfield notes the ways in which Cyprian's work is distinct from the other works Favez considered in that it was earlier than the others, was not addressed to or about an individual, was not in the epistolographic or epideictic traditions, and was harsher and more demanding than the others.[159] He identifies the purpose of the text as follows: "Cyprian is concerned to combat the undermining of religious convictions and appropriate Christian behavior that the plague has caused."[160]

At the heart of deliberative oratory was concern to persuade people to adopt a future course of action that was advantageous or resist a future course of action that was disadvantageous based on what was expedient or impractical and honorable or dishonorable.[161] In *De mortalitate* Cyprian wanted those in his community who had succumbed to doubts and fears brought about by the pandemic to make a fresh commitment to their faith and to be untouched and unmoved by the disaster swirling around them. Thus, he was less concerned about bringing comfort to those in mourning over the loss of loved ones than he was to bring comfort to those who lived with anxiety about their own destinies. This does not make the work other than consolatory, but consolatory as understood in a somewhat, but not altogether different, way from what those in the wider Greco-Roman world held it to be. Indeed, as we noted in the extract provided above, Pontius used the verb *console* when referring to this pamphlet,[162] thereby identifying a consolatory element to it. What makes Cyprian's consolation different from any classical antecedent is that he was not focusing as much on the attitude of the living concerning their dead loved ones as on the attitude of the living concerning their own lives. His consolation was of the more confronting variety. Yet, while I agree with the main thrust of Scourfield's comment that "loss, and the grief resulting from it, are of minimal significance, sympathy and consolation are thus not called for," I think he uses consolation in a modern, soft sense.[163] This he justifies by noting that not only does Cyprian show no compromise in rejecting grief as appropriate for Christians, but that non-Christian consolation literature, despite its emphasis on the irrationality of grief, did indulge in it in practice.[164] Thus, he characterizes Cyprian's work as more correctly *anticonsolatio*.[165] I would not go as far as Scourfield in making quite such a contrast, given that, as he noted, there are similarities between Cyprian and classical consolation literature in that grief is something in which not in indulge. Cicero in his *Tusculanae disputationes* and the younger Seneca in his *De consolatione ad Marciam*, for example, did present this harsh, rational kind of consolation, even if not as extreme as Cyprian did. While it is true that "his comfort is the cool, cerebral comfort of Christian truth,"[166] we should not undervalue that the comfort offered in the classical tradition was at times the cool comfort of Stoicism. The uncompromising nature of Cyprian's attitude was different in degree rather than in kind from the rest of consolation literature. If Cyprian did not turn to as many of the commonplaces of consolation rhetoric as used by earlier, non-Christian writers, it was because, in the face of widespread and overwhelming disease, he wanted to highlight a contrast between the attitudes a Christian ought to have, informed from the scriptures, and those held by the non-Christians around them. It was an unyielding faith in Christian promise that Cyprian sought to reiterate that left no room for sorrow and regret.

STRUCTURE OF THE PAMPHLETS

If we accept that Cyprian brough his rhetorical skills to bear in composing his pamphlets and that *Ad Demetrianum* has a forensic purpose and *De mortalitate* a deliberative one, we can discern a structure for both works that reflects what would have been devised by the author himself.[167]

A. *Ad Demetrianum*

The structure of this pamphlet has not been the subject of much scholarly hypothesizing. Earlier English translations offered nothing by way of comment on the work's structure. In his recent English translation, Allen Brent divides the pamphlet into various sections, but does not offer an explanation about how those various sections are related in a coherent whole.[168] He groups sections 1–2 together, 3–4, 5–11, 12–16, 17–20, and 21–26 as a conclusion. Gallicet offered nothing by way of proposal about the overall structure of the work, although he noted that the work is structured around addressing two points: that the world is old that and God punishes the non-Christians for the evil they have committed, most of which he considers under the heading of idolatry.[169] Fredouille discerns a preamble (1–2) and a three-part main body (3–16, 17–22, and 23–26). In the first part the charges that the Christians were the cause of evil in the world because they had forsaken the gods were refuted (3–11) and non-Christians denounced for satisfying their hatred in persecution (12–16). He sees the second part as a description and explanation of Christian patience in the face of persecution and completes the refutation of the charges and the denunciation of persecution (17–22). The third part is a typical but lengthier apologetic call to conversion.[170]

What I offer here is a structure that reflects Cyprian's rhetorical training and sees each part in relation to the whole as part of a forensic argument.

The work opens with an *exordium* (1–2a) in which Cyprian, acting on behalf of his fellow Christians, defended a position that would be seen by Demetrian as discreditable (*turpe*), in that something Cyprian considered honorable (the Christians) was under attack.[171] Addressing Demetrian directly in the opening words of the pamphlet could suggest that he was its imagined reader and that Cyprian was trying to persuade him alone. Yet, Cyprian attacked Demetrian as a vexatious, ignorant, and argumentative individual. Such an approach was hardly likely to repair a long-time acquaintance with whom one had fallen out over Cyprian's adoption of Christianity. It would make sense instead that Cyprian's imagined addressees were all of Carthage's non-Christian population; they, more than Demetrian, were to be the judges of the Christian bishop's persuasiveness. To try to obtain some goodwill from this audience, perhaps Cyprian sought to drive a wedge between Demetrian and his fellow non-Christians, whom Cyprian thought could be persuaded.

If Cyprian could create the impression of Demetrian's obstinacy and pertinacity as a prosecutor and of his own reasonableness and temperance as a defendant in the minds of other non-Christians, whom he also wanted to paint as fair and reasonable in contrast with Demetrian, then Cyprian had a chance to make them attentive and even sympathetic.[172] The fact that the two individuals were of the same social standing and knew each other gave some plausibility to the veracity of Cyprian's assertions about Demetrian's temperament.

There is no more than a passing *narratio* in this pamphlet (2b). Cyprian acknowledged that there were wars, disease, famine, and drought and that the non-Christians held Christians responsible for the presence of these plights (through their lack of participation in the approved religious rituals of empire). Cyprian also acknowledged that a failure on his part to reply to those accusations could give the appearance of agreeing with them.

Then follows the *partitio* or *propositio* (3a), whereby a defense orator outlined the charges against his client and the position he was going to take with regard to those charges, thereby determining the point at issue (*status*), which in this instance would be conjectural: were the Christians responsible for the problems experienced in the world? Cyprian's position was that they were not.[173] What is to be noted, however, is that Cyprian only stated his own position implicitly at this stage in the pamphlet. It is to be noted further that these charges were of a fairly generic nature; they could have been employed at any time during Cyprian's episcopacy. On only a few occasions throughout this work did Cyprian specify that the particular trigger for this outburst of non-Christian antagonism and aggression was the pestilence (10b).

The main body of the pamphlet consists, as one would expect, of *confirmatio* and *refutatio* (3b–22). As is the case with many of Tertullian's works, the two parts are not always clearly distinguished in Cyprian.[174] The focus in the pamphlet is definitely on *confirmatio* rather than *refutatio*; he did not deal with Christian innocence directly but rather with non-Christian guilt. To assert Christian innocence of the charge of being responsible for the ills of the world, Cyprian identified someone else to blame as the central argument in his *confirmatio*. This was not a completely different approach than that used by Tertullian in *Apologeticum*, although Cyprian's work is far from being merely a rehash of Tertullian's.

In that earlier work, Tertullian had announced his *partitio* or *propositio* as being to demonstrate Christian blamelessness and to lay the blame at the feet of non-Christians.[175] The main body is an alternating pattern of *refutatio* and *confirmatio* (4–45) of the four main charges against Christians: Thyestean feasts (cannibalism and, to compound the charge, infanticide)[176] and incest (7–9), sacrilege (10–27), and treason (28–45).[177] The first two are dealt with conjecturally and the second two qualitatively.[178] With the first two charges, Tertullian showed that the basis of the accusation against Christians was merely rumor (7–8) and that non-Christians were the ones responsible for such atrocities (9). To the charge of sacrilege Tertullian retorted that Christians did not worship the gods because they were not gods[179] and to shift the blame onto the non-Christians, non-Christians already knew that they were not gods so their worship of them was hypocritical.[180] On the positive side, Tertullian sought to demonstrate that the Christians worshipped the one, true God (17–21). As to the last charge, Tertullian sought to prove that Christians were indeed loyal to the empire in many ways, just not by sacrifice, and that non-Christians, by offering sacrifice to a man, were in fact showing disrespect to their supposed gods and that even in offering sacrifice non-Christians could still be treasonous (36).

In Cyprian's work, he engaged primarily in *confirmatio*, shifting the blame for the woes of the world onto something or someone else. In terms of his engagement with Tertullian's *Apologeticum*, sections 40 to 45 of that work had the most influence on what Cyprian wrote, but Cyprian reshaped what he read to suit a different purpose.

According to *Rhetorica ad Herennium*, the anonymous handbook on rhetoric written during the last generations of the Roman republic, comparison (*conlatio*) was one of the six issues that an orator could employ in a conjectural issue for a forensic case.[181] Arguing for the defense, an orator would try to show by using comparison that no one else could have done what is alleged or that it is more likely to have benefitted others rather than the defendant. All of this would be to show that someone else could have been responsible. In *De inventione*, the near-contemporary youthful work of Cicero, the division of arguments to be employed in these two parts of a forensic speech are listed as attributes either of a person or of an action.[182] In a conjectural case, under the cause of the action (motive) there are arguments for and against shifting the blame, which amounts to something similar to comparison.[183]

In our pamphlet, Cyprian quickly shifted the blame: Christians were not responsible; these events were a natural part of the world growing old (*senectus mundi*) (3b–4). The disasters occurring in the world were signs. Quintilian, in particular, had written about how an orator would use signs to construct an argument.[184] For Cyprian, the negative changes that were occurring in the world in each of the four seasons, to take but one example, were signs not of Christian culpability but of the in-built path to obsolescence that every educated person, particularly those steeped in Stoicism, knew to be part of the design of creation. Even uneducated people would accept the validity of this argument when they looked at the weakness and growing decrepitude of elderly people (4). As with people, so with the world itself. This contrasts with Tertullian, who, when he considered the natural world, developed an argument that it was Christian prayers that kept the world going and was preventing or delaying its inevitable annihilation.[185]

Cyprian's next argument was along the same lines, but he offered a different suspect. He attempted to shift the blame off Christians and to place it on God or, more precisely, on non-Christians for not worshipping the true God, whose response, as promised in the scriptures, was to punish those responsible (5–22). This effort occupies most of the pamphlet. What Cyprian contended was not that God committed a crime by inflicting these ills upon the world, but that God was delivering justice for the offenses committed by non-Christians. We see Cyprian begin by turning to another of the six issues mentioned by the author of *Rhetorica ad Herennium*: presumptive proof (*argumentum*).[186] This examines other matters, not sufficient in themselves to prove guilt or innocence but, when added to other evidence, could increase certainty. Such presumptive proof could come from the time before, during, or subsequent to the act. So, after some introductory comments (5), by turning to the scriptures, Cyprian was attempting to show that God: had long promised (time before) punishment for those who failed to worship the only God, which had come to pass (time during) (6–7a); had long anticipated (time before) that those punished would fail to respond as they ought, which had come to pass (time during) (7b–8); and had vowed (time before) that when they would respond, while in the punishment of the next world, it would be too late (a yet unfulfilled time subsequent) (9). The idea that non-Christians deserved to be punished for failing to worship God is found in Tertullian's *Apologeticum* (40–41), but the idea that God had long promised such punishment is much more developed in Cyprian, by reference to the scriptures, than in Tertullian. The latter delighted more in presenting the clever retort that if it were the gods who were inflicting ills because of their neglect by the Christians, then they were being unfair in punishing their own worshippers as well.[187]

Of course, this is where Cyprian's argument was at its weakest. Demetrian's response to Cyprian's appeal to Scripture would simply have been to show that the scriptures were unreliable, not independent, and were not a record of divine revelation but fictitious. Given that the jury as envisaged in this instance consisted of non-Christians, already predisposed against accepting the validity of Christianity as an authentic expression of belief in the divine, this would not have been at all difficult for Demetrian to accomplish.[188]

Then follows a more thorough examination of the reasons in this presumptive proof argument for why God is justified in punishing the world. Up until this point the comments had been general ones about failure to worship God; from here on they were more specifically about the persecution of Christians (12–13) and non-Christian idolatry (14–22). He began by highlighting the complaints made by non-Christians. Such complaints had been mentioned in 7, 8, and 9 but here they are fleshed out in more detail. It begins with a deliberative call to action to stop complaining about Christians and realize their own culpability (10a). Among those complaints is the pestilence being caused by Christians, but it is only one among several and is not overly emphasized (10b). This is one of the reasons why I consider this pamphlet to have been written early in the pandemic, before *De mortalitate.* The experience of the outbreak of deadly contagion was not so overwhelming as to be the only topic for discussion. It certainly receives more than a passing reference, in that Cyprian observed that because of the health crisis the true, despicable, and uncaring character of some non-Christians was revealed in their actions. They would have nothing to complain about if only they realized how sinful they were. Cyprian argued that even if God were not punishing non-Christians, things would not be any better because their self-centeredness or sinfulness was damaging to the world and God was not intervening to stop it (10b–11).

This reading differs from that of Gallicet, who argued that in section 10 the complaints of the non-Christians were the results of the effects of the pestilence (and not just other complaints that non-Christians had against Christians). For him this was a sign that the pestilence had been around for some time, longer than we see in *De mortalitate.*[189] I would think that a close reading of what Cyprian wrote at this point indicates that food shortages and inflation were seen not as a result of labor shortages due to the ravages of disease but due to drought, an event not actually caused by the pandemic. I think the more vivid description of the impact of the outbreak that is found in section 14 of *De mortalitate* comes from the longer existence of the pestilence than was the case at the time of writing *Ad Demetrianum.*

Their persecution of Christians is perhaps the most significant demonstration of their sinfulness, offering presumptive proof of non-Christian responsibility for bringing the wrath of God down upon the world (12–13). In *Apologeticum* 44, Tertullian moved from the complaints non-Christians made about the things they had lost to the complaint that they should have made but did not: the loss to society that resulted from the persecution of innocent Christians. However, most of Tertullian's comments about persecution are found in the *exordium*, where he made much of the irrational legal procedure used against Christians (2.10–19). Most defendants denied the charges against them and needed to be tortured in order to confess, but only Christians, who admitted the charge of being Christian but denied the charges of other crimes, were tortured to deny the identity charge. What is more, not only were they not tortured to confess to specific crimes, but those other crimes were accepted as proved simply because of the confession of the name and the torture was ultimately in order for them to deny rather than confess to those crimes! Christians were held to be both the worst of people and deserving of rescue through torture! If they would deny being Christian, there would be no torture at all! For Cyprian it was not so much the inconsistencies of the legal approach that interested him, as it did Tertullian, as much as it was the fact that by committing such an outrage against the Christians, non-Christians showed that truly they deserved divine punishment.[190]

Given that Cyprian knew Tertullian's *Apologeticum*, it is not surprising that he wanted to incorporate as many of the arguments Tertullian had utilized even though they were not all appropriate or necessary for the case he was building against Demetrian. Indeed, given that the memory of what the Christian community had experienced under Decius was still very fresh in the minds of that community, it is little wonder that Cyprian chose to dwell on this topic at some length.

He started by linking persecution with the failure to worship the true God (12a). Then Cyprian employed another of the six topics for dealing with conjectural matters: probability (*probabile*).[191] It was divided into motive and manner of life. Cicero, in looking at arguments from inference, had divided his material into cause of action, character of person, and nature of the act.[192] Quintilian followed suit, dividing the arguments of artificial proof into those concerned with person and those with thing or action.[193] Under action, Quintilian thought that an orator needed to address four questions: why (motive), where (place), when (time), and how (manner). In dwelling on the topic of non-Christian persecution of Christians, Cyprian turned to some of these questions to shape his comments. Cyprian presents arguments from manner (12b) and motive—where he used Tertullian, *Apologeticum* 2 (13).

From here Cyprian turned to the issue of the non-Christian failure to worship the true God as the justification for the divine punishment being inflicted upon the world (14–22), arguing that if the gods existed, they could defend themselves and did not need non-Christians persecuting Christians on their behalf (14). The fact that non-Christians took it upon themselves to punish Christians while the gods did not would seem to indicate that non-Christians were more powerful than their gods. Further, the gods were, in fact, so impotent (as demons) that Christians could and did vanquish them (15). Of course, the two topics of persecution and idolatry are linked and intertwined, and so it is little wonder that Gallicet and Fredouille see sections 12–16 as forming a unity, although I would divide them somewhat differently.[194]

Having laid out his argument that the non-Christian failure to worship God was the reason for the world's calamities, Cyprian inserted a deliberative call to them to change that and to avoid further punishment by converting to Christianity, which was the only way to fulfill their human condition, and by stopping persecutions (16).

This punishment of non-Christian sinfulness was not exacted by the victims of that sin and persecution but by God. Indeed, innocent Christians were nonretaliatory (17–22).[195] Such patience must surely be because they believed that God would punish those actually guilty. The point essentially is about divine punishment for sin rather than just Christian patience in the face of hostility. There was a related issue that needed to be addressed: If God were punishing non-Christians, what was wrong with Christians that they were caught up in it? Even though Christians experienced the same events that non-Christians did, Cyprian regarded these events not as punishment for Christians but a means for them to prove their faith. While Cyprian wanted to assert that God's justice was swift (and there is the veiled reference to the death of Decius in 17 being just such an example), Christians were assured that it would take place in the next life if not in this. This contrasted them with non-Christians, who saw nothing beyond this world (21). All of this was predicted in the scriptures (22). The reward in the next life for Christian patience lived in this leads naturally to the call for the non-Christian to do likewise.

Thus, in this main body of the pamphlet we find two explanations for the coming end of the world that are crafted into arguments to exonerate Christians from charges of being responsible for current disaster: the world is coming to an end as a natural event and/or as a divine punishment for non-Christian failures.

Brent sees section 21–26 as a conclusion, and there certainly is a sense that what we read in 23–26 summarizes arguments presented already.[196] Our anonymous late-republican rhetorical handbook, *Rhetorica ad Herrenium*, stated that the *peroratio* (*conclusio* was the term employed in this work) was the place to summarize, amplify, and appeal to the pity of judge/jury.[197] It begins with another deliberative call for non-Christians to change their ways (23) so that they do not become victims of the divine day of punishment (24–26). It is not a typical forensic *peroratio* in that the arguments for Christian innocence or even non-Christian guilt are not repeated. Instead, the advantages of a non-Christian change of attitude and behavior are held out, as one would expect in a work of a deliberative nature.[198]

B. *De Mortalitate*

Scourfield makes comments about structural elements of this pamphlet without determining a complete framework. He identifies chapters 2 to 6 as dealing with the audience's attitude to their own deaths. Chapters 8 and 9 treat the fact that Christians and non-Christians alike have been falling victim to disease, and that the Christians ought to react with patience and fortitude (10–14). The grief of those left alive is to the fore from chapter 20 on, with a final summary in chapters 25–26.[199]

No other commentator on the work has offered a complete structure either, except for Hannan, and Deferrari, who follows her.[200] Apart from an introduction (1) and conclusion (25–26), they identified two middle sections devoted to death not being feared but welcomed (2–19) and the dead not being mourned (20–24). For them, Cyprian's method of argumentation was simple: he would find relevant passages of Scripture and comment on them and apply them to the topic under discussion. Ruggiero does not offer a structure so much as a summary of the chapters.[201] On such readings, the development of the argument appears somewhat haphazard and random. I think we can find something a little more sophisticated and in tune with Cyprian's approach to argumentation, namely, a rhetorical structure.

The work opens with a brief *exordium* (1a). Its purpose was to win the goodwill of the audience and in deliberative oratory needed only to be brief, according to Quintilian.[202] The opening sentence of the pamphlet is addressed to the entire community and Cyprian wants to praise most of them for having the right attitude. It is probable that the distinction between most and some is exaggerated rather than literal because he wanted to stress that the majority already did what he was going to advocate, indicating that he was right and that the majority would support him. He wanted most of his audience to be on-side from the beginning, even if, as the address unfolded, it became clear to some of them that they were also among the ones being targeted. A positive frame of mind would help them accept criticism rather than reject it.

There is no *narratio* in *De mortalitate*, something Quintilian noted need not be part of deliberative oratory.[203] There is a brief *partitio* (sometimes called *propositio*), that part of a speech where one set out the question to be answered, the position one was going to take, and/or the topics to be discussed (1b). In this instance Cyprian only stated the position he was supporting and promoting: "Let the cowardice of a frivolous mind be curbed with full vigor and by an address derived from the Lord's Scriptures and let the one who has begun already to be a man of God and Christ be considered worthy of God and Christ." There was to be a change of attitude and a change of behavior. This is the action he advocated: a change of attitude; and this was the advantage he was offering if they did as he advocated: God would consider them worthy of eternal life.

From here starts the main body of the pamphlet, divided into a *confirmatio* (2–7) and *refutatio* (8–24). In the first part he sets forth his positive arguments to prove that the person of faith should not be disturbed by the pandemic because such things had been predicted by Jesus and the fact that they are occurring should only perturb the faithless (2–3). His concern is not with the fate of those who died but the attitude of those still living and, in particular, not with their feelings for those who had died but with their concern for themselves and their own fate. Here he sets out the principal advantage of having the correct attitude toward the presence of pestilence: with the world passing away, paradise would be more quickly available for all Christians (2). Thus, there are reasons for a Christian to want to leave this world and there are reasons for a Christian to want to join the next world. At times throughout the pamphlet one perspective may be more to the fore than the other, although both receive due consideration. The just (that is, those who will experience paradise) live by faith (Rom 1:17, quoting Hab 2:4). Simeon from Luke 2 is offered as the scriptural proof that the person of faith welcomes death as the means of gaining access to eternal peace and rest (3). This is contrasted with those who do not have such faith and who cling to life in this world. Rather than speak about the external challenge that civic persecution presents to the living Christian, Cyprian speaks about the internal moral persecution and challenge to a person's character from the devil's temptations to commit the deadly sins as being what living Christians had to face. The implication is that having to face temptations caused anxiety and that if only they were more like Simeon, a man of faith ready to depart this world, they could avoid that anxiety (4). To reinforce the fact that Simeon had the right attitude about longing for a quicker death, Cyprian returns to other scriptural passages for support. John 16:20 contains the teaching of Jesus that joy will be ours when we see Christ, which will only happen after death (5). The problem for some Christians was that they did not trust that the promises of God revealed in the words of Jesus were true (6). The greatest scriptural example of the benefits of leaving this world is Christ himself, who told his disciples to rejoice in his departure from the world (7).

In the second half, Cyprian counters the arguments he heard around him. First, there were those who complained that the pandemic did not discriminate between good (Christian) and bad (non-Christian) people (8), to which Cyprian replies that such trials are tests of endurance for Christians (9–16). The human condition and the vicissitudes of life are shared in common by all, no matter their religious identity, and must be borne with patience and acceptance, especially by Christians, who are under more pressure than non-Christians because of their struggles against the devil. He agrees that believers are to suffer at least as much as nonbelievers and argues that this is proved by the scriptures. He appeals to several scriptural figures (Sirach, Job, Tobit, Abraham, Paul) (9–10, 12–13) and other scriptural passages against grumbling about God (11). Since it has been proved that suffering and sorrow do not discriminate, the Christian is to endure such opportunities for demonstrating their faith, like those examples of old, without complaint or grumbling.

Cyprian then applies the lesson from those scriptural examples to the present condition (14–16), showing that Christians must bear the test of the pestilence not only without complaint but in a welcoming spirit. After a few graphic comments about the impact of the pandemic, Cyprian urges his readers to give thanks for the opportunity the disease presents and not be afraid (14), and to see the death brought by such ravages as a liberation just like the others who embrace the disciplines of Christian living, including those who face persecution (15). In fact, the sweeping illness provides Christians with opportunities to display their virtues.

Second, there were those who complained that those carried off by disease were robbed of the opportunity for martyrdom (17a), to which Cyprian replies that fidelity to God's will is as good as martyrdom (17b–19). God knows the strength of conviction of those claiming to be prepared for future martyrdom, so even if that could not be proved to the rest of the church, that is not important. To demonstrate that God knows what is in the inner depths of a person (their kidneys and heart as Cyprian writes, or heart and mind as we would understand it today, or will and intellect, to avoid the corporeal imagery altogether), he turns to the scriptural passage of the murder committed by Cain (17b). Not only does God know the inner depths of the human person, but it is for people to do the will of God rather than their own, so that they should not have an expectation of martyrdom but an expectation to do whatever it may be that God intends (18). In a direct challenge to the assertion of the imagined objector, Cyprian claims that, in reality, most people when faced with death (and he did not specify martyrdom here) as an expression of God's will are reluctant to embrace it. Cyprian offers the contemporary example of a bishop struck down by the deadly pestilence who prayed for his life to be spared only to be rebuked by the vision of some youth, probably an angel, for his reluctance or cowardice in the face of God's summons through death. No summons from God, even if it were not through martyrdom, was to be ignored or circumvented (19).

Finally, in what appears to be the *refutatio* of a new topic (20–24), Cyprian offers reasons why the dead themselves, who now live with God, are not to be mourned. The fate of the deceased who believe is not a tragedy but a triumph, not a departure but an arrival. Christians could be accused of hypocrisy if they did not actually rejoice when one of their members passes from death into the next life, which was at the heart of Christian belief (20). This belief and the hope it produces is expressed in seven scriptural passages: 1 Thessalonains 4:13–14; John 11: 25–26 (21); Philippians 3:20–21 (22); Genesis 5:24; Wisdom 4:11 and 14; Psalm 83[84]:2–3 (LXX) (23); and 1 John 2:15–17 (24), the last of which warns of the consequences for those whose rejoicing is in this life rather than the next.

The whole work finishes with a *peroratio* (25–26) in which the main points are revisited and the final appeal to agree with his perspective offered. Using the metaphors of the crumbling house and the battered ship, the latter of which had appeared at the start of the pamphlet, Cyprian could remind his readers that the deadly pestilence was proof that the world was coming to an end and that they should be glad of the opportunity to escape from it (25). Switching from departure to destination, Cyprian reminds his readers of the joyful reunion with loved ones that awaits them in the next life.

THE TEXT OF THE PAMPHLETS

This is the first English translation of these two treatises of Cyprian from the 1976 text of Simonetti provided in CCL apart from Brent's translation of *Ad Demetrianum*. While the text of *De mortalitate* does not differ in too many respects from the 1868 text of Hartel in CSEL, a new translation and commentary is desirable because of the advances in Cyprian studies since Hannan's translation of 1933 (reprinted in the 1958 FC volume), which was based upon Hartel's and used the Rheims-Douay translation of Scripture. Prior to that we depended upon the translation of Ernest Wallis found in the 1868 vol. 8 of Roberts and Donaldson's Ante-Nicene Christian Library series (in vol. 5 of Coxe's 1886 American reprint in Ante-Nicene Fathers), which followed the text in Migne.[204] I am forever grateful to the diligent work conducted by Hannan in her dissertation of nearly a century ago. Many of my comments are built upon hers, although most of the comments about the differences between Cyprian's late Latin and more classical expressions have been omitted here.

In this translation I have been able also to consult the three Italian translations of Ruggiero, Cerretini, and Gallicet and the French translation of Fredouille. There is extensive commentary offered in them, only a little of which I have been able to incorporate here.

Numbers in square brackets in the translation indicate the pages in CCL 3A. Words in square brackets have been added where required for sensible English expressions.

TO DEMETRIAN

(Ad Demetrianum)

[35] 1. I had paid no heed to you, Demetrian,[1] while you were barking and shouting frequently against God, who is one and true, with your sacrilegious mouth and irreverent words, judging it more restrained and better to spurn one ignorant through error with silence than to provoke the frenzy of the deranged by speaking.[2] And I was not doing this without the authority of divine instruction, since it is written, *Refuse to say anything in the ear of a fool lest he ridicule your intelligent words when he has heard them.*[3] And again, *Refuse to answer a fool according to his foolishness lest you become like him.*[4] Also, we are directed to preserve within our personal knowledge[5] whatever is holy and not expose it to be trampled upon by swine and dogs, as the Lord utters, saying, *Do not give holy things to the dogs nor cast your pearls before swine, lest they trample them under their feet.*[6]

For when you came to me, often with more enthusiasm for contradicting than with a pledge to learn,[7] and preferred shamelessly to force your own point of view, bellowing with thunderous utterances rather than patiently to listen to our own,[8] it appeared silly to engage[9] with you, because it would be easier and less burdensome to quell the agitated waves of a turbulent sea[10] by roaring than to curb your ferocity with discussion.[11] Without doubt, to offer light to the blind, speech to the deaf, and wisdom to the irrational is a useless undertaking with no result, given that the irrational is not able to understand, the blind is not able to receive light, and the deaf is not able to hear.[12] 2. Considering these things, often I fell silent and conquered impatience with patience, because I was not able to teach the unteachable nor restrain the irreverent with divine scruples,[13] nor hold back the furious person with moderation.

However, the truth is that when you say that many are complaining, laying the fault on us[14] because wars are developing one after another,[15] because scourges,[16] because famines rage,[17] and because long cloudless days hold back the showers and rain,[18] it is not right to be silent any longer, lest the fact that we are silent[19] begin now to be a matter not of restraint[20] but of reticence, and lest, while we avoid refuting false accusations, we seem to acknowledge the crime.[21]

Therefore, I respond to you, Demetrian, [36] and equally to the others whom perhaps you have incited[22] and whom, by sowing hatred against us by your slanderous utterances,[23] you have made many companions for yourself who have sprouted from you, the root and origin.[24] Still, I believe they will admit[25] the rationality of our speech. For the one roused to evil after being deceived by a lie will be roused to good much more by the truth.

3. You said that all those things by which the world[26] is shaken and oppressed[27] have come about through us and that the fault ought to be laid on us because your gods were not being worshipped by us.[28]

In the first place, you, who in this regard are a stranger to divine inquiry and a foreigner to the truth,[29] ought to know that the present age now has grown old[30] and does not maintain that strength that it had maintained previously and does not thrive with the same vigor and firmness by which it prevailed before.[31] Even with us being silent and producing no examples from the sacred scriptures and from divine foretellings, the world itself says this and attests to its decline by the proof of its collapsing situation. In winter the number of showers is insufficient to nourish seeds.[32] In summer the usual scorching heat of the sun is insufficient to ripen crops.[33] Thus, neither are the springs pleasing with regard to their temperature,[34] nor are the autumns truly abundant with trees bearing fruit.[35] Slabs of marbles are mined less from overgouged and worn-out mountains,[36] exhausted mines furnish fewer resources of silver and gold, and the meager veins are reduced day by day.[37] And the farmer in the fields is decreasing in number and disappearing,[38] [so too] the sailor on the sea, the soldier in the camp, integrity in the forum,[39] justice in the court, harmony in friendships,[40] expertise in the trades,[41] control in behavior.[42]

Do you suppose that the nature of a thing ebbing away is able to present itself as robust as it was able previously when still young and in youthful vigor? Whatever is sinking to its twilight and last moments with its end now close must be diminishing.[43] Thus, the sun in its setting shines with less radiance and burning splendor.[44] Thus, the moon, with its horns fading, wanes as its path fades away.[45] The tree, which before had been verdant and fruitful, later, when its branches have withered, becomes barren, deformed by old age. The fountain, which previously used to cascade forth in abundance from its overflowing channels, barely trickles with a drop of moisture in its failing old age. This judgment has been passed on the world. This is the law of God,[46] that [37] everything begotten perish and everything matured grow old[47] and the strong be weakened and the great be diminished, and that when they have been weakened and impaired they are at an end.

4. You lay the fault for everything being diminished as the world grows old on the Christians. What if the elderly also laid the fault on the Christians that they have less strength in old age, that, similarly, they are not as vigorous in the hearing of their ears as before, in the speed of their feet, in the sharpness of their eyes, in the firmness of their strength, in the vitality of their internal organs, in the strength of their limbs?[48] And that, whereas once the longevity of human life proceeded beyond eight or nine hundred years, now it is barely able to reach a total of one hundred?[49] We see gray hair in children, hair falls out before it grows, the span of life does not end with old age but begins with old age.[50] Thus, even in its begetting, birth hastens to its end;[51] thus, whatever now is born degenerates with the old age of the world, such that no one ought to be surprised that everything in the world has begun to fail when the whole world itself is now in collapse and at its end.[52]

5. In addition, you ought to know that this was predicted: that wars follow one after another; that barrenness and famine increase anxiety; that good health is broken by raging disease;[53] that the human race is devastated by the ravages of the scourge;[54] and also, within the last days,[55] evils are multiplied and obstacles are diversified.[56] Now, with the day of judgment approaching, the reproval of an aggrieved God[57] is roused more and more to the affliction[58] of the human race.[59] For these things eventuate, as your false complaints and ignorant unfamiliarity with the truth boast and shriek, not because your gods were not being worshipped by us,[60] but rather because God is not being worshipped by you.[61]

For God[62] is lord and director of the world,[63] and all things are governed by the divine[64] will and command, and nothing is able to happen except that which God has done or has allowed to happen.[65] Certainly, when those things happen that show the anger of an aggrieved God, they happen not on account of us, by whom God is worshipped, but are imposed by your faults and culpable actions, through which God is neither sought nor feared at all.[66] Nor is true attentiveness to God[67] learned [by you] nor the empty cults[68] forsaken, in order that only the one who is the one God for everyone be worshipped and petitioned by everyone.

6. Indeed,[69] hear God[70] speaking, God [38] instructing us with the divine voice and warning, *You shall pay homage to the Lord, your God,* God says,[71] *and serve only God.*[72] And again, *There shall not be other gods for you apart from me.*[73] And again, *You must not go about after foreign gods in order to serve them and do not pay homage to them and do not incite me regarding the work of your hands to destroy you.*[74] The same prophet, filled with the Holy Spirit, bears witness and threatens the anger of God, saying, *The Lord, the almighty, says this, "Because my house has been abandoned, while each of you follows his own house, for this reason heaven will withhold the dew and earth will take away its productiveness, and I shall bring a sword upon the earth and upon the grain and upon the wine and upon the oil and upon people and upon the flocks and upon the labors of their hands."*[75] Another prophet recalls this and says, *"And I shall make it rain upon one city and upon one city I shall make it not rain. One part shall be rained upon and the part upon which I shall not have made it rain will wither. And two and three cities will assemble in one city in order to drink water and will not be satisfied. And you are not turning to me," says the Lord.*[76]

7. Behold, the Lord is indignant and irate[77] and threatens because you are not turning to God.[78] And you are dumbfounded or complain in this stubbornness[79] and contempt of yours if the rain falls from above infrequently, if the earth is encrusted by a deposit of dust,[80] if the barren soil barely produces hungry and pale grass,[81] if the pelting hail damages the vine,[82] if the destructive swirling tempest[83] topples the olive tree, if drought halts the fountain, if a noxious[84] stench contaminates the atmosphere, if sickly illness devours humankind.[85] Yet, all those things come as a result of sin.[86]

In addition, God is enraged more when such numerous and significant events accomplish nothing.[87] For the same God declares in the holy writings that those things happen either for the correction[88] of the disobedient or the punishment of evil people,[89] saying, *In vain I have struck your children; they have not undertaken correction.*[90] And the prophet, who was devoted and dedicated[91] to God, responded to these the same way and said, *You have beaten them and they have not felt remorse, you have whipped them and they have not wished to accept correction.*[92] Behold, [39] afflictions have been imposed from heaven but there is no fear of God. Behold, beatings and whippings from above are not absent but there is no panic, no dread. What if even that reproval did not intervene in human affairs? How much greater yet would human audacity be, untroubled in the immunity of its outrages?[93]

8. You complain that the overflowing fountains, the wholesome atmosphere, the frequent rain, and the fertile earth now render less servility[94] to you because the elements[95] are not devoted in this way to your advantage and delight.[96] For [actually] you are slave to the God through whom all things are devoted to you and you attend to the one at whose signal the universe attends to you.[97] You yourself exact servitude from your slave and you compel a person to yield to and obey you, a person. Although you share the same fate with regard to being born,[98] the one situation with regard to dying,[99] an identical bodily composition, a common rationality of souls,[100] and either you may come into that same world or pass from the world afterward by an equal right and the same law, yet, unless he serves you according to your will,[101] unless he yields in servility to your inclination,[102] you, as the overbearing and ruthless extorter of servitude, whip, you beat, you afflict and mistreat with hunger, thirst, nakedness, and frequently with the sword and imprisonment. And you do not acknowledge God as master while you yourself enforce mastery in such a way, do you?

9. Therefore, it is right that neither the whippings nor beatings of God are absent in the assaulting afflictions.[103] Although these things accomplish nothing here nor turn individuals to God by means of such terror of carnage, afterward the eternal prison and the everlasting flame and perpetual punishment awaits.[104] And the moaning of supplicants[105] will not be heard there because here was not heard the terror of the indignant God, who declares and says: *Hear the word of the Lord, children*[106] *of Israel, because the judgment of God is against the inhabitants of the earth insofar as there is neither mercy nor truth nor knowledge of God upon the earth. Curse and lie and murder and theft and adultery have spread upon the earth, they mix blood with blood. Therefore, the earth will grieve with all its inhabitants, with the beasts of the farm, with the serpents of the earth, with* [40] *the birds of the sky, and the fish of the sea will fail. Let no one give judgment, let no one object.*[107]

God says that the divine self[108] is indignant because there is no knowledge of God on earth, and God is not known or feared. God rebukes and rejects the faults of lying, lust, fraud, cruelty, lack of respect, and fury, yet no one is turned to integrity.[109] Behold, those things are taking place that were foretold before by the words of God, yet no one is persuaded, on account of faith in the present moment, to consider the future. Among those troubles themselves, by which the constricted and confined soul[110] barely breathes, there is room for people to be evil and in such great dangers as not to appraise themselves but the other. You are indignant[111] that God is indignant, as if you deserved something good by living badly, as if all those things that occur still are less burdensome than your sins.

10. You who judge others, be also a judge of yourself before it is too late. Inspect the recesses of your conscience.[112] More to the point, examine yourself, you who yourself are seen as transparent and naked by others, because already there is actually no shame about doing wrong and thus sin is committed as if there is more satisfaction through the sins themselves. For you are either puffed up with pride or grasping with greed or raging with resentment or generous with gambling or wasted from wine or malevolent with malice or polluted with passion or violent with viciousness.[113]

Are you amazed that the anger of God grows in the punishment[114] of the human race when what is punished grows daily?[115] You complain that an enemy bestirs itself as if, although an enemy be lacking, peace would be able to exist among the toga wearing.[116] You complain that an enemy bestirs itself as if, although foreign arms and the dangers from barbarians be subdued,[117] the weapons of domestic onslaught from false accusations and the injustice of powerful citizens would run riot more fiercely and oppressively from within. You complain about the barrenness and famine as if drought produces a more extensive famine than rapacity, as if the blaze of destitution does not grow more monstrously from seizing increases in the grain supply[118] and from the escalation in price.[119] You complain that the sky is obstructed from producing showers, although the storehouses on earth are obstructed in the same way.[120] You complain that less is being produced as if what has been produced is being made available to the needy. You blame [us] for the curse and scourge [of the pestilence], although the offenses of individuals either are detected or increased by means of the curse and scourge themselves, while mercy is not shown to the weak and greed and robbery drool in anticipation over the deceased.[121] In the observance of respect,[122] the same people [41] are timid, reckless in irreverent profit, fleeing the corpses of the dying[123] and grasping for the pickings from the dead, such that it is evident that the wretched have been abandoned in their affliction, perhaps even for this [very] purpose, that they may not be able to evade [death] by being treated, for he who takes possession of the property of the dying wished the afflicted to expire.

11. So great a terror of carnage is unable to impart training[124] in integrity and, among a people dying from repeated havoc, no one considers themself to be mortal. Everywhere there is running about, there is snatching, there is taking possession; there is no hiding of the pillaging, no hesitation, as if it were permitted, as if it were the right thing to do, as if the one who does not snatch experiences his own damage and loss.[125] Thus, each one hastens to snatch.

Among thieves at any rate, there is some shame for their transgressions. They prefer remote gorges and forsaken wilderness[126] and so offenses are committed in those places, such that the outrage of the offending nevertheless is concealed by darkness and night.[127] [By contrast, here] greed rages in the open and, protected by its very audacity, flaunts the weapons of its uncontrolled craving into the light of the marketplace. As a result, scammers,[128] poisoners, murderers in the middle of the city plunge into sinning as they sin without consequence.[129] The crime is admitted by the guilty, but no innocent person is found who would seek vindication.[130] There is no fear of the accuser or the informer.[131] The evil achieve immunity while the restrained are silent, witnesses are afraid, and those who are to pass judgment are able to be bought.

And therefore, let the truth of the matter be brought out into the open through the prophet by means of the divine spirit and by inspiration. It is demonstrated by a reliable and obvious account that God is able to prevent difficulties, but the just deserts of those sinning cause God not to intervene. *Can it be, he says, that the hand of God does not prevail to produce safety, or the ear be overpowered that God does not hear? But your sins make the separation between you and God, and on account of your faults God averts the divine face from you lest there be mercy.*[132] And so, let the sins and faults be reflected upon, let the wounds to the conscience be pondered. And each one would stop complaining about God [42] or us, if one were to understand that what one suffers is deserved.

12. Behold, this is the very issue itself, about which the discussion with us exists: that you attack us,[133] the innocent, that you assail and oppress the servants of God in derision of God.[134] It is of little importance that your life is tainted by a variety of crazed vices, by the wickedness of fatal[135] crime, by acquisition from bloodstained robbery, that true divine scruples are toppled by false superstitions,[136] that God is neither sought nor feared at all.[137]

Even more, you demand[138] unjust persecutions against the servants of God, who are dedicated to God's[139] majesty and divine will. It is not enough that you yourself do not worship God, even more you persecute with sacrilegious attacks those who do worship. You neither worship God nor permit God to be worshipped at all.[140] Although others who not only venerate those stupid idols of yours and images made by human hands[141] but also certain oddities and monsters[142] are pleasing to you; only the worshipper of God displeases you. Everywhere the ashes of sacrificial victims and the funeral pyres of animal flocks smolder in your temples and the altars of God do not exist or are hidden.[143] Crocodiles, baboons, stones, and serpents are worshipped,[144] and only God is either not worshipped on earth or is not worshipped without punishment.[145]

You deprive the innocent, the just, and those precious to God of a home, you strip their inheritance, you clasp them in chains, you lock them in prison, you punish them with beasts, sword, and fires. You are not even content with acquisitions from our suffering and with the simple and swift brevity of the punishments. You add lengthy torments by mutilating the bodies, you increase the extent of the trauma by tearing at the vital organs.[146] Your brutality and inhumanity is not able to be satisfied by the usual torments; your ingenious cruelty contrives new punishments.[147]

13. What is this insatiable madness for butchery? What is this unquenchable lust for savagery? Why not choose for yourself one of the two: either to be a Christian is a crime or it is not. If it is a crime, why do you not kill the one who confesses it?[148] If it is not a crime, why do you persecute the innocent? For I ought to be tortured if I were to deny it. If, afraid of your punishment, I were to conceal by a beguiling lie what I had been before[149] and that I had not worshipped your gods, then I ought to have been tortured,[150] [43] then I ought to be driven to the confession of the crime[151] by the impact of pain, just as in other investigations those who deny that they ought to be held accountable for the crime of which they are accused are tortured in order that the truth of the outrage, which is not disclosed by the informing voice, be extracted by the suffering of the body.

Now, however, when I confess and declare and testify willingly with the constant and continuously repeated words that I am a Christian, why do you add torments to the one who confesses and to the one who refutes your gods not in hidden and secret places[152] but openly and publicly, in the forum itself in the hearing of magistrates and governors?[153] Even if your earlier charges against me had been insufficient, that which you ought to hate and punish more has grown,[154] because, while I proclaim myself a Christian in a crowded place with people gathering around, I am upsetting both you and your gods through a plain and public proclamation. Why do you turn your attention to the infirmity of the body, why do you concern yourself with the feebleness of earthly flesh? Engage with intellectual vigor, overcome the mind with strength, demolish the faith, conquer by debate if you can, conquer by reason.[155]

14. Indeed, if there is some divinity and power in your gods, let them present their own redress themselves, let them defend themselves with their own divine dignity.[156] Failing that, what are they able to supply to their worshippers if they are not able to avenge themselves on those who are not worshippers?[157] For if the one who avenges is more powerful than the one who is avenged, you are greater than your gods. However, if you are greater than those whom you worship, you ought not to worship them but to be worshipped by them. Thus, your redress defends them when they have been offended, just as also your guardianship[158] protects the enclosed[159] lest they be destroyed. You should be ashamed to worship those whom you yourself defend. You should be ashamed to hope for guardianship from those whom you guard.

15. O, if only you would wish to hear and see them when they are compelled by oath by us, sent spinning by spiritual lashes, and flung out from possessed bodies by the bombardment of words, when, shrieking and moaning from a human voice and experiencing whippings and beatings from the divine power, they confess the judgment about to come.[160]

Come and learn that what we declare is true. Since you say that you worship the gods in such a way, at any rate believe in those whom you worship. Or, if you wish to believe yourself also, the one who now has possessed your breast[161] and who now has blinded your mind with the nocturnal darkness of ignorance will speak from within you yourself[162] with you hearing it. You will see that we are petitioned by those [44] whom you petition, feared by those to whom you pay homage. You will see that they, whom you admire and venerate as lords, stand bound and tremble as captives under our hands. Certainly, thus also will you be able to be bewildered in those errors of yours when you see and hear that your gods immediately abandon what they are through our interrogation and that, although in your presence, they are not able to disguise those deceptions and their tricks.

16. Therefore, what weakness of mind is it, or rather, what blind and stupid derangement of the foolish,[163] not to come from darkness to light[164] and, bound with the snares[165] of eternal death, refuse to accept the hope of immortality and not to dread the threatening words of God: *He who sacrifices to the gods, unless it is to the Lord alone, shall be totally destroyed*[166] and again: *They have paid homage to those whom their own fingers have made, and the human being has been bowed down and the man has been debased. And I shall not relent toward them?*[167] For what reason do you debase and bend yourself to false gods? For what reason do you bow your captive body down before stupid images and earthly inventions?

God made you upright and, although other animals are bent over and reach down to the earth in a low, sinking position, there is an exalted condition for you and his expression is raised to heaven and to his[168] Lord.[169] Gaze in that direction, direct your eyes in that direction, search for God above. In order that you may be free from the things below,[170] lift up your fretful breast to the celestial heights.[171] For what reason do you lie prostrate with the serpent whom you worship in the fall of death?[172] For what reason do you sink into catastrophe through and with the devil? Protect the exalted position with which you were born. Preserve yourself in such a way as you were made by God.[173] Align your intellect[174] with the condition of your mouth and body. In order that you may know God, know yourself first.[175] Abandon the idols, which human error invented.[176] Turn to God who will rescue if you implore. Believe in Christ whom the Father sent to revivify and renew us.[177] Stop striking the servants of God and of Christ, whom divine redress defends when they are offended, through your persecutions.

17. For that is why when detained none of ours resists, nor do our people, although so numerous and plentiful,[178] take their own retribution themselves against your unjust violence.[179] Assurance in the redress that is to come makes us patient.[180] The innocent submit to the guilty, the harmless give way to the punishments and ill treatments certain and assured that whatever we endure does not remain unpunished [45] and that, however great the injustice of the persecution, the more just and serious the vengeance for the persecution will be.[181] Nor does the transgression of the irreverent ever take action against our name[182] that is not followed immediately by vengeance from heaven.

Let us pass over the ancient histories in silence and not refer back with any publicity of words to the often repeated redresses on behalf of the worshippers of God.[183] The example of a recent event is enough that our defense, which recently followed so swiftly—and in such swiftness so powerfully—is [shown] in the catastrophe of human affairs, in the squandering of resources, in the loss of soldiers, in the depletion of military camps.[184] Let no one suppose that this happened by some accident or regard it as fortuitous, since the divine Scripture already long ago recorded and said: *"Vengeance is mine, I shall repay," says the Lord,*[185] and let the Holy Spirit forewarn again and say: *Do not say, "I shall avenge myself against my enemy," but wait for the Lord that he may help you.*[186] From this it is clear, as well as obvious, that all these things, which befall us from the indignation of God, happen not through us but for us.

18. For that reason, while they themselves also seem to be impaired by the assault of the events, do not let anyone think that Christians are not avenged when these things have happened.[187] It is the one whose every joy and renown[188] is in the world who experiences the punishment that comes from the troubles of the world. That one, for whom it is not possible for things to go right after this present age, mourns and weeps,[189] if it were to go wrong for him in the present age. For that one, the enjoyment of everything in life is contained in this place; for that one, solace reaches its limit in this place; for that one, a perishable and brief life includes moments of sweetness and delight in this place. When that one has gone away from this place, all that remains is only punishment leading to suffering.

Yet, there is no suffering from the assault of the present evils for those who have trust in future good things. In point of fact, we are not overwhelmed by troubles, neither are we broken, nor do we suffer, and we do not mutter either in any events of carnage or in any illness of our bodies.[190] Living by the spirit more than by the flesh,[191] [46] we conquer the weakness of the body by the strength of the soul.[192] We know and trust that we are being tested and strengthened by the very things that harrow and overwhelm you.

19. Do you think that we endure these troubles equally with you when you see that the same troubles are not withstood equally by us and by you? With you there is always rowdy and whining impatience, with us there is a strong and scrupulous[193] patience, always calm and always grateful to God. It does not avenge itself here in any joyful or profitable way, but, meek and mild[194] and steadfast[195] against all the swirling tempests[196] of the wave-tossed world,[197] it waits for the time of the divine promise.[198] In as much as we share this body in common

with others, it is necessary that its bodily situation be common[199] and it is not allowed for those of the human race to be separated from one another[200] unless one is passing away from this side of the present age. Meanwhile, we are confined, good and evil, within one house.[201] Whatever might have come into the house we endure with equal allocation until, when the limit of the temporal age has been reached, we are distributed to the lodgings either of eternal death or of immortality.

Therefore, on that account, we are not your partners and equals even though, having been placed in that world and this flesh, we come up against the disadvantages of the world and of the flesh equally with you. For, since everything is punished with a sense of suffering, it is obvious that the one whom you see does not suffer with you does not share in your punishment.[202]

20. The strength of hope and the firmness of faith[203] thrive among us and, among the very catastrophes of the present age of decline, the mind is raised and courage is fixed[204] and patience is never not joyful and the intellect[205] is always assured concerning its God. It is just as the Holy Spirit says and exhorts through the prophet, fortifying the firmness of our hope and faith through the heavenly voice. *The fig tree,* he says, *will not produce fruit and nothing will be growing in the vineyards. The operation of the olive will be deceptive and the open lands will not supply food. Sheep will have nothing for grazing and there will be no cattle in the feedlots. I,*
[47] *however, will exalt in the Lord and rejoice in my saving*[206] *God.*[207]

He denies that the person of God and the worshipper of God, relying on the truth of hope and established on the steadfastness of faith, is disturbed by the houndings of this world and of the present age. Although the vine may disappoint and the olive may mislead and the open field may wither with its grasses dying from the burning drought, what is this to Christians?[208] What is this to the servants of God whom paradise[209] summons, whom every grace and asset of the heavenly kingdom awaits? They always exalt in the Lord and are glad and rejoice in their God and live bravely with the evils and troubles of the world while they look forward to future good and favorable things. For we, after abandoning our earthly birth,[210] are revived and renewed by the Spirit[211] and now we live not for the world but for God and unless we have come to God, we shall not take possession of the gifts and promises of God.[212]

Nevertheless, for the hindering of enemies and for the successful petitioning of showers and for the removal or moderating of opponents we petition always and pour forth prayers, and we pray continually and insistently soothing and appeasing God by day and by night for your peace and salvation.[213]

21. Thus, let none flatter themself in the meantime, because of the equality of the flesh and the body,[214] that there is a common condition for us and the outsiders,[215] the worshippers of God and the opponents of God, in the struggles of the present age, such that they think from this that not all those things that happen are imposed upon you. This is because, by the foretelling of God's very self[216] and by prophetic testimony,[217] it has been foretold earlier that the anger of God would come upon the unjust, that persecutions, which injure us on the human level, would not be lacking, but also that redresses to protect those injured would follow on the divine level.

22. And how great are the things that are happening for us here in the meantime! Let a particular example be given in order that the anger of God as avenger be recognized.[218] However that may be, the day of judgment is coming, which the holy scriptures announced saying: *Howl! For the day of the Lord is near and demolition will arrive from God. For behold, the day of the Lord, unstoppable*[219] *in its indignation and anger, comes to render the globe forsaken and to destroy the sinners from it.*[220] And again: *Behold the day of the Lord comes blazing like an oven and all those who do not belong*[221] *and all the wicked will be like straw, and the day coming* [48] *sets them on fire, says the Lord.*[222]

The Lord prophesies that those who do not belong will be set on fire and burned, that is, those who do not belong and are outsiders to the divine race, those not renewed spiritually and not created children[223] of God. For in another place, God mentions that only those who have been renewed and signed with the sign of Christ are able to escape.[224] When sending his angels for the devastation of the world as well as the human race, [God] threatens more seriously about the last day,[225] saying: *Go and strike down*[226] *and you must not avert your eyes. You must not have mercy on the elderly or the young, slaughter the unmarried girls and the married women and the small children in order that they be annihilated. However, all who have the sign written on them, you shall not touch.*[227]

Moreover, what this sign is and where on the body it is put, God reveals in another place, saying: *Cross through the middle of Jerusalem and you will observe the sign on the forehead of the men who are moaning and mourning on account of the wicked deeds that are committed among them.*[228] And that this sign relates to the suffering and blood of Christ and that whoever is discovered with this sign is preserved safe and unharmed is proved also by the testimony of God who says: *And the blood upon the houses in which you will be in that place will be a sign for you, and I shall see the blood and shield you. When I target the land of Egypt the afflictions*[229] *of contraction will not be upon you.*[230] What went before in the guise[231] of the slain lamb is fulfilled in reality in the Christ who came later.[232] Just as then, when Egypt was targeted, the Jewish people were not able to escape except through blood and the sign of the lamb, so also when the world begins to be devastated and targeted only whoever will be discovered with the blood and sign of Christ will escape.

23. Therefore, while there is time, consider true and eternal salvation.[233] Since the end of the world now is near,[234] turn your minds to God through fear of God. Do not let that powerless and empty domination of yours take pleasure in the present age with regard to the just and the meek, [49] when even in the field the weeds and oats dominate among the cultivated and fertile crops.[235] Nor should you say that evil things take place because your gods are not worshipped by us, but you should know that this is the anger of God, this is the censure <of God>, such that the one who is not understood from kindnesses indeed may be understood from afflictions. Seek God, even this late, because some time ago already God, forewarning through the prophet, urged and said: *Seek God and your soul will live.*[236] Recognize God, even this late because the coming Christ advises and teaches this, saying:[237] *This moreover is eternal life, that they may recognize you as the only and true God and Jesus Christ whom you have sent.*[238] Believe in the one who does not deceive at all. Believe in the one who foretold all these things as going to happen. Believe in the one who will give to those who believe in God the reward of eternal life.[239] Believe in the one who will impose on unbelievers the eternal traumas in the blazes of Gehenna.[240]

24. What glory there will be then for fidelity,[241] what punishment for treachery when the day of judgment will come! What joy for believers, what sorrow for the treacherous[242] who previously were unwilling to believe in this place and now are unable to return in order to believe! Gehenna, always blazing, and its unappeasable punishment will incinerate the doomed in its unending flames, from which it will not be the case that the torments will be able ever to have rest or limit.[243] Souls are kept with their bodies in an endless harrowing of suffering.

The one who here watched us for a time will be watched always by us there. The brief enjoyment by cruel eyes in the persecutions that took place will be counterbalanced by the perpetual vision [of you] according to the faith of the holy scriptures, which say: *Their worm will not die and their fire will not be extinguished, and they will be in the vision of all flesh.*[244] And again: *Then the just will stand with great resolution against those who have crushed them and who have swept away their toils. Seeing this, they will be flustered by a terrible fear and will be bewildered by the suddenness of this unexpected safety [for the just], saying among themselves, having regret*[245] *and moaning through their crushed spirit, "These are those whom we held* [50] *in derision at one time and as a model of insult. We the irrational regarded their lives as madness and their end as dishonorable. In what way have they been counted among the children of God and their fate among the holy? Therefore, we have wandered from the path of truth and the light of justice has not shone for us and the sun has not risen for us. We have exhausted ourselves on the path of wicked deeds and destruction and have walked in troublesome wilderness while we were ignorant of the path of the Lord. What has pride gained for us or what has boasting in riches brought to us? All these things have passed from existence like a shadow.*[246]

Then the suffering of punishment will be without the fruit of regret,[247] wailing will be pointless, and pleading will be ineffectual. They believe in eternal punishment too late who have refused to believe in eternal life.

25. Therefore, provide for your assurance and life while it is permitted. We offer you the helpful service of our intellect and advice. And because it is not permitted for us to hate, and thus we please God more by paying back nothing in exchange for injury,[248] we exhort, while the opportunity is available, while something of the present age survives, to make amends[249] with God and emerge into the radiant light of true divine scruples[250] from the depths of gloomy superstition.[251] We are not jealous of your advantages, nor do we keep [you] in the dark about divine benefits.[252] We pay back your hatred[253] with kindness and, instead of the torments and traumas with which you inflict us, we show the passage of salvation.[254] Believe and live[255] and rejoice with us for eternity, you who are persecuting us for a time. By the time there has been a passing away from here, there is no place for regret,[256] no accomplishment of redress. Here, life is either lost or held; here, eternal salvation is provided for by the worship of God and the fruit of faith. May no one be delayed either by sins or years that they may not come to the acquisition of salvation. For the ones still remaining in this world, no penitence[257] is too late.

Access to the pardon[258] of God is open and, for those seeking and understanding the truth, admittance is easy. Although you entreat and implore God, who is one and true, by admitting and trusting in knowledge of God,[259] on behalf of your own faults at the end of life and at the sunset of time, forgiveness is given to the one admitting, and saving pardon is granted to the one believing by means of the divine [51] tenderness, and there is a passing over to immortality at the moment of death itself.

26. Christ imparts this grace, he presents this gift of his mercy by conquering death with the victory of the cross, by buying back[260] the believer for the price of his own blood, by reconciling the human person with God the Father, by bringing mortals back to life by heavenly regeneration.[261] Let all of us follow this one if it is possible to do, let us be counted through his oath[262] and sign. This one opens the way of life for us, this one brings about the restoration to paradise, this one leads to the kingdoms of heaven.[263] With him we shall live always, having been made children of God through him, with him we shall rejoice always, having been renewed by his blood. We Christians shall be glorious with Christ at the same time as blessed from God the Father, rejoicing from perpetual delight always in the sight of God and giving thanks to God always. For no one will be able to be other than always happy and grateful who, having been liable to death, has been given assurance through immortality.

THE DEADLY PESTILENCE

(De mortalitate)

[17] 1. Among most of you,[1] most beloved brethren,[2] there is an unyielding resolve,[3] a constant faith, and a committed spirit[4] that is not disturbed at the extent of the present deadly pestilence[5] but rather, like a solid and steadfast rock,[6] smashes the tempestuous assault of the world and the violent waves of the present age[7] and is not itself smashed and is not conquered but proved[8] by testing.[9]

Nevertheless,[10] since I notice that some among the people stand less bravely and do not demonstrate the divine and invincible firmness in their heart either through a fragility of spirit,[11] a paucity of faith, the pleasures of life in the present age, softness of gender,[12] or, more importantly, uncertainty about the truth,[13] the situation ought not to be ignored or left unmentioned but, to the extent our meager ability is capable,[14] let the cowardice of a frivolous mind[15] be curbed with full vigor and by a speech[16] derived from the Lord's scriptures[17] and let the one who has begun already to be a person of God[18] and Christ be considered worthy of God and Christ.[19]

2. For the one who is a soldier for God[20] and who now exudes[21] divine things since he has been stationed in the heavenly camp, most beloved brethren,[22] ought to come to know himself again in order that there be no terror, no turmoil[23] for us at the storms and swirling tempests[24] of the world, since the Lord foretold through the urging of his prophetic utterance, which was instructing and teaching and preparing and also fortifying[25] the people of his church to endure everything that would happen, that these things would eventuate. He foreshadowed and predicted that wars, famines, earthquakes, and pandemics would reach everywhere.[26] He forewarned[27] earlier that difficulties would become more and more frequent in the last times, lest an unexpected, new[28] fear of damaging situations shake us.[29]

See, the things spoken about are happening! Since the things foretold earlier are happening, whatever has been foretold will follow as well, as the Lord himself promises, saying, *Further, when you see that these things are happening, you will know since the reign of God is near.*[30] The reign of God, most beloved brethren,[31] has begun to be near. [18] The reward[32] of life, the joy of eternal salvation, perpetual happiness, and possession of paradise lost in our own time[33] arise now by means of the passing away of the world.[34] Now heavenly things are replacing earthly ones, great things the small, and eternal things the temporary.

What place is here for anxiety and concern? Who is alarmed and gloomy in the midst of this except the one who abandons hope and faith?[35] For it is theirs to fear death who do not want to go to Christ. It is theirs to not want to go to Christ who do not believe themselves to be beginning to reign with Christ.[36] 3. It is written that *the just person lives by faith.*[37] If you are just and live by faith, if you believe truly in God, you who are going to be with Christ and who are confident in the promise of the Lord, why do you not welcome the fact that you are called to Christ and do not give thanks that you are free from the devil?

Indeed, Simeon,[38] that just man who was truly just, who kept the commandments of God with complete faith, when the answer from heaven had been given to him that he would not die before he had seen the Christ and when the infant Christ had come into the temple with his mother,[39] recognized in his spirit that the Christ now was born, about whom he had been foretold earlier. When he had seen him, he knew that he was going to die before long. And so, glad about the nearness of death and welcoming being summoned[40] soon, he took the child in his hands and, blessing God, he lifted his voice and said, *Now you are sending your servant away in peace, Lord, according to your word, because my eyes have seen your salvation.*[41] This certainly proves and is evidence that at that moment there is peace for the servants of God, at that moment freedom, at that moment still calmness, when, once rescued from those swirling tempests[42] of the world, we make for home and the safety of an eternal harbor and when, once stung with death,[43] we come to immortality. For that is our peace, that is our certain stillness, that is our steadfast, firm, and perpetual safety.[44]

4. For the rest,[45] what is waged daily in the world except a fight against [19] the devil?[46] What is contested except with incessant struggles against its javelins and spears?[47] The battle for us is with greed, with impurity, with anger, with ambition. The unending and incessant conflict is with sins of the flesh, with the enticements of this present age.[48] The human resolve, having been assailed on every front by the

damage[49] of the devil and having been hemmed in, hardly puts up a single fight, hardly resists.[50] If greed is knocked out of the way, the libido swells. If the libido is constrained, ambition takes its place. If ambition is disregarded, anger irritates, pride inflates, intoxication beckons, spite[51] splits harmony, jealousy tears apart friendship.[52] You are forced to blaspheme, which the divine law prohibits.[53] You are compelled to swear your allegiance, which is not permitted.[54] 5. The intellect[55] suffers daily such a great number of persecutions,[56] the heart is hit by such a great number of perils. Does it even cherish remaining here at length among the devil's swords?

Instead, it ought to long for and wish to hasten to Christ through being helped by a sooner death. He himself instructs us saying, *Amen, amen, I say to you, since you will weep and mourn, while the present age*[57] *will rejoice. You will be sad, but your sadness will turn to joy.*[58] Who would not want to be without sadness? Who would not hurry to come to joy? However, about the time when our sorrow turns to joy, the Lord himself once more declares, saying, *I shall see you again, and your heart will rejoice and no one will steal your joy from you.*[59] Therefore, since to see Christ is to rejoice, and since our joy is unable to exist unless one has seen Christ,[60] what blindness of spirit, or what madness[61] it is to love the oppressions and punishments and tears of the world and not prefer to hurry to the joy that may never be stolen!

6. But this occurs, most beloved brethren,[62] because faith is abandoned, because no one believes that the things the truthful God promises are true. God's word is eternal and constant for those who believe.[63] If an important[64] and praiseworthy man were promising you something, you would have confidence in his promise and would not [20] believe yourself to be cheated or to be misled by him whom you would know to stand by his words and deeds.[65] God is talking to you and are you tossed about on the waves,[66] deceitful in your unbelieving resolve?[67] God promises immortality and eternity when you depart this world[68] and are you doubting? This is not to accept God at all. This is to offend Christ, the teacher of what to believe, by the sin of disbelief. This is, for one who has been established in the church, not to have faith in the house of faith.[69]

7. Christ himself, the teacher of our salvation and advantage, shows how much of a benefit it is to escape[70] from the present age.[71] It was he, when his disciples were depressed[72] because he told them that now he was about to depart, who spoke to them, saying, *If you had loved me you would rejoice since I am going to the Father.*[73] He was teaching

and showing that when the loved ones we cherish escape[74] from the present age we should rejoice more than grieve. Mindful of this, the apostle Paul sets it down in his letter and says, *To me, to live is Christ and to die is profit.*[75] He was calculating that the greatest profit is now not to be possessed by the snares of the present age, is now not to be taken as guilty of the sins and vices of the flesh, since we have been released from the throttling oppression and freed from the venomous jaws of the devil to go forth into the joy of eternal salvation when Christ calls.[76]

8. But it disturbs some[77] that[78] the illness from such a disease sweeps away our people equally with nonbelievers,[79] as if a Christian in this situation were to believe that, immune from contamination[80] from evil things, one may enjoy happily the world and present age[81] and, without having endured all adversity here, be destined for future joy. It disturbs some that we share such a deadly pestilence with others. In fact, what do we have in this world that we do not share with others inasmuch as we continue to share this flesh according to the law of our first birth?[82] As long as we are here in the world we are joined[83] with the human race[84] by an equality of the flesh, [although] separated in spirit. And so, until this perishable nature puts on imperishability and this mortal nature receives immortality[85] and the Spirit leads us to God the Father,[86] whatever the maladies of the flesh are, we share them [21] with the human race. Thus, when the earth is barren because of a meager crop,[87] famine excludes no one. Thus, when some city has been seized because of hostile attacks, captivity devastates everyone together. And when bright clouds[88] hold back the rain, the same drought is there for all.[89] And when the jagged rocks[90] wreck a ship, the shipwreck is shared without exception by those sailing. And eye complaints, bouts of fever, and all illness in the limbs we share with others inasmuch as that shared flesh is borne in the present age.[91]

9. In fact, instead, if Christians[92] were to recall and comprehend in what agreement and in what law they have believed, they would know that they must be adversely affected more than others in the present age[93] and must grapple more with the onslaught[94] of the devil. The divine Scripture teaches and forewarns, saying, *Son, when you come into the service of God, stand firm in justice and fear and prepare your spirit for testing.*[95] And further, *Continue in sorrow and in your humility be patient because gold and silver are proved in fire.*[96]

10. Thus, Job, after the loss of property, after the burial of his children, and also having been afflicted severely with wounds and worms, was not conquered but proved.[97] It is he who shows in his struggles and

sorrows themselves the patience of his committed resolve and says, *I emerged naked from my mother's womb. I shall go naked as well into the ground. The Lord gave and the Lord swept away. As it seemed to the Lord, so it happened. May the name of the Lord be blessed.*[98] When his wife also was pushing him in order that, impatient at the intensity of his sorrow,[99] he might say something against God to speak with complaining and loathing utterance, he responded and said, *"You have spoken as though you were the same as the foolish women. If we have received good things from the hand of God, shall we not put up with bad?" In everything that happened to him Job did not sin with his lips in the sight of God.*[100] And so, the Lord God gives witness, saying, *Have you noticed Job, my servant? For there is no one like him on earth, a man without complaint, a true worshipper of God.*[101]

Tobit, after his excellent works, after the many glorious demonstrations of his mercy, suffering [22] blindness, fearing and praising God in his difficulties, grew in praise through the very carnage to his body. His wife too attempted to test him saying, *Where are your works of justice? See what you are suffering!*[102] But he was steadfast and firm[103] in his fear of God and was armed for all endurance of suffering by the faith of his religion. He did not yield in his sorrow to the testing by his weak wife but instead gained God by his intense patience. Later, the angel Raphael commends him and says, *It is honorable to reveal and acknowledge the works of God. For when you*[104] *and Sarah prayed, I offered the memory of your prayer in the presence of the radiance of God. Since you buried the dead without qualification and because you did not delay to rise and forego your lunch and go out and inter the dead,*[105] *I was sent also to test you. God sent me a second time to cure you and Sarah, your daughter-in-law, for I am Raphael,*[106] *one of the seven holy angels, we who stand and dwell before the radiance of God.*[107]

11. The just have always had this endurance. The apostles possessed this discipline from the law of the Lord: not to grumble in their difficulties[108] but to accept bravely and patiently whatever happens in the present age,[109] although the Jewish people always violated this because frequently they were muttering against God, as the Lord God attests in Numbers, saying, *Let their muttering finish before me and they will not die.*[110] We must not mutter in our difficulties, most beloved brethren,[111] but must bear whatever will happen patiently and bravely, since it is written, *A broken spirit is the sacrifice to God. God does not despise a broken and humble heart.*[112] In Deuteronomy let the Holy Spirit advise through Moses and say, *The Lord your God will harass you and will inflict you with famine and will examine in your heart if you have observed his*

commands or not.[113] And again, *The Lord your God tests you in order to know if* [23] *you love the Lord your God with your whole heart and with your whole soul.*[114]

12. Thus, Abraham pleased God because, in order that he might please God, he did not fear to lose his son nor did he refuse to engage in parricide.[115] You who cannot lose your son by the law and the lottery of the deadly pestilence, what would you do if you were ordered to kill your son? The fear of God and faith ought to make you ready for everything. Even though it may be from the loss of one's possessions, it may be from the unrelenting and bloody aggravation of your limbs from the damaging[116] disease, it may be from a funerary and sorrowful rupture from your wife, your children, or loved ones passing over,[117] but let them be hostile encounters not offensive to you.[118] Do not let them cripple or break a Christian's faith, but rather let them reveal courage[119] in the bout, since every injustice from the present evils ought to be disregarded by a trust in the good things to come. Unless the fight has come first there cannot be a victory. When there has been victory in the conflict of the fight, then a crown is given as well to the winners. A helmsman is singled out in the violent weather, in the battleline a soldier is proved.[120] Boasting is frivolous when there is no peril, the struggle in adversity is the proof of truth. A deep-rooted tree is not disturbed by the howling winds[121] and a solidly constructed ship is struck by waves but not shattered.[122] And when the threshing-floor separates the harvest, the firm and solid seeds disregard the wind, the hollow husks are carried off by the supporting breeze.[123]

13. Thus also the apostle Paul, after his shipwrecks,[124] after his whippings,[125] after the many painful tortures of his flesh and body,[126] says that he is not aggravated but improved by adversity, in order that, while he is afflicted more painfully, he may be proved more genuinely. *A thorn in my flesh,* he says, *was given to me, an angel of Satan who beats me lest I be exalted. Three times I begged the Lord about it in order that it may leave me, and he said to me, "My grace is sufficient for you. For courage*[127] *is being completed in frailty."*[128] Therefore, when some frailty and fragility and devastation runs riot,[129] then your courage is being completed, then faith is crowned if it has withstood being tested, just as it is written, *The furnace proves the potter's vessels and* [24] *the test of tribulation [proves] just people.*[130]

Finally, this is the difference between us and those ignorant of God: that they complain and mutter in adversity. Adversity does not divert us from the truth of courage and faith but confirms us in sorrow.

14. This results in a demonstration of faith because the bowels, having been loosened in diarrhea, discharge the strength of the body, because the burning fever that comes from deep within surges up[131] into ulcers in the throat, because the intestines convulse with continual vomiting, because the eyes burn[132] with the throbbing of blood, because the feet of some or some other parts of limbs are removed by the infection of sickly[133] putrefaction, because by means of the feebleness[134] that takes over, through the losses and deprivations of the body, either the ability to walk is crippled or the ability to hear is blocked or the ability to see is blinded.[135]

It is such an intensity of feeling to battle against so great an attack of devastation and death with an unshaken[136] courage[137] of spirit and it is such a nobleness of character to stand up straight among the ruins of the human race and not lie prostrate with those who have no hope in God, to give thanks instead, and to embrace the opportunity of these times, because, while we are displaying our faith firmly[138] and, by having put up with that hardship, are proceeding to Christ along Christ's narrow path,[139] we may grasp the reward[140] of his life and faith according to his own judgment.[141]

Clearly, one may fear to die who, not having been reborn from water and the Spirit,[142] is surrendered to the fires of Gehenna.[143] One may fear to die who is not registered with the cross and suffering of Christ. One may fear to die who will traverse from this death to a second death. One may fear to die whom the eternal flame will torture[144] with perpetual punishments when one departs from the present age.[145] One may fear to die to whom this is bestowed after a longer delay, such that their anguish and groaning is deferred in the meantime.[146]

15. Many of us are dying in this deadly pestilence, that is, many of us are being freed from this present age.[147] This deadly pestilence is a curse for Jews and Gentiles[148] and the enemies of Christ. It is a passing over[149] to salvation for the servants of God. With regard to the fact that the just also are dying with the unjust without any discrimination in the human race, you ought not to think that violent death is common to bad and good. The just are called to refreshment, the unjust are carried off to torment.[150] Protection is given more rapidly to the faithful, punishment to the deceitful. We are unthinking and ungrateful, most beloved [25] brethren,[151] about the divine kindnesses nor do we recognize what is being bestowed upon us. See the virgins passing over[152] in peace, protected by their glory, not fearing the threats, allurements, and brothels[153] of the coming[154] antichrist.[155] Boys are

evading the peril of the vulnerable age.[156] They are coming happily to the reward[157] for their restraint and innocence. Now a refined[158] wife does not fear tortures since, by her speedy death, she has been spared the fear of persecution and the hands and the cruelty of the torturer.[159] Through panic at the deadly pestilence and these times, the frightened are enflamed, the inattentive are held in check,[160] the cowardly are enlivened, the deserters are compelled to return,[161] the nonbelievers[162] are forced to believe, the old people among the faithful are called to rest, and a fresh and numerous army with a stronger firmness is being assembled at the battle line and, having been added to the campaign in the time of the deadly pestilence, will fight without fear of death when the hostile encounter comes.[163]

16. Further, most beloved brethren,[164] what a remarkable thing that is, how relevant, how necessary that such a curse and scourge,[165] which seems awful and fatal,[166] investigates the justice of each person and examines the resolve of the human race to see whether the healthy tend the frail, whether people cherish their relatives dutifully, whether masters are compassionate toward their flagging slaves, whether doctors are not neglecting the ill who call out for help, whether the cruel constrain their violence, whether the rapacious extinguish the ever insatiable intensity of their ferocious greed even through fear of death, whether the proud bend their necks,[167] whether the outrageous moderate their audacity, and whether the rich when near death give generously and donate when their dying loved ones leave them heirless![168] Even if this deadly pestilence has bestowed nothing else, its greatest benefit to Christians and servants of God is that we begin to desire martyrdom gladly,[169] while we learn not to fear death. Those things are training exercises for us, not burial rites. They give the glory of fortitude to the spirit. They prepare for the crown by a contempt for death.[170]

17. But possibly someone may object and say, "This then depresses me regarding the present deadly pestilence, that I, who had been prepared for confession and had vowed myself to the endurance of suffering with my whole heart and full courage,[171] am robbed of my martyrdom since I am preempted [26] by death."[172] In the first place, martyrdom is not in your power but in the special favor of God[173] and you are not able to say that you have lost that which you do not know whether you deserve to receive. Then, in the next place, God is the searcher of the kidneys and of the heart[174] and the observer and investigator of secret things,[175] [God] sees you and praises and approves

you and [God], who perceives that courage has been prepared in you, gives a reward for your courage.[176]

Surely Cain had not slain his brother when he offered his tribute already to God?[177] And yet God with foresight condemned the fratricide[178] before it was conceived in his mind. Just as in that case the evil thought and destructive plan was anticipated by a foreseeing God, so also in the servants of God, with whom confession is considered and martyrdom is conceived in the mind, the spirit dedicated to good is crowned by God as judge.[179] It is one thing that the desire for martyrdom is absent, it is another thing that martyrdom was absent for the desire.[180] The Lord also judges in the same way as he finds you when he calls, since it is God indeed who testifies and says, *And all the churches will know that I am the searcher of the kidneys and of the heart.*[181] For God does not seek our blood but our faith. For neither Abraham, Isaac, nor Jacob was killed and yet, honored for the merits of their faith and justice, they have deserved to be first among the patriarchs to whose banquet is gathered whoever is found faithful, just, and praiseworthy.[182]

18. We ought to remember that we ought to do not our will but God's, in accordance with what the Lord ordered us to pray daily.[183] How distorted it is and how perverse, that, although we ask that the will of God be done, when God calls and summons us from this world, we do not submit immediately to the sovereignty of [God's] will![184] We struggle and resist and, in the custom of stubborn slaves, we are led into the presence of the Lord with sadness and mourning, departing[185] from here by means of the chain of necessity, not the acquiescence of inclination.[186] And we want to be honored with heavenly rewards[187] by the one to whom [27] we are coming reluctantly. Therefore, why do we pray and demand that the kingdom of heaven come if earthly captivity entices? Why do we ask and beg by means of frequently repeated prayers that the day of the kingdom hasten if there are greater desires and stronger commitments[188] to serve the devil here than to reign with Christ?[189]

19. Finally, in order that the proofs of divine providence may be made clear more plainly that the Lord, having foreknowledge of future things, looks out for the true salvation of his own: when one of our colleagues and fellow bishops,[190] weak from sickness and apprehensive about his approaching death, implored for a reprieve[191] for himself, a young man, venerable in honor and majesty, of upright bearing and radiant appearance, whom human vision of the one standing near

him was scarcely able to behold with fleshly eyes, except the one about to withdraw from the present age[192] who now was able to see, stood next to the one praying who was now almost dead.[193] And not without some anger in his mind and voice he yelled and said, "Are you afraid to suffer? Do you not wish to escape? What shall I do with you?" The rebuking and admonishing voice, which is attentive[194] to persecution and untroubled about being summoned, does not consent to the present desire but considers the future.[195] Our brother and colleague about to die heard what he was to say to others. For he who heard when he was about to die, heard for this purpose in order that he speak: he heard it not for himself but for us. For what might he learn at that time when about to pass over? On the contrary, he learned for those remaining behind in order that, now we have discovered that the bishop[196] who was begging for more time was rebuked, we may recognize what benefits everyone.

20. To us ourselves, the least and last, how often it has been revealed, how frequently and obviously it has been commanded from the special favor[197] of God, so that I may be called to witness continually and so that I might proclaim publicly: that our brethren[198] who have been freed from the present age[199] by being summoned by the Lord are not to be lamented, since we know that they are not lost but sent ahead;[200] that the departing[201] precede, as travelers, as navigators are accustomed to do; that they ought to be missed not mourned; nor ought black garments to be put on here [28] since they have obtained white robes there;[202] [and] that no opportunity be given to the nonbelievers[203] that they blame us deservedly and justly insofar as we lament those who we say live with God as wiped out and lost, and insofar as we do not demonstrate by means of the testimony of heart and breast[204] the faith, which we produce in speech and utterance![205] We are violators of our hope and faith when those things that we say seem to be make-believe, false, and contrived. There is no benefit in exhibiting courage with words and in demolishing truth with actions.[206]

21. Indeed,[207] the apostle Paul disapproves of, reproves, and blames any who may be depressed by the passing over[208] of those close to them. *We do not wish,* he says, *that you be ignorant, brethren,*[209] *about those sleeping, lest you be depressed just like the others who do not have hope. For, if we believe that Jesus has died and rose again, thus also God will bring those who sleep in Jesus with him.*[210] He says that they who do not have hope are depressed by the passing over[211] of those close to them. However, we who live in hope and believe in God and trust that Christ

suffered for us and rose, who remain in Christ, and who rise through him and in him, why either do we not wish to depart from the present age[212] here or do we mourn and grieve our departing ones[213] as if lost?

Christ himself, our Lord and God, exhorts [us] by saying: *I am the resurrection. The one who believes in me, although he die, will live and everyone who lives and believes in me will not die for ever.*[214] If we believe in Christ let us have faith in his words and promises in order that we who are not to die for ever may come with joyful safety to Christ with whom we are always both to conquer and to reign.[215]

22. Since we die in the meantime, we cross over[216] from death to immortality, and eternal life is not able to come next unless it were granted one to escape[217] here. This is not the end but a transition[218] and, with the passage of time [29] having run its race, a crossing[219] to eternity. Who would not hurry to better things? Who would not long to be changed and reshaped into the likeness of Christ and speedily into the dignity of heavenly grace?[220]

The apostle Paul announces, *Our residence, however,* he says, *is in heaven, from where also we are waiting for the Lord, Jesus Christ, who will transfigure the body belonging to our lowly state and give it a form like that of his own radiant body.*[221] Christ the Lord also promises us that we are going to be such, when he entreats the Father for us, in order that we be with him and that we may rejoice with him in the eternal home and heavenly kingdom, saying, *Father, I want those whom you have given to me such that where I shall be they will be with me also and that they may see the radiance that you have given to me before the world was made.*[222]

The one who is to come to the home of Christ, to the radiance of the heavenly kingdom, ought not to lament and mourn but rather, according to the promise of the Lord, according to faith in the truth, rejoice in this, their going forth[223] and change of abode.

23. Thus finally, we find also that Enoch, who pleased God, had his abode changed, just as divine Scripture testifies and says in Genesis, *And Enoch pleased God and was not found afterward because God transported him.*[224] It was this to have been pleasing in the sight of God: to have deserved to be transported from this infection of the present age.[225] But the Holy Spirit also teaches through Solomon that they who please God are released from here earlier and are liberated sooner lest, while they stay longer in this world, they are polluted by the contaminations of the world: *He was carried off lest wickedness alter his understanding. For his spirit was pleasing to God. On account of this, [God] hurried to draw him out from the midst of iniquity.*[226] Thus also in Psalms the spirit committed

to its God with spiritual faith hurries to God, as it is written, *How highly beloved are your lodgings, God of power. My spirit desires and hurries to the courtyards of God.*[227]

24. It is the wish of one whom the world pleases, [30] whom the blandishing and deceiving present age[228] entices by the spell of earthly delights,[229] to remain in the world a long time. In addition, since the world hates the Christian, why do you love that which hates you and do not follow Christ instead, who has redeemed[230] and loved you? In his letter John declares, says, and urges, lest, pursuing desires of the flesh, we love the world. *Refuse,* he says, *to love the world and the things that are in the world. If anyone will love the world, the affection*[231] *of the Father is not in that person, since all that is in the world is the longing of the flesh and the longing of the eyes and the ambition of the world,*[232] *which is not from the Father but is from the longing of the world.*[233] *Both the world and its longing will pass away. However, the one who will do the will of God remains forever, just as God too remains forever.*[234]

Instead, most beloved brethren,[235] with complete resolve, with firm faith [and] with steadfast courage, we ought to be ready for the entire will of God. Having excluded the fear of death, let us think about the immortality that follows. Let us show that this is what we believe, in order that we may not lament the departure of our loved ones and that we may come unhesitatingly and willingly to the Lord who calls us when the day of our own summons will come.

25. While this always ought to have been done by servants of God, now, with the world already falling apart and beset by the swirling tempests[236] of damaging[237] evils, it ought to happen much more, in order that we, who discern that serious things already have begun and who know that more serious things threaten, may reckon it the greatest gain if we should depart most swiftly from here.[238]

If the walls of your residence were giving way from age, the roof above were shaking, [and] the house, already worn out and already exhausted, were showing signs of collapse before long with the structure having subsided with extreme age, would you not change residence with all speed?[239] If tempestuous and stormy weather,[240] with violent waves having been whipped up, were announcing in advance future shipwrecks to you while sailing, would you not head for port more swiftly? Behold, the world is giving way and subsiding and testifies to its collapse not now from extreme age but from the end of things, and are you not [31] thanking God, are you not congratulating yourself that, having been taken away by a timely exit, you are deprived of collapses and shipwrecks and afflictions?[241]

26. We ought to consider, most beloved brethren,[242] and to ponder frequently that we have renounced the world and wait here in the meantime as guests and foreign travelers.[243] Let us embrace the day, which assigns each their dwelling, which, having snatched us away from here and having released us from the snares of the present age,[244] restores us to paradise and the reign [of God].[245] Who would not rush to return to their residence after having been stationed abroad?[246] Who would not wish more eagerly for a favorable wind to sail quickly to their family in order to be able to embrace their loved ones more swiftly?[247] We reckon paradise as our homeland and have already begun to hold the patriarchs as parents.[248] Why are we not rushing and hurrying in order to see our homeland, in order to be able to greet our parents?

There a great company of our loved ones awaits us: parents, siblings, children. A numerous and abundant crowd yearns for us, secure in their safety, yet concerned for our salvation.[249] How great a shared joy it is both for them and us to come into their sight and their clasp! There what great delight in the heavenly kingdom without the fear of dying and with an eternity of living, which is the highest and perpetual happiness! There the glorious band of apostles! There the exultant company of prophets! There the innumerable multitude of martyrs crowned on account of the glory and victory of their contest and suffering![250] [There] the triumphant virgins who have conquered the desires of the flesh and body by the power of self-control![251] [There] the recompensed merciful who have accomplished works of justice by food and distributions to the poor, who obey the precepts of the Lord and have transferred earthly patrimony to heavenly vaults![252]

To these, most beloved brethren,[253] let us rush with eager enthusiasm and let us desire that it comes to pass speedily that we be with them, that speedily we come to Christ. [32] May God see this as our intention. May Christ, who is going to give more rewards[254] from his charity to those whose desire for him has been greater, behold this proposal of resolve and faith.

NOTES

INTRODUCTION

1. See Anthony Birley, *Marcus Aurelius: A Biography*, 2nd ed. (London: B. T. Batsford, 1987); and Michael Grant, *The Antonines: The Roman Empire in Transition* (London: Routledge, 1994).

2. Kyle Harper, *The Fate of Rome: Climate, Disease, and the End of an Empire* (Princeton, NJ: Princeton University Press, 2017), 98–115. See also R. P. Duncan-Jones, "The Impact of the Antonine Plague," *JRA* 9 (1996): 108–36; and Irwin W. Sherman, *The Power of Plagues*, 2nd ed. (Washington, DC: ASM Press, 2017), 61–62.

3. Harper, *The Fate of Rome*, 65–98.

4. See D. R. Hopkins, *The Greatest Killer: Smallpox in History* (Chicago: University of Chicago Press, 1988); D. A. Koplow, *Smallpox: The Fight to Eradicate a Global Scourge* (Berkeley: University of California Press, 2003); and Michael B. A. Oldstone, *Viruses, Plagues, and History*, 2nd ed. (Oxford: Oxford University Press, 2010), 53–101.

5. Lucretius, *Nat.* 6.1100–1286. See H. S. Commager, Jr., "Lucretius' Interpretation of the Plague," *HSCP* 62 (1957): 105–18; D. E. Bright, "The Plague and the Structure of *De rerum natura*," *Lat* 30 (1971): 607–32; J. H. Dircks, "Pestilence Narratives in Classical Literature: A Study in Creative Imitation: I. Homer, Sophocles, Thucydides, and Lucretius," *American Journal of Dermatopathology* 22 (2000): 197–202; Fernando Rosa, "Lucrezio e il senso della malattia nel *De rerum natura*," *Medicina nei Secoli* 19 (2007): 763–81; and Hunter H. Gardner, *Pestilence and the Body Politic in Latin Literature* (Oxford: Oxford University Press, 2019), 79–112.

6. See Rebecca Flemming, "Galen and the Plague," in *Galen's Treatise Περὶ Ἀλυπίας (*De indolentia*) in Context: A Tale of Resilience*, ed. Caroline Petit, Studies in Ancient Medicine 52 (Leiden: Brill, 2019), 219–44.

7. Eutropius, *Brev.* 8.12.

8. Aelius Aristides, *Or.* 48.

9. Ammianus Marcellinus, *Rerum gestae* 23.6.24.

10. Cassio Dio, *Hist. Rom.* 72.14.3.

11. See Kyle Harper, "Pandemics and Passages to Late Antiquity: Rethinking the Plague of *c.* 249–270 Described by Cyprian," *JRA* 28 (2015):

223–60, who surveys the breadth of evidence about this outbreak beyond Cyprian.

12. See Géza Alföldy, "The Crisis of the Third Century as Seen by Contemporaries," *GRBS* 15 (1974): 89–111. On the reassessment of recent scholarly reaction against the use of the word *crisis* see Wolf Liebeschuetz, "Was There a Crisis of the Third Century?," in *Crises and the Roman Empire*, ed. Olivier Hekster, Gerda de Kleijn, and Daniëlle Slootjes, Proceedings of the Seventh Workshop of the International Network Impact of Empire (Nijmegen, June 20–24, 2006), Impact of Empire 7 (Leiden: Brill, 2007), 11–20; and Clifford Ando, *Imperial Rome AD 193 to 284: The Critical Century*, Edinburgh History of Ancient Rome (Edinburgh: Edinburgh University Press, 2012). See also Caillan Davenport and Christopher Mallan, "Dexippus' *Letter of Decius*: Context and Interpretation," *Museum Helveticum* 70 (2013): 57–73.

13. Harper, *The Fate of Rome*, 122–36.

14. Harper, *The Fate of Rome*, 137. Cf. Tim G. Parkin, *Demography and Roman Society* (Baltimore: Johns Hopkins University Press, 1992), 63–64, on the extent of casualties.

15. Sabine R. Huebner, "The 'Plague of Cyprian': A Revised View of the Origin and Spread of a 3rd-c. CE Pandemic," *JRA* 34 (2021): 151–74. Much of the argument against Harper rests on the question of the dating of Eusebius's letters, which she places about a decade later.

16. Zosimus, *Hist. nov.* 1.26.

17. Eutropius, *Brev.* 9.5. Hostilian, a younger son of Decius, was emperor in the second half of 251, co-ruling with Trebonianus Gallus (251–53), with the latter's son, Volusian, as Caesar. He became Augustus after the death of Hostilian and ruled with his father from 251 to 253 until they were both killed by their own troops before facing the next clamant, Aemilian, who only lasted a few months in 253. Orosius, *Hist. adv. pag.* 7.21.4–6 (CSEL 5.479–80), mistakenly identified Volusian as Hostilian's son. He indicated that the pandemic hit as punishment for Decius's decree, that it occurred while Gallus and Volusian were emperors, and that there was hardly a home in any province of the empire that was not emptied of its inhabitants. Hostilian himself might have died from this disease, as Aurelius Victor, *De Caes.* 30 and the later *Epit. de Caes.* 30 say that Hostilian died from the pandemic (*pestilentia*), although Zosimus, *Hist. nov.* 1.25.2, recorded that Gallus had Hostilian killed in order to promote Volusian. Huebner, "The 'Plague of Cyprian,'" 158, dates Hostilian's death to late August and is undecided about his cause of death.

18. Harper, *The Fate of Rome*, 142–43. This is supported by Amber Lynn Kearns, "A Plague in a Crisis: Differential Diagnosis of the Cyprian Plague and Its Effects on the Roman Empire in the Third Century CE" (master's thesis, University of Arizona, 2018). See Oldstone, *Viruses, Plagues, and History*, 199–206, who does not provide an historical approach. Much of Harper's research is endorsed by Tomasz Skibiński and Maciej Książyk, "Postawa chrześcijan wobec Zarazy Cypriana w świetle źródel epoki," *VP* 78 (2021): 121–40.

19. See William H. McNeill, *Plagues and Peoples* (Garden City, NY: Doubleday, 1976), 136–37; Dionysios Ch. Stathakopoulos, *Famine and Pestilence in the Late Roman and Early Byzantine Empire: A Systematic Survey of Subsistence Crises and Epidemics*, Birmingham Byzantine and Ottoman Monographs 9 (London: Routledge, 2004), 95; and Sherman, *The Power of Plagues*, 62–64.

20. See Lester K. Little, ed., *Plague and the End of Antiquity: The Pandemic of 541–750* (Cambridge: Cambridge University Press, 2007); with caution, William Rosen, *Justinian's Flea: The First Great Plague and the End of the Roman Empire* (London: Penguin, 2007), and Geoffrey D. Dunn, "'For it is improper to be addicted to the tedium of affliction': Christian Responses to Pandemic in Late Antiquity and the Early Middle Ages," *VP* 77 (2021): 247–84.

21. Among the vast wealth of literature, see Rosemary Horrox, *The Black Death* (Manchester: Manchester University Press, 1994); David Herlihy, *The Black Death and the Transformation of the West* (Cambridge, MA: Harvard University Press, 1997); Ole J. Benedictow, *Black Death 1346–1353: The Complete History* (Woodbridge, UK: Boydell Press, 2004); and Joseph P. Byrne, *The Black Death*, Greenwood Guides to Historic Events of the Medieval World (Westport, CT: Greenwood Press, 2004).

22. Pontius, *V. Cyp.* 9 (CSEL 3/1.xcix). My own translation.

23. Eusebius, *Hist. eccl.* 7.22.4–6.

24. Eusebius, *Hist. eccl.* 7.22.7.

25. Harper, *The Fate of Rome*, 137.

26. Thucydides 2.47.3–54.

27. David J. DeVore, "'The Only Event Mightier Than Everyone's Hope': Classical Historiography and Eusebius' Plague Narrative," *Histos* 14 (2020): 12–13 and 19–25. Cf. G. W. Clarke, *The Letters of St. Cyprian of Carthage*, 3: *Letters 55–66*, ACW 46 (New York: Newman Press, 1986), 6, who accepts a later date in the 260s for Dionysius's letters.

28. G. W. Clarke, "Some Observations on the Persecution of Decius," *Antichthon* 3 (1969): 63–76; G. W. Clarke, "Two Measures in the Persecution of Decius? Two Recent Views," *Bulletin of the Institute of Classical Studies* 20 (1973): 118–23; and A. R. Birley, "Decius Reconsidered," in *Les empereurs illyriens. Acts du colloque de Strasbourg (11–13 octobre 1990)*, ed. E. Frézouls and H. Jouffroy, Contributions et Travaux de l'Institut d'Histoire Romaine, Université de Strasbourg 8 (Strasbourg: Civi Romaine, 1998), 57–80.

29. J. B. Rives, "The Decree of Decius and the Religion of Empire," *JRS* 89 (1999): 135–54. See also J. B. Rives, *Religion and Authority in Roman Carthage from Augustus to Constantine* (Oxford: Clarendon Press, 1995). Cf. David S. Potter, *The Empire at Bay, AD 180–395*, Routledge History of the Ancient World, 2nd ed. (London: Routledge, 2014), 622 n. 111, misreads Rives on this point. Cf. Paul Keresztes, "The Decian *libelli* and Contemporary Literature," *Lat* 34 (1975): 761–81, who takes Eusebius at face value and does consider this to have been targeted directly against Christians, as does Reinhard Selinger,

The Mid-Third Century Persecutions of Decius and Valerian, 2nd ed. (Frankfurt am Main: Peter Lang, 2004), who, on 31, explicitly rejects Rives's position.

30. Rives, "The Decree of Decius," 151.

31. Kyle Harper, "Another Eye-Witness to the Plague Described by Cyprian and Notes on the 'Persecution of Decius,'" *JRA* 29 (2016): 473–76.

32. Huebner, "The 'Plague of Cyprian,'" 156–59.

33. As I do with Tertullian, I prefer to describe these writings as pamphlets. I do not mean they are brief and trifling, but in the eighteenth-century sense of a persuasive piece of literature dealing with a current, topical issue. "Treatise" tends to suggest something more comprehensive, systematic, and balanced. I think of the works of authors like Tertullian and Cyprian as something more like blogs rather than handbooks.

34. See Ronald Syme, *Emperors and Biography: Studies in the* Historia Augusta (Oxford: Clarendon Press, 1971); Timothy D. Barnes, *The Sources of the* Historia Augusta, Collection Latomus 155 (Brussels: Latomus, 1978); André Chastagnol, *Histoire Auguste. Les empereurs romains des IIe et IIIe siècles* (Paris: Bouquins, 1994); A. R. Birley, "Rewriting Second- and Third-century History in Late Antique Rome: The *Historia Augusta*," *Classica* 19 (2006): 19–29; and David Rohrbacher, "The Sources of the *Historia Augusta* Re-examined," *Histos* 7 (2013): 146–80.

35. *Hist. Aug. Divus Claudius* 12.2.

36. *Hist. Aug. Divus Claudius* 11.3–4.

37. Cyprian, *Ep.* 56 (CCL 3B.296–99).

38. Cyprian, *Ep.* 56.2.2 (CCL 3B.29).

39. See Cyprian, *Ep.* 55 (CCL 3B.256–95). On the synod see Joseph A. Fischer, "Die Konzilien zu Karthago und Rom im Jahr 251," *AHC* 11 (1979): 263–86; Geoffrey D. Dunn, "The Carthaginian Synod of 251: Cyprian's Model of Pastoral Ministry," in *I concili della cristianità occidentale secoli III–V*. XXX Incontro di studiosi dell'antichità Cristiana, Rome, 3–5 May 2001, SEAug 78 (Rome: Institutum Patristicum Augustinianum, 2002): 235–57; and Geoffrey D. Dunn, *Cyprian and the Bishops of Rome: Questions of Papal Primacy in the Early Church*, ECS 11 (Strathfield, NSW: St Pauls Publications, 2006), 43–48.

40. Cyprian, *Ep.* 56.2.2 (CCL 3B.298).

41. For more detail on the lapsist controversy see Charles A. Bobertz, "Cyprian of Carthage as Patron: A Social Historical Study of the Role of Bishop in the Ancient Christian Community of North Africa" (PhD diss., Yale University, 1988); J. Patout Burns, *Cyprian the Bishop*, Routledge Early Church Monographs (London: 2002); and Allen Brent, *Cyprian and Roman Carthage* (Cambridge: Cambridge University Press, 2010).

42. See Bobertz, "Cyprian of Carthage as Patron."

43. Geoffrey D. Dunn, "Cyprian's Rival Bishops and Their Communities," *Aug* 45 (2005): 61–93.

44. Cyprian, *Ep.* 58 (CCL 3C.319–35). See Nienke Vos, "A Universe of Meaning: Cyprian's Use of Scripture in Letter 58," in *Cyprian of Carthage:*

Studies in His Life, Language, and Thought, ed. Henk Bekker, Paul van Geest, and Hans van Loon, LAHR 3 (Leuven: Peeters, 2010), 65–93.

45. Cyprian, *Ep.* 57 (CCL 3B.300–10).

46. Clarke, *The Letters of St. Cyprian*, 3.4–17, argues that Trebonianus Gallus did not issue any new decree on this matter, although this did not preclude a local campaign against Christians.

47. Cyprian, *Epp.* 57.1.2 (CCL 3B.302); 58.1.2 and 7.1 (CCL 3C.320 and 329); and 60.5.1 (CCL 3C.379). See Clarke, *The Letters of St. Cyprian*, 3.218, n. 9.

48. Cyprian, *Ep.* 57.2.1 (CCL 3B.302). Clarke, *The Letters of St. Cyprian*, 3.219, n. 12, does not seem to consider the pandemic as one of these signs or warnings.

49. Later events, with the formation of break-away communities of laxists and rigorists, and then the controversy about how those who wanted to move between communities were to be received (the so-called "rebaptism" controversy) need not concern us here.

50. Clarke, *The Letters of St. Cyprian*, 3.211, n. 12.

51. Clarke, *The Letters of St. Cyprian*, 3.213–16; Joseph A. Fischer, "Das Konzil im Frühjahr 253," *AHC* 13 (1981): 12–26; Geoffrey D. Dunn, "*Censuimus*: Cyprian and the Episcopal Synod of 253," *Lat* 63 (2004): 672–88; Yvette Duval, *Les chrétientés d'Occident et leur évêque au IIIe siècle.* Plebs in ecclesia constituta *(Cyprien, Ep. 63)*, CEASA 176 (Paris: Institut d'Études Augustiniennes, 2005), 124–25; and Dunn, *Cyprian and the Bishops of Rome*, 102–6. This would mean that the information in *Epp.* 59 and 64 (CCL 3C.336–73 and 418–25), which are of a completely different tone, about the activity of another episcopal synod are best dated to 252. See Joseph A. Fischer, "Das Konzil zu Karthago im Mai 252," *AHC* 13 (1981): 1–11; Clarke, *The Letters of St. Cyprian*, 3.302–303; Geoffrey D. Dunn, "Cyprian and His *Collegae*: Patronage and the Episcopal Synod of 252," *JRH* 27 (2003): 1–13; Duval, *Les chrétientés d'Occident*, 122–23; and Dunn, *Cyprian and the Bishops of Rome*, 90–102.

52. Edward White Benson, *Cyprian: His Life, His Times, His Work* (London: Macmillan, 1897), 258.

53. Mary Louise Hannan, *Thasci Caecili Cypriani—De Mortalitate: A Commentary, with an Introduction and Translation*, CUAPS 36 (Washington, DC: Catholic University of America Press, 1933), 3.

54. Hugo Koch, *Cyprianische Untersuchungen*, Arbeiten zur Kirchengeschichte 4 (Bonn: A. Marcus and E. Weber, 1926), 140–45.

55. This interpretation of there being a second imperial decree, this one from Gallus, ordering another round of sacrifices to be offered is rejected by Clarke, *The Letters of St. Cyprian*, 3.246–47; the most he will concede is that there could have been a local decree.

56. Roy J. Deferrari, *Saint Cyprian: Treatises*, FC 36 (Washington, DC: Catholic University of America Press, 1958), 195–96.

57. Deferrari, *Saint Cyprian*, 165. On a date for the death of Decius later than March 251 see G. W. Clarke, "Dating the Death of the Emperor Decius," *Zeitschrift für Papyrologie und Epigraphik* 37 (1980): 114–16. Potter, *The Empire at Bay*, 242, dates the battle of Abritus, in which Decius was killed, to the summer of 251. Michael M. Sage, *Cyprian*, Patristic Monograph Series 1 (Cambridge, MA: Philadelphia Patristic Foundation, 1975), 267, dates the death of Decius and his elder son and co-emperor, Herennius Etruscus, to June 251. On the significance of the battle see Aleksander Bursche, "The Battle of Abritus, the Imperial Treasury and Aurei in Barbaricum," *Numismatic Chronicle* 173 (2013): 151–70.

58. Giuseppina Stramondo, *Studi sul De mortalitate di Cipriano: Studi, testo e traduzione, index verborum omnium* (Catania: Università di Catania, 1964), 36.

59. Sage, *Cyprian*, 377.

60. Sage, *Cyprian*, 378.

61. Sage, *Cyprian*, 381.

62. Sage, *Cyprian*, 380–81.

63. Sage, *Cyprian*, 273 and 275.

64. Sage, *Cyprian*, 280–81.

65. G. Alföldy, "Der heilige Cyprian und die Krise des römischen Reiches," *Historia* 22 (1973): 486.

66. M. Simonetti, "Sancti Cypriani De Mortalitate," in *Sancti Cypriani episcopi opera*, ed. M. Simonetti and C. Moreschini, CCL 3A (Turnhout: Brepols, 1976), 16; and M. Simonetti, "Sancti Cypriani Ad Demetrianum," in Simonetti and Moreschini, *Sancti Cypriani*, 34.

67. Ezio Gallicet, *Cipriano. A Demetriano*, CP 4 (Turin: Società Editrice Internazionale, 1976), 53.

68. Gallicet, *Cipriano*, 54.

69. Gallicet, *Cipriano*, 56–57.

70. Gallicet, *Cipriano*, 54 n. 5.

71. Antonio Quacquarelli, "S. Cipriano: 'La pestilenza' e la 'Lettera ai Tibariti' sulla preparazione al martirio," in *Morte e immortalità nella catechesi dei padri del III–IV secolo*. Convegno di studio e aggiornamento Facoltà di Lettere cristiane e classiche (Pontificium Institutum Altioris Latinitatis), Rome, 16–18 March 1984, Biblioteca di Scienze Religiose 66 (Rome: Libreria Ateneo Salesiano, 1985), 35.

72. Quacquarelli, "La pestilenza," 37. Reference is made to G. Lomiento, "Cipriano per la preparazione al martirio dei Tibaritani (Ep. 58)," *Annali della Facoltà di Magistero dell'Università di Bari* 3 (1962): 3–35.

73. Quacquarelli, "La pestilenza," 29–30.

74. Clarke, *The Letters of St. Cyprian*, 3.8–14, 204–206, and 213–16.

75. Clarke, *The Letters of St. Cyprian*, 3.11 and 245–47.

76. Clarke, *The Letters of St. Cyprian*, 3.7–8.

77. Clarke, *The Letters of St. Cyprian*, 3.8.

78. Clarke, *The Letters of St. Cyprian*, 3.13.

79. Clarke, *The Letters of St. Cyprian,* 3.215–16. Paul Keresztes, "Two Edicts of the Emperor Valerian," *VC* 29 (1975): 81, accepts that, while there was some targeting of Christians under Gallus, this did not extend to Africa.

80. Mario Ruggiero, *Cipriano, Paolino di Nola, Uranio: Poesia e teologia della morte,* 2nd ed., CTP 42 (Rome: Città Nuova, 1997), 14.

81. Antonella Cerretini, *Cipriano: Trattati,* CTP 175 (Rome: Città Nuova, 2004), 27.

82. Jean-Claude Fredouille, ed., *Cyprien de Carthage. A Démétrien,* SC 457 (Paris: Les Éditions du Cerf, 2003), 13.

83. Fredouille, *Cyprien,* 15.

84. Fredouille, *Cyprien,* 32–33.

85. Clarke, *The Letters of St. Cyprian* 3.228–29, n. 5, suggests the two pamphlets were written before *Epp.* 58 and 57.

86. One can suggest an explanation for why he did not. Since *Ep.* 58 is addressed to the laity in Thibaris, perhaps Cyprian did not expect them to be familiar with his two pamphlets. Perhaps he did not want to return to the question of the pandemic, having dealt with it already. Simply acknowledging it as one of the signs and warnings he had received, he wanted to focus on its implications and requirements for the remaining repentant *lapsi.*

87. Cyprian, *Ep.* 57.1.1 (CCL 3B.301).

88. Cyprian, *Ep.* 57.2.2 (CCL 3B.303).

89. Cyprian, *Ad Deme.* 2 (CCL 3A.35).

90. Cyprian, *Ad Deme.* 5 (CCL 3B.37).

91. Cyprian, *Ad Deme.* 7 and 10 (CCL 3A.38 and 40). In the second of those passages, it must be noted, there is something of an extended reflection on the impact of disease within the local community.

92. See Cyprian, *Ad Deme.* 18 (CCL 3A.45–46), for the sole exception.

93. See Stanley F. Bonner, *Education in Ancient Rome: From the Elder Cato to the Younger Pliny* (Berkeley: University of California Press, 1977); Graham Anderson, *The Second Sophistic: A Cultural Phenomenon in the Roman Empire* (London: Routledge, 1993); George A. Kennedy, *A New History of Classical Rhetoric* (Princeton: Princeton University Press, 1994); M. L. Clarke, *Rhetoric at Rome: A Historical Survey,* 3rd ed., rev. D. H. Berry (London: Routledge, 1996); William J. Dominik, ed., *Roman Eloquence: Rhetoric in Society and Literature* (London: Routledge, 1997); Stanley E. Porter, ed., *Handbook of Classical Rhetoric in the Hellenistic Period 330 B.C.–A.D. 400* (Leiden: Brill, 1997); Erik Gunderson, *The Cambridge Companion to Ancient Rhetoric* (Cambridge: Cambridge University Press, 2009); and Michael J. MacDonald, ed., *The Oxford Handbook of Rhetorical Studies* (Oxford: Oxford University Press, 2017).

94. Pontius, *V. Cyp.* 2 (CSEL 3/1.xci).

95. Pontius, *V. Cyp.* 1 (CSEL 3/1.xc).

96. G. W. Clarke, "The Secular Profession of St. Cyprian of Carthage," *Lat* 24 (1965): 633–38. His point was that appearing in court on behalf of a client simply made one an advocate (legal orator) rather than a lawyer

(legal expert). This does not depend upon the question of how long after his conversion Cyprian became bishop. See Bobertz, "Cyprian of Carthage as Patron," 75–129, who establishes Cyprian as a member of the upper echelons of the local African aristocracy (and on 94 agrees with Clarke about Cyprian's profession as advocate); and Mattias Gassman, "Cyprian's Early Career in the Church of Carthage," *JEH* 70 (2019): 1–17.

97. See S. F. Bonner, *Roman Declamation in the Late Republic and Early Empire* (Liverpool: University of Liverpool Press, 1949).

98. Pontius, *V. Cyp.* 7 (CSEL 3/1.xcvii): *Per quem gentiles blasphemi repercusses in se quae nobis ingerunt vincetentur? A quo Christiani mollioris affectus circa amissionem suorum aut, quod magis est, fidei parvioris consolarentur spe futurorum?*

99. On Tertullian's *Apol.* as forensic, see Louis J. Swift, "Forensic Rhetoric in Tertullian's *Apologeticum*," *Lat* 27 (1968): 864–77; Robert Dick Sider, *Ancient Rhetoric and the Art of Tertullian* (London: Oxford University Press, 1971), 22–23; R. F. Evans, "On the Problem of Church and Empire in Tertullian's *Apologeticum*," in *SP*, vol. 14/3, ed. Elizabeth A. Livingstone, papers presented at the Sixth International Conference on Patristic Studies, Oxford 1971 (Berlin: Akademie-Verlag, 1976), 21–36 (who, probably correctly, sees it as a forensic work with a deliberative twist); Timothy David Barnes, *Tertullian: A Historical and Literary Study*, rev. ed. (Oxford: Clarendon Press, 1985), 107–12; and Geoffrey D. Dunn, *Tertullian*, The Early Church Fathers (London: Routledge, 2004), 45. Cf. Paul Keresztes, "Tertullian's *Apologeticus*: A Historical and Literary Study," *Lat* 25 (1966): 124–33.

100. Augustine, *Serm.* 313C (Guelf. 26).2 (German Morin, *Miscellanea Agostiniana. Testi e studi*, vol. 1: *Sancti Augustini Sermons post Maurinos reperti* [Rome: Tipografia Poliglotta Vaticana, 1930], 531).

101. See Mary B. Cunningham and Pauline Allen, eds., *Preacher and Audience: Studies in Early Christian and Byzantine Homiletics*, A New History of the Sermon 1 (Leiden: Brill, 1998); O. C. Edwards Jr., *A History of Preaching* (Nashville: Abingdon Press, 2004); and Anthony Dupont, Shari Boodts, Gert Partoens, and Johan Leemans, eds., *Preaching in the Patristic Era: Sermons, Preachers, and Audiences in the Latin West*, A New History of the Sermon 6 (Leiden: Brill, 2018).

102. On Scapula see A. R. Birley, "Caecilius Capella: Persecutor of Christians, Defender of Byzantium," *GRBS* 32 (1991): 81–82; and A. R. Birley, "Persecutors and Martyrs in Tertullian's Africa," *IAB* 29 (1992): 53.

103. See Geoffrey D. Dunn, "Rhetorical Structure in Tertullian's *Ad Scapulam*," *VC* 56 (2002): 47–55.

104. Lactantius, *Inst.* 5.4.3–7 (CSEL 19.412). On Lactantius and Cyprian see John A. McGuckin, "Does Lactantius Denigrate Cyprian?," *JTS* n.s. 39 (1988): 119–24.

105. Jerome, *Ep.* 70.3 (CSEL 54.703).

106. Gallicet, *Cipriano*, 63.

107. Gallicet, *Cipriano,* 63.

108. See Stephen Benko, *Pagan Rome and the Early Christians* (Bloomington: Indiana University Press, 1984); Robert M. Grant, *Greek Apologists of the Second Century* (Philadelphia: Westminster Press, 1988); Avery Dulles, *A History of Apologetics* (San Francisco: Ignatius Press, 2005); and Jörg Ulrich, Anders-Christian Jacobsen, and Maijastina Kahlos, eds., *Continuity and Discontinuity in Early Christian Apologetics,* Early Christianity in the Context of Antiquity 5 (Frankfurt am Main: Peter Lang, 2009).

109. There is a vast literature about the emergence of a Christian identity from or alongside Judaism and of the extent of engagement between them. See, for example, Miriam S. Taylor, *Anti-Judaism and Early Christian Identity: A Critique of the Scholarly Consensus,* Studia Post-Biblica 46 (Leiden: Brill, 1995); Adam H. Becker and Annette Yoshiko Reed, eds., *The Ways That Never Parted: Jews and Christians in Late Antiquity and the Early Middle Ages,* Texts and Studies in Ancient Judaism (Tübingen: Mohr Siebeck, 2003); James D. G. Dunn, *The Partings of the Ways between Christianity and Judaism and Their Significance for the Character of Christianity* (London: SCM Press, 2006); and Geoffrey D. Dunn, *Tertullian's* Aduersus Iudaeos*: A Rhetorical Analysis,* North American Patristics Society Patristic Monograph Series 19 (Washington, DC: Catholic University of America Press, 2008).

110. Mark Edwards, Martin Goodman, Simon Price, and Christopher Rowland, "Introduction," in *Apologetics in the Roman Empire: Pagans, Jews, and Christians,* ed. Mark Edwards, Martin Goodman, Simon Price, with Christopher Rowland (Oxford: Oxford University Press, 1999), 1.

111. Simon Price, "Latin Christian Apologetics: Minucius Felix, Tertullian, and Cyprian," in Edwards et al., *Apologetics in the Roman Empire,* 113.

112. Hannan, *Thasci Caecili Cypriani,* v.

113. Hannan, *Thasci Caecili Cypriani,* 2–3.

114. Sage, *Cyprian,* 273.

115. Ruggiero, *Cipriano,* 15.

116. See Han Baltussen, "Introduction," in *Greek and Roman Consolations: Eight Studies of a Tradition and Its Afterlife,* ed. Han Baltussen (Swansea: Classical Press of Wales, 2013), xiv, who offers the following: "a philosophically informed written crystallization of social practice."

117. See F. H. Sandbach, *The Stoics,* 2nd ed. (Bristol: Bristol Press, 1989); Brad Inwood, ed., *The Cambridge Companion to the Stoics* (Cambridge: Cambridge University Press, 2003); Steven Strange, ed., *Stoicism: Traditions and Transformations* (Cambridge: Cambridge University Press, 2004); Tad Brennan, *The Stoic Life: Emotions, Duties, and Fate* (Oxford: Oxford University Press, 2005); and John Sellars, *Stoicism,* Ancient Philosophies 1 (Berkeley: University of California Press, 2006).

118. Michel Meyer, *Philosophy and the Passions: Toward a History of Human Nature,* trans. Robert F. Barsky (Philadelphia: Penn. State University Press, 2000).

119. Thucydides 2.34.

120. Thucydides 2.36–42.

121. Thucydides 2.43–44.

122. James A. Mackin, Jr., "Schismogenesis and Community: Pericles' Funeral Oration," *QJS* 77 (1991): 251–62; C. Sicking, "The General Purport of Pericles' Funeral Oration and Last Speech," *Hermes* 123 (1995): 404–25; A. B. Bosworth, "The Historical Context of Thucydides' Funeral Oration," *JHS* 120 (2000): 1–16; and Julia L. Shear, "'Their Memories Will Never Grow Old': The Politics of Remembrance in the Athenian Funeral Orations," *CQ* 63 (2013): 511–36.

123. Cicero, *Div.* 2.1.

124. Cicero, *Tusc.* 1.9–33.

125. Cicero, *Tusc.* 3.26–28.

126. See Ingo Gildenhard, Paideia Romana: *Cicero's Tusculan Disputations*, Cambridge Classical Journal Proceedings of the Classical Philological Society Supplementary Series 30 (Cambridge: Cambridge Philological Society, 2007).

127. See Susan Treggiari, *Terentia, Tullia and Publilia: The Women of Cicero's Family* (London and New York: Routledge, 2007).

128. See Amanda Wilcox, "Sympathetic Rivals: Consolation in Cicero's Letters," *AJP* 126 (2005): 237–55. One thinks of the letter from Sulpicius Rufus to Cicero on the death of Tullia (*Fam.* 4.5 [248]).

129. Cicero, *Fam.* 4.6 (249).

130. Cicero, *Att.* 12.14 (251).

131. Cicero, *Att.* 12.15 (252).

132. Cicero, *Att.* 12.16 (253); 12.18 (254); and 12.38a (279).

133. Han Baltussen, "Cicero's *consolatio ad se*: Character, Purpose and Impact of a Curious Treatise," in Baltussen, *Greek and Roman Consolations*, 67.

134. Jochen Sauer, "*Consolatio ad Marciam*," in *Brill's Companion to Seneca: Philosopher and Dramatist*, ed. Gregor Damschen and Andreas Heil (Leiden: Brill, 2014), 135–39.

135. Seneca, *Marc.* 2–3.

136. Seneca, *Marc.* 6.

137. Seneca, *Marc.* 12–19.2.

138. Seneca, *Marc.* 19.3–25. Whether he had gone to a painless something or a painless nothing is not clear from Seneca.

139. See Jochen Sauer, "*Consolatio ad Helviam*," in Damschen and Heil, *Brill's Companion to Seneca*, 171–73.

140. Seneca, *Helv.* 1.

141. Seneca, *Helv.* 4.

142. Seneca, *Helv.* 1.

143. Seneca, *Helv.* 5 and 9–12.

144. Seneca, *Helv.* 6–8.

145. Seneca, *Helv.* 13.

146. Jochen Sauer, "*Consolatio ad Polybium*," in Damschen and Heil, *Brill's Companion to Seneca*, 167–69. Given that Polybius could help end Seneca's exile could explain a lot.

147. Seneca, *Poly.* 2.

148. Seneca, *Poly.* 7–8. Again, not far below the surface must be the suggestion that if Polybius did not have enough work to do, helping Seneca secure his recall could be added to the list. Despite what he had said to his mother about a Stoic being able to bear anything anywhere, he did not simply accept whatever fate presented him without making an effort to change misfortune.

149. Seneca, *Poly.* 18.

150. Han Baltussen, "Personal Grief and Public Mourning in Plutarch's *Consolation to His Wife*," *AJP* 130 (2009): 67–98.

151. Baltussen, "Personal Grief and Public Mourning," 82.

152. Abraham J. Malherbe, *Moral Exhortation: A Greco-Roman Sourcebook*, Library of Early Christianity 4 (Philadelphia: Westminster Press, 1986), 124.

153. Malherbe, *Moral Exhortation*, 124–25. This is stated in the context of explaining the difference between *paraenesis* and *protepsis*, the former of which is broader in scope. Stanley K. Stowers, *Letter Writing in Greco-Roman Antiquity*, Library of Early Christianity 5 (Philadelphia: Westminster Press, 1986), 92, instead uses "*protreptic* in reference to hortatory literature that calls the audience to a new and different way of life, and *paraenesis* for advice and exhortation to continue in a certain way of life. The terms, however, were used in this way only sometimes and not consistently in antiquity." See Diana M. Swancutt, "Paraenesis in Light of Protepsis: Troubling the Typical Dichotomy," in *Early Christian Paraenesis in Context*, ed. James Starr and Troels Engberg-Pedersen, Beihefte zur Zeitschrift für die neutestamentliche Wissenschaft und die Kunde der älteren Kirche 125 (Berlin: Walter de Gruyter, 2004), 113–56, who places *paraenesis* within *protrepsis*. This was not a debate that engaged Latin rhetorical thinkers such as Cicero and Quintilian, so we can leave it aside here.

154. Charles Favez, *La consolation latine chrétienne* (Paris: J. Vrin, 1937).

155. In verse 13, the question is whether Paul was calling for Christians not to grieve (*lupeō*) or not to grieve as those without Christian faith do. In other words, in English, should our translation read "do not grieve, like the rest who have no hope" or "do not grieve like the rest, who have no hope"? The comma makes all the difference. See J. Chapa, "Consolatory Patterns? 1 Thess 4:13–18," in *The Thessalonian Correspondence*, ed. R. F. Collins, Bibliotheca Ephemeridum Theologicarum Lovaniensium 87 (Leuven: Peeters, 1990), 220–28; and David Luckensmeyer, *The Eschatology of First Thessalonians*, Novum Testamentum et Orbis Antiquus 71 (Göttingen: Vandenhoeck and Ruprecht, 2009), 192–211. On 1 Thess as consolatory, see David Luckensmeyer and Bronwen Neil, "Reading First Thessalonians as a Consolatory Letter in Light of Seneca and Ancient Handbooks on Letter-Writing," *NTS* 62 (2015): 31–48.

156. See Hans Boersma, "'Numbed with Grief': Gregory of Nyssa on Bereavement and Hope," *Journal of Spiritual Formation and Soul Care* 7 (2014): 46–59.

157. George A. Kennedy, *New Testament Interpretation through Rhetorical Criticism* (Chapel Hill: University of North Carolina Press, 1984), 76.

158. J. H. D. Scourfield, "Towards a Genre of Consolation," in Baltussen, *Greek and Roman Consolations*, 1–36.

159. J. H. D. Scourfield, "The *De mortalitate* of Cyprian: Consolation and Context," *VC* 50 (1996): 13.

160. Scourfield, "The *De mortalitate* of Cyprian," 14.

161. Quintilian, *Inst.* 3.8.

162. See n. 98 above.

163. Scourfield, "The *De mortalitate* of Cyprian," 30.

164. Scourfield, "The *De mortalitate* of Cyprian," 18–19.

165. Scourfield, "The *De mortalitate* of Cyprian," 31.

166. Scourfield, "The *De mortalitate* of Cyprian," 32.

167. On rhetorical structure as discerned in the writings of Tertullian, the Carthaginian layman whose writings Cyprian much admired, see Sider, *Ancient Rhetoric and the Art of Tertullian*; and Dunn, *Tertullian's* Aduersus Iudaeos.

168. Allen Brent, *St. Cyprian of Carthage. On the Church: Select Treatises*, Popular Patristics Series 32 (Crestwood, NY: St. Vladimir's Seminary Press, 2006), 6–95.

169. Gallicet, *Cipriano*, 225–26.

170. Fredouille, *Cyprien*, 20 and 55–56.

171. *Rhet. Her.* 1.3.5.

172. *Rhet. Her.* 1.5.8.

173. See Quintilian, *Inst.* 3.6.1–104 and 7.2.1–57.

174. Sider, *Ancient Rhetoric and the Art of Tertullian*, 31.

175. Tertullian, *Apol.* 4.1 (CCL 1.92).

176. See Andrew McGowan, "Eating People: Accusations of Cannibalism against Christians in the Second Century," *JECS* 2 (1994): 413–42.

177. See Robert D. Sider, *Christian and Pagan in the Roman Empire: The Witness of Tertullian*, Selections from the Fathers of the Church 2 (Washington, DC: Catholic University of America Press, 2001), 5–6, for a rhetorically informed structure of *Apol.*

178. Sider, *Ancient Rhetoric and the Art of Tertullian*, 6, 45–49, and 76–78.

179. Tertullian, *Apol.* 10.2 (CCL 1.105).

180. Tertullian, *Apol.* 10.3 and 24.2 (CCL 1.105–106 and 133).

181. *Rhet. Her.* 2.4.6.

182. Cicero, *Inv. rhet.* 1.24.34–1.18.43. See also Quintilian, *Inst.* 5.8.4, who placed these two attributes under artificial proofs.

183. Cicero, *Inv. rhet.* 2.7.24–2.8.28.

184. Quintilian, *Inst.* 5.9.1–16.

185. Tertullian, *Apol.* 32 (CCL 1.142–43).

186. *Rhet. Her.* 2.5.8.

187. Tertullian, *Apol.* 41.2 (CCL 1.155–56). Of course, one could rebut Tertullian's retort by pointing out that if it were God who was punishing the world because of non-Christian failure to worship God, then God was being unfair in punishing Christians as well. Tertullian anticipated this objection by stating in 41.3–6 (CCL 1.156) that since God promised that Christians and non-Christians would be mixed until the final judgment, Christians would be treated the same as non-Christians, although it was an admonition for Christians but a punishment for non-Christians. The idea of the mixed condition in this life is from the parables of Matthew 13. See Geoffrey D. Dunn, "Ecclesiology in Early North African Christianity: The Parable of the Wheat and the Weeds," *Aug* 57 (2017): 371–401.

188. See Fredouille, *Cyprien*, 38–44.

189. Gallicet, *Cipriano*, 54.

190. Of course, how to deal with evidence from torture made frequent appearances in classical rhetorical guides. See, for example, Quintilian, *Inst.* 5.4.1–2.

191. See *Rhet. Her.* 2.2.3.

192. Cicero, *Inv. rhet.* 2. 5.17–2.8.28 (cause); 2.9.28–2.11.37 (person); and 2.12.38–2.13.45 (action).

193. Quintilian, *Inst.* 5.10.23–52.

194. Gallicet, *Cipriano*, 225–26; and Fredouille, *Cyprien*, 20.

195. Tertullian, *Apol.* 41.3–6 (CCL 1.156), had focused on the willingness of Christians to endure non-Christian injustice, while Cyprian here was more interested in stressing the divine retribution.

196. Brent, *On the Church*, 90. I do not see 21 as part of the general conclusion but more as a conclusion to the lengthy section that runs from 6 to 21.

197. *Rhet. Her.* 2.30.47–2.31.50. Cicero, *Inv. rhet.* 1.52.98–1.56.109, substituted the rousing of indignation against the opponent for amplification. Quintilian, *Inst.* 6.1.1–55, offered two types of *peroratio*, one that dealt with fact and one with emotions.

198. Fredouille, *Cyprien*, 21, is right to see that there is more than just a forensic purpose to the work.

199. Scourfield, "The *De mortalitate* of Cyprian," 15–18.

200. Hannan, *Thasci Caecili Cypriani*, 6–7; and Deferrari, *Saint Cyprian*, 197–98.

201. Ruggiero, *Cipriano*, 15–17.

202. Quintilian, *Inst.* 3.8.6 and 10.

203. Quintilian, *Inst.* 3.8.10.

204. J.-P. Migne, ed., *Patrologia Latina* 4: *S. Cypriani tomus unicus* (Paris: J.-P. Migne, 1844). This was taken from Étienne Baluze, ed., *Sancti Caecilii Cypriani episcopi Carthaginiensis et martyris opera* (Paris: Ex typographia regia,

1726). See Pierre Petitmengin, "Un monument controversé, le 'Saint Cyprien' de Baluze et Dom Maran (1726)," *RHT* 5 (1975): 97–136.

TO DEMETRIAN

1. We know nothing about Demetrian. Much has been speculated from very little evidence. Ernest Wallis, "The Treatises of Cyprian," in *The Ante-Nicene Fathers,* vol. 5: *Hippolytus, Cyprian, Caius, Novatian,* Appendix, ed. Alexander Roberts and James Donaldson, rev. A. Cleveland Coxe (Buffalo, NY: Christian Literature Co., 1886), 457, asserted that he was proconsul of Africa. Benson, *Cyprian,* 250, rejected that but suggested instead that he was an aged magistrate, one of five *primores* responsible for investigating Christians and "a harsh enforcer of the penal statutes." This was on the basis of Cyprian, *Ad Deme.* 10 (CCL 3B.40), where Demetrian is referred to as judging others. However, the reference need not be taken as indicating any official position. Sage, *Cyprian,* 276, critical of the wild assertions of others, suggests he could have been employed in the proconsul's court or as a local magistrate. Yet, he also asserted that Demetrian attended Christian meetings, although this opening section of the pamphlet describes an encounter that seems to have entailed only Cyprian and Demetrian (see n. 7 below). Sage's position is adopted uncritically by Allen Brent, *Cyprian and Roman Carthage* (Cambridge: Cambridge University Press, 2010), 99. Ezio Gallicet, *Cipriano. A Demetriano,* CP 4 (Turin: Società Editrice Internazionale, 1976), 58, saw Demetrian as an exponent and spokesman of the rich bourgeois of Carthage. Charles A. Bobertz, "Cyprian of Carthage as Patron: A Social Historical Study of the Role of Bishop in the Ancient Christian Community of North Africa" (PhD diss., Yale University, 1988), 52–53, whose arguments about Cyprian's high status in Carthage are accepted here (see n. 96 of the introduction), argues that in this pamphlet Cyprian was urging Demetrian to act favorably toward his clients (the Christians of Carthage) and that Demetrian, if not in an official position, was close enough to those who were to be able to make a difference. More reasonably, David E. Wilhite, *Ancient African Christianity: An Introduction to a Unique Context and Tradition* (London: Routledge, 2017), 149, says that he was of the local elite. The most we can say is that Demetrian and Cyprian seem to have belonged to the same prominent social class, knew each other for some time, and disagreed vehemently about the value of Christianity.

2. In a normal forensic episode, the speech or written text was addressed to a third party (a jury or a judge) whose responsibility it was to determine guilt or innocence. Here, Cyprian's work is addressed explicitly to Demetrian as prosecutor and judge. This does not mean necessarily that Demetrian held any formal appointment within the North African apparatus of government since this was not a formal proceeding but a debate. Cyprian sought to change Demetrian's mind and those of his fellow non-Christians about the guilt of Christians in bringing this pestilence to the empire. The

first two paragraphs constitute the *exordium,* in which Cyprian attacked Demetrian as prosecutor for his pigheadedness and troublesomeness, thereby hoping to drive a wedge between him and his fellow non-Christians who were also the judges of this debate. While Demetrian and other non-Christians within Carthage who thought as he did were the imagined audience, were there others for whom this pamphlet was intended? The option would be the Christian community itself, whom Cyprian wished to inform about his efforts on their behalf and to arm for their own responses to the non-Christians they met and mixed with who would accuse them in a similar fashion with being responsible for all the ills of their society.

3. Prov 23:9. This is found in Cyprian, *Ad Quir.* 3.50 (CCL 3.138), although with *subsannet* ("sneer") instead of *inrideat* ("ridicule"). See Michael A. Fahey, *Cyprian and the Bible: A Study in Third-Century Exegesis* (Tübingen: Eberhard-Karls Universität, 1971), 167. On Cyprian's use of passages from the Hebrew scriptures to indicate to non-Christians the antiquity of Christianity, see Ezio Gallicet, "L'Antico Testamento nell'*Ad Demetrianum* di Cipriano," *Aug* 22 (1982): 199–202.

4. Prov 26:4. See Fahey, *Cyprian and the Bible,* 167. This is not in Cyprian, *Ad Quir.*

5. *Conscientia*: Cyprian is not writing about "conscience" as a moral force but more in tune with the general sense of the Latin terms as "consciousness."

6. Matt 7:6. This is found in Cyprian, *Ad Quir.* 3.50 (CCL 3.138), although with the addition of "perhaps" (*forte*) and the conclusion of the verse, "and turn and destroy you" (*et conversi elidant vos*). See Fahey, *Cyprian and the Bible,* 167.

7. There is no indication here of anything other than private discussion between Cyprian and Demetrian.

8. Not only was the content of Demetrian's tirades objectionable to Cyprian, but his method of delivery was as well. Quintilian, *Inst.* 7.1.44, had noted that it was characteristic of the uneducated speaker to rant and rave, and that those who disdained method were "booming inarticulately" (*Inst.* 2.11.4). He was contemptuous of those whose success at public speaking was due to pandering to the crowd's love of abusive and rash speaking (*Inst.* 2.12.4–5). Loud and frenzied speech accompanied by wild gesticulation was best avoided as uncouth, uneducated, and violent rather than persuasive (*Inst.* 2.12.9–11). Was Cyprian accusing Demetrian of being uneducated or, worse, having forgotten his training? Cyprian would go on to write a pamphlet about patience, *De bono,* based heavily on Tertullian's earlier *De pat.*

9. *Congredi*: Bobertz, "Cyprian of Carthage as Patron," 52, translates this as "meet." I do not think that Cyprian and Demetrian stopped meeting each other, for the next section describes further encounters.

10. The image of dangerous waves on a rough sea appears also in Cyprian, *De mort.* 1, 6, 12, and 25 (CCL 3A.17, 20, 23, and 30).

11. Seneca, *Ira* 3.12.4, linked impatience with turbulent waves.

12. From Isa 32:3 and 5; Matt 11:5; and Luke 7:22, Cyprian would have known that the Christian mission was indeed to bring sight to the blind and hearing to the deaf. The irrational is not found in the scriptures and its addition probably was aimed directly at Demetrian. Fahey, *Cyprian and the Bible*, 302 and 343, has no reference to these gospel passages. If Cyprian intended this pamphlet to be read not only by Demetrian but also by his Christian community, then this scriptural allusion was no doubt to convince them that such miracles could only work with those open to the activity of God and that his own failure to convert Demetrian was not his fault but Demetrian's. Gallicet, *Cipriano*, 138, notes a similar tripartite reference in Cyprian, *De laps.* 23 (CCL 3.234).

13. *Religio*: It is clear that the Romans did not understand this word to mean, as it does today, a system of faith belief. For them it was the supernatural forces that bound them into a way of life, exemplified by cultic practices. Clifford Ando, *The Matter of the Gods: Religion and the Roman Empire*, The Transformation of the Classical Heritage 44 (Berkeley: University of California Press, 2008), 126, suggests "religious scruples" as a translation. See G. R. De Villiers and E. Germiquet, "*Religio and Superstitio* in Early Christianity and Graeco-Roman Society: Christian Perspectives on Paganism," *Acta Patristica et Byzantina* 9 (1998): 52–69; René Gothóni, "*Religio* and *Superstitio* Reconsidered," *Archiv für Religionspsychologie* 21 (1994): 37–46; Jörg Rüpke, "*Religio* and *Religiones* in Roman Thinking," *Les Études Classiques* 75 (2007): 67–78; and Asher Ovadiah, "*Deisidaimonia, Superstitio* and *Religio*: Graeco-Roman, Jewish and Early Christian Concepts," *Liber Annuus* 64 (2014): 417–40.

14. This paragraph and the next mark the short *narratio* of the pamphlet. The practice of blaming Christians for disasters that befell the empire was nothing new in North Africa. In *Apol.* 40.2 (CCL 1.153), Tertullian mentioned that Christians were blamed for flooding of the Tiber, for the lack of flooding of the Nile, for drought, earthquake, famine, and pestilence, leading for calls for them to be thrown to the lions. In *Ad Scap.* 3.1–3 (CCL 2.1129), Tertullian took a different tack, warning the African proconsul that the shedding of Christian blood was the reason why bad things like floods, fires, and eclipses happened. The path forward was clear: stop persecuting Christians and the bad things would stop (at least for a time; Tertullian does refer briefly and without comment to the final destruction of the world).

15. Gordian III (238–44) defeated the Sassanids led by Shapur I (c. 240–70) at the battle of Resaena (near modern Ceylanpınar in southeastern Türkiye on the border with Syria) in 243. In 244, however, he died while on another campaign against the Sassanids. See Michael H. Dodgeon and Samuel N. C. Lieu, eds., *The Roman Eastern Frontier and the Persian Wars (AD 226–363): A Documentary History* (London: Routledge, 1994), 34–46; and Potter, *The Roman Empire at Bay*, 232–36. Philip I (244–49) had forced the Carpi back across the Danube in 246. Decius and his son, Herennius Etruscus, were both killed at the battle near Abritus (modern Razgrad in northeastern Bulgaria) in the

province of Moesia Inferior in summer 251, when the Goths and others (called Scythians in Zosimus) under Cniva defeated the Romans. They had been victorious over the Goths the previous year at the battle of Nicopolis ad Istrum (modern Nikyup in northern Bulgaria), but not sufficiently to prevent them from continuing to Philippopolis (modern Plovdiv in southern Bulgaria). While pursuing the Goths, Decius's army was surprised and defeated at the battle at Beroe (modern Stara Zagora in central Bulgaria), allowing Cniva to capture Philippopolis in summer 251. The battle near Abritus occurred while the Goths were withdrawing from Philippololis with their loot. See Aurelius Victor, *De Caes.* 29; Eutropius, *Breu.* 9.4; Zosimus, *Hist. nov.* 1.23; Ivanov Teofil and Stojanof Stojan, *ABRITUS: Its History and Archaeology* (Razgrd: Cultural and Historical Heritage Directorate, 1985); Herwig Wolfram, *History of the Goths*, trans. Thomas J. Dunlap (Berkeley: University of California Press, 1988), 43–46; and Bursche, "The Battle of Abritus," 151–70. Of course, there had been many battles within the empire over the previous generation as emperors clashed with usurpers, but the deaths of Gordian III and Decius had been major shocks to the empire. Ammianus Marcellinus, *Rerum gestae* 31.5.16–17, highlights just how severe the plight of the Balkans was at this time. From a later Christian perspective, Lactantius, *De mort.* 4 (CSEL 72/2.178), saw the death of Decius as fitting punishment for an enemy of God, without actually acknowledging divine responsibility. Under Gallus, hostilities would break out again with the Goths in 253, news of which probably reached North Africa after *Ad Deme.* had been written. Shapur I defeated the Romans at Barbalissos (near modern Aleppo in Syria) in 252 or 253, news of which might have reached North Africa before Cyprian wrote this pamphlet, depending upon how early this battle took place and how late the pamphlet was written. See Dodgeon and Lieu, *The Roman Eastern Frontier*, 50–57; and Peter Edwell, *Rome and Persia at War: Imperial Competition and Contact 193–363 CE* (Abingdon: Routledge, 2021). On Roman views of the Sassanids in later centuries, see Scott McDonough, "Were the Sasanians Barbarians? Roman Writers on the 'Empire of the Persians,'" in *Romans, Barbarians, and the Transformation of the Roman World*, ed. Ralph W. Mathisen and Danuta Shanzer (Farnham: Ashgate, 2011), 55–65; and Jan Willem Drijvers, "A Roman Image of the 'Barbarian' Sasanians," in Mathisen and Shanzer, *Romans, Barbarians, and the Transformation of the Roman World*, 67–76.

16. *Lues*: Cyprian, *De mort.* 16 (CCL 3A.25), used this term for the deadly pestilence. See n. 165 in the translation of *De mort.* Can we make anything from the fact that Cyprian did not use the term *mortalitas* for the pestilence in this pamphlet in terms of determining the sequence of the two pamphlets? One could suggest that *lues* was sufficient as a term early in the outbreak but, as things grew worse, *mortalitas* captured this seriousness better, but it is only a suspicion.

17. See Peter Garnsey, *Famine and Food-Supply in the Graeco-Roman World: Responses to Risk and Crisis* (Cambridge: Cambridge University Press, 1988);

and Stathakopoulos, *Famine and Pestilence*, for later evidence. Famine was a result of bad harvests, which could be caused by drought and/or a shortage of workers, which could have resulted from an outbreak of disease. Another consequence of a bad harvest was an increase in food prices. See A. H. M. Jones, *The Later Roman Empire 284–602: A Social, Economic, and Administrative Survey* (Oxford: Blackwell, 1964), 445–46 and 818–11.

18. In *De mort.* 8 (CCL 3A.21), Cyprian wrote about the impact of famine and drought being shared equally by Christians and non-Christians. Was Demetrian's accusation what prompted Cyprian to use the image in *De mort.* (thereby dating *Ad Deme.* before it)? It is hard to say but, given Cyprian's familiarity with these topics from Tertullian (see n. 14 above), it seems unlikely, particularly since Tertullian, *Apol.* 40.14 (CCL 1.155), used this very image of rainless clouds. Kyle Harper, *The Fate of Rome: Climate, Disease, and the End of an Empire* (Princeton, NJ: Princeton University Press, 2017), 131, turns to Cyprian as evidence of drought in North Africa, but supports that on 133–34, with evidence of repeated failures of the Nile inundations in the 240s. While Cyprian was repeating the complaints passed on and endorsed by Demetrian, one could note that the events about which they complained reminds one of Luke 21:10–11, a passage used in *De mort.* 2 (CCL 3A.17) about things foretold by Jesus to take place, the occurrence of which ought not to surprise Christians. See n. 26 in the translation of *De mort.* I do not see information here that would help determine the sequence of the two pamphlets.

19. One may note Cyprian's use of the plural here. While the Roman jurist Paul, a generation older than Cyprian, reported that silence is neither consent nor denial (Justinian, *Dig.* 50.17.142), Cyprian here seems to be endorsing the more popular maxim of unknown origin about silence giving consent (*qui tacet consentire videtur*).

20. Patience and silence in the face of illness and disease was important to Stoics, as Seneca, *Ep.* 78.19, reveals. That Demetrian could not bear the world's suffering without complaint was a betrayal of the Stoic principles with which he must have been familiar, and that Cyprian could not bear Demetrian's criticism without replying needed some self-justification.

21. *Crimen*: In Roman law this could be understood as a legally punishable action or the accusation that such an action had occurred. See Miroslav Frýdek, "Terminology of Roman Criminal Law: *Crimen et delictum*," *Journal on European History of Law* 1 (2010): 69–72; and Jill Harries, *Law and Crime in the Roman World* (Cambridge: Cambridge University Press, 2012).

22. *Concitasti*: The Romans had no law against incitement, but using such a word, which sounds legal at least to modern ears, is what one would expect in a piece of forensic oratory, and I believe it should have that flavor in this translation. See Edward Watts, "Introduction: Freedom of Speech and Self-Censorship in the Roman Empire," *RBPH* 92 (2014): 159; and Antonio Duplá Ansuategui, "Incitement to Violence in Late Republican Political

Oratory," in *Political Communication in the Roman World*, ed. Cristina Rosillo-López, Impact of Empire 27 (Leiden: Brill, 2017), 179–200.

23. There is a contrast with the use of the verb *maledico* in Cyprian, *De mort.* 4 (CCL 3A.19), where, used for a Christian readership, the sense of "blaspheme" is more to the fore. See n. 53 of the translation of that pamphlet. Elsewhere, the term could simply refer to unacceptable verbal assaults even within the Christian community. See Cyprian, *Ep.* 13.5.2 (CCL 3B.77), which G. W. Clarke, *The Letters of St. Cyprian of Carthage*, 1: *Letters 1–27*, ACW 43 (New York: Newman Press, 1984), 85 translates as "backbiting."

24. *Radices*: Demetrian is held to be the root for this present attitude against the Christians and Cyprian's expression is influenced perhaps by Isa 11:1. We find the image in Cyprian, *De unit.* 5 (CCL 3.253) and Cyprian, *Ep.* 48.3.1 (CCL 3B.229).

25. The referent here is to those like Demetrian, in contrast with those non-Christians addressed by Cyprian, whom he was attempting to portray as more reasonable, all in an effort to make his words more persuasive to them.

26. Cyprian often employs *mundus* and *saeculum* synonymously. See the pleonastic use in Cyprian, *De laps.* 17 (CCL 3.230) and Cyprian, *De mort.* 8 (CCL 3A.20). Á. P. Orbán, *Les dénominations du monde chez les premiers auteurs chrétiens*, Graecitas Christianorum Primaeva 4 (Nijmegen: Dekker and van der Vegt, 1970), 188, concludes that Cyprian used *saeculum* most often in a pejorative sense, while *mundus* was used as a more neutral term (221–22). On 191, with reference to this passage, Orbán comments that Cyprian could use *mundus* as well as *saeculum* pejoratively, although less frequently so, and that as pejorative terms they are basically synonymous for him. On the difficulty of distinguishing Tertullian's use of the two words, see Jaroslav Pelikan, "The Eschatology of Tertullian," *CH* 21 (1952): 108–22.

27. In *De mort.* 2 (CCL 3A.17), in commenting on the wars, famines, earthquakes, and disease of Luke 21:10–11 (see n. 18 above), Cyprian's point had been to reassure his readers that these terrible experiences (using the verbs *exurgere* and *quatere*) had been predicted by Christ himself. Here, realizing that reference to the gospels would not persuade Demetrian, he omits the reference to the gospel prediction but still describes the experience using similar verbs (*quatere* and *urgere*).

28. On the charge and response that Christians deserved to be punished because they did not worship the gods see Tertullian, *Apol.* 10–28 (CCL 1.105–40). This sentence forms the brief *partitio/propositio* of the pamphlet.

29. *Veritatis alienus*: Cyprian described himself as "a foreigner to the truth and the light" in *Ad Dona.* 3 (CCL 3A.4).

30. A similar idea, although with a different emphasis, is found in Cyprian, *De mort.* 2 and 25 (CCL 3A.18 and 30). See nn. 34 and 240 in the translation of *De mort.* The idea is scriptural: Isa 43:18–19; 65:17; Ezek 36:26; Rom 6:4; 2 Cor 5:17; Eph 4:22–24; 2 Pet 3:10; 1 John 2:17; and Rev 21:1 and 4–5. It has a long history in Christian thinking. See James M. Dean, *The World*

Grown Old in Later Medieval Literature (Cambridge, MA: Medieval Academy of America, 1997). It contrasts with Ambrose's idea, expressed more than a century later, that there is progress in the world. See Alex Fogleman, "'Since Those Days All Things Have Progressed for the Better': Tradition, Progress, and Creation in Ambrose of Milan," *HTR* 113 (2020): 440–59. Cyprian's choice of *saeculum* instead of *mundus* here could be an indication that he was distinguishing between the natural environment and the human contribution to its degradation. However, the fact that he returns to using the word *mundus* and describes the changes to the natural environment as part of God's plan would instead suggest that, at least in this section, *mundus* and *saeculum* were being synonymously. See Gallicet, *Cipriano*, 149–63.

31. *Vigore et robore*: both nouns appear in Cyprian, *De mort.* 1 (CCL 3A.17). With this sentence Cyprian began the *confirmatio/refutatio* of the pamphlet (3b–22), in which he sought to demonstrate Christian innocence of the charge of being responsible for the world's troubles because they fail to worship the gods by shifting the blame. In the first instance (3–4) the blame belongs to the very nature of the world: it is growing old and falling apart. The argument about the obsolescence of the world contrasts with Tertullian, *Apol.* 32 (CCL 1. 142–43), who argued that Christian prayer preserved the world.

32. On climate change and the impact on North African agriculture and the importance of grain from North Africa for the food supply of the empire, see Rhoads Murphey, "The Decline of North Africa since the Roman Occupation: Climatic or Human?," *Annals of the Association of American Geographers* 41 (1951): 116–32; Susan Raven, *Rome in Africa*, 3rd ed. (London: Routledge, 1993), 79–99; Brent D. Shaw, *Environment and Society in Roman North Africa*, Variorum Collected Studies (Aldershot: Ashgate, 1995); Arbia Hilali, "Rome and Agriculture in *Africa Proconsularis*: Land and Hydraulic Development," *RBPH* 91 (2013): 113–25, whose evidence would indicate that Cyprian's claims of a decline (a recent decline?) in climatic conditions was exaggerated; Daniel Hoyer, "Public Feasting, Elite Competition, and the Market Economy of Roman North Africa," *Journal of North African Studies* 18 (2013): 574–91; Matthew S. Hobson, *The North African Boom: Evaluating Economic Growth in the Roman Province of Africa Proconsularis (146 B.C.–A.D. 439)*, *Journal of Roman Archaeology* Supplementary series 100 (Portsmouth, RI: Cambridge University Press, 2015); and Dennis Kehoe, "Agriculture in Roman North Africa," in *A Companion to Ancient Agriculture*, ed. David Hollander and Timothy Howe, Blackwell Companions to the Ancient World (Chichester: Wiley Blackwell, 2020), 499–516.

33. On the ripening power of the sun, see Virgil, *Georg.* 1.67.

34. Here I have followed Jean-Claude Fredouille, ed., *Cyprien de Carthage. A Démétrien*, SC 457 (Paris: Les Éditions du CERF, 2003), 77, rather than previous English translations in making *sua* agree with *temperies* rather than with the earlier *fruges*. This preserves the fact that spring and autumn do not refer back to the crops.

35. The four seasons was a popular topic for mosaic decoration in Roman North Africa. Rather than being cyclical, Cyprian was highlighting the seasons as being in a downward spiral. See David Parrish, "Two Mosaics from Roman Tunisia: An African Variation of the Season Theme," *American Journal of Archaeology* 83 (1979): 279–85; David Parrish, *Seasons Mosaics of Roman North Africa*, Archaeologica 46 (Rome: Giorgio Bretschneider, 1984); Michèle Blanchard-Lemée, Mongi Ennaïfer, Hédi Slim, and Latifa Slim, *Mosaics of Roman Africa: Floor Mosaics from Tunisia*, trans. Kenneth D. Whitehead (London: British Museum Press, 1996), 37–63; and Katherine M. D. Dunbabin, *Mosaics of the Greek and Roman World* (Cambridge: Cambridge University Press, 1999), 101–29. Cicero, *Senec.* 15.51–53, writes about the pleasure for the old, himself included, in cultivating fields of wheat and grapes. There is no suggestion from him that the world has grown weary and unproductive.

36. On marble production in the Roman empire, see Mosche Fischer, "Marble Imports and Local Counterparts: Luxury Business in Roman Palestine," *Topoi. Orient-Occident Supplément* 8 (2007): 249–69; Alfred Michael Hirt, *Imperial Mines and Quarries in the Roman World: Organizational Aspects 27 BC–AD 235* (Oxford: Oxford University Press, 2010); Anna Gutiérrez Garcia-M., "The Exploitation of Local Stone in Roman Times: The Case of North-Eastern Spain," *World Archaeology* 43 (2011): 318–41; F. Antonelli et al., "Petrographic Characterization and Provenance Determination of the Crystalline Marbles Used in the Roman City of *Banasa* (Morocco): New Data on the Import of Iberian Marble in Roman North Africa," *Archaeometry* 57 (2015): 405–25; and Wissem Gallala et al., "A Multi-Analytical Approach for Determining the Provenance of the Marbles from Ruspina Roman Batha (Monastir, Tunisia)," *Archaeological and Anthropological Sciences* 9 (2017): 1275–85. The complaint remains current (albeit in the eastern Mediterranean rather than the southern), suggesting Cyprian's exaggeration. See Ahmed Mohammed Abu Haneih, Sadiq Abdelall, and Afif Hasan, "Sustainable Development of Stone and Marble Sector in Palestine," *Journal of Cleaner Production* 84 (2014): 581–88.

37. On silver and gold production in the Roman empire, see Aubrey L. Hillman et al., "Lead Pollution Resulting from Roman Gold Extraction in Northwestern Spain," *Holocene* 27 (2017): 1465–74.

38. The translation captures Cyprian's alliteration at this point.

39. The forum in Carthage was atop the Byrsa Hill, on a platform the Romans constructed by demolishing Punic remains in the area late in the first century BCE. The hill lay at the intersection of the two major roads in Roman Carthage, the *decumanus* and *cardo maximus*, and contained the main administrative buildings of the provincial government, such as basilicas, temples, and library, which surrounded the open space of the colonnaded forum. The old forum, down close to the sea, operated as a marketplace. See Edith Mary Wightman, "The Plan of Roman Carthage: Practicalities and Politics," in *New Light on Ancient Carthage*, ed. John Griffiths Pedley (Ann

Arbor: University of Michigan Press, 1980), 29–46; P. Gros and J. Deneauve, "Hypothèses sur le centre monumental de la Carthage romaine, d'après les recherches récentes sur la colline de Byrsa, par MM. Pierre Gros et Jean Deneauve," *CRAI* 124 (1980): 299–332; P. Gros, "Colline de Byrsa: les vestiges romains," in *Pour sauver Carthage. Exploration et conservation de la cite punique, romaine et byzantine*, ed. Abdelmajid Ennabli (Paris: UNESCO/INAA, 1992), 99–103; and Jean-Paul Morel, "Mission archéologique de Carthage-Byrsa," *Les Nouvelles de l'archéologie* 123 (2011): 39–43. Much of the current archaeological interest is with the Punic rather than Roman remains here.

40. Cyprian, *De unit.* 14 (CCL 3.259), saw such harmony in the Christian community being ordered by Christ. The fact that it was to be found less in the wider society provides an implicit point of contrast.

41. In *Ep.* 41.1.2 (CCL 3B.196), Cyprian wrote of the help that ought to be given to Christians during the time of Decius's religious revival efforts in order for them to be able to practice their *artes*, which G. W. Clarke, *The Letters of St. Cyprian of Carthage*, 2: *Letters 28–54*, ACW 44 (New York: Newman Press, 1984), 59, translates as "trades."

42. *Disciplina*: see Rolf Noormann, Ad salute consulere*: Die Paränese Cyprians im Kontext antiken und frühchristlichen Denkens*, Forschungen zur Kirchen- und Dogmengeschichte 99 (Göttingen: Vandenhoeck and Ruprecht, 2009). We find Cyprian using this term in *De habi.* 1 (CCL 3F.283); *De laps.* 6 (CCL 3.223); *Epp.* 4.1.2 (CCL 3B.18); 15.4 (CCL 3B.89); 38.1.3 (CCL 3B.184); and 39.5.1 (CCL 3B.191). More generally, the term means "instruction" and "orderly behavior" or even "correction." See Clarke, *The Letters of St. Cyprian*, 1.174, n. 8 and Gallicet, *Cipriano*, 167–68.

43. On Roman attitudes to old age in people, see M. I. Finley, "The Elderly in Classical Antiquity," *Greece & Rome* 28 (1981): 156–71; Tim G. Parkin, *Old Age in the Roman World: A Cultural and Social History* (Baltimore: Johns Hopkins University Press, 2003), 57–90; and Karen Cokayne, *Experiencing Old Age in Ancient Rome*, Routledge Classical Monographs (London: Routledge, 2003).

44. Cicero, *Senec.* 16.57, wrote of the warmth of the sun or a fire being a comfort to an old man. Cyprian plays with the image of the setting sun to conjure images of the decrepitude of the world. His point to Demetrian, of course, was that the Christians could in no way be held responsible for the aging of the world.

45. See Ovid, *Met.* 7.531. In the last quarter of the lunar phase, only the ever-diminishing crescent of the moon (characterized by its horns) is visible. In the northern hemisphere the waning horns point to the right, while in the southern hemisphere they point to the left. The weakness of the passage of the sun and the phases of the moon as metaphors for the aging of the world is that they were cyclical and that just as the sun set it would rise and just as the moon waned it would wax. On Roman astronomy, see Alexander Jones, "Greco-Roman Astronomy and Astrology," in *The Cambridge History of Science*,

ed. Alexander Jones (Cambridge: Cambridge University Press, 2018), 374–401; and Giulio Magli, Antonio César González-García, Juan Belmonte Aviles, and Elio Antonello, eds., *Archaeoastronomy in the Roman World,* Historical and Cultural Astronomy (Cham: Springer, 2019).

46. *Dei lex: In De mort.* 25 (CCL 3A.30), Cyprian has expressed to the Christian community the fact that the world is coming to an end (and the deadly pestilence could be taken as proof of that) not because of its old age but because it has reached its divinely allotted end. See n. 240 in the translation of that pamphlet. Here, this law of God is mentioned, but only in passing. Yet, there seems to be a clear statement that even Stoicism served God's will. The emphasis is on the wearing out of the world, a familiar enough topic for educated Romans to consider, rather than to a divine eschatological plan. See Lucretius, *Nat.* 5.240–47 and 318–23, although in 5.330–37, he stated his belief that the world was young enough to still be developing and had not yet reached its apogee. Further, at 5.380–415, he suggested that the world will end not because of its old age but because of a battle between the elements, although the old age idea reappears at 5.821–36, but as part of a continuous cycle. For the classical tradition on the *senectus mundi,* see Peter Burke, "Tradition and Experience: The Idea of Decline from Bruni to Gibbon," *Daedalus* 105/3 (Summer 1976): 137–52; Gerhard Bartelink, "Le thème du monde vieilli," *Orpheus* 4 (1983): 342–54; F. Gerald Downing, "Cosmic Eschatology in the First Century: Pagan, Jewish and Christian," *L'Antiquité Classique* 64 (1995): 99–109; Natale Spineto, "L'escatologia nel mondo classico," *Annali di Storia dell'Esegesi* 16 (1999): 7–20; Jocelyn Groisard, "Catastrophe and Cyclical Time in Ancient Thought," *The Journal of Social Sciences and Humanities* 514 (2018): 183–98; and Alessandro Schiesaro, "Lucretius' Apocalyptic Imagination," *Materiali e discussion per l'analisi dei testi classici* 84 (2020): 27–93. On Cyprian's use of Lucretius, see Carlo Pascal, "Lucrezio e Cipriano," *Rivista di Filologia e d'Istruzione Classica* 31 (1903): 555–57; Luigi Castagna, "Vecchiaia e morte del mondo in Lucrezio, Seneca e San Cipriano," *Aevum Antiquum* 13 (2000): 239–63; and Susanne Gatzemeier, *Ut ait Lucretiurs: Die Lukrezrezeption in der lateinischen Prosa bis Laktanz,* Hypomnemnata 189 (Göttingen: Vandenhoeck and Ruprecht, 2013). Interestingly, the divine law is a judgment (*senentia*) passed by God, a point emphasized by Sophie Lunn-Rockliffe, "Cyprian on the Senescence of the World," *Revue des Études Tardo-antiques* Supplement 5 (2018): 267–76, who identifies it as being passed with the expulsion of Adam and Eve from paradise, where death is the punishment for sin, on the basis of comments made in Cyprian's other works, most notably *De bono* 17 (CCL 3A.128) and *Ep.* 64.5.2 (CCL 3C.424). That this pamphlet was addressed ostensibly to a non-Christian would explain why Cyprian did not spell this out.

47. *Omnia orta occident et aucta senescant:* In Sallust, *Ad Caes.* 1.5.2, we find *omnia orta intereunt,* while in Sallust, *Iug.* 2.3, we find *omniaque orta occidunt et aucta senescunt.* In Minucius Felix, *Oct.* 34.2 (CSEL 2.48), we read *omnia quae orta, occidere, quae facta sunt, interire.*

48. Fredouille, *Cyprien*, 143, notes that this is a *reductio ad absurdum*. See Seneca, *Ira* 12.10.1, where it is pointed out that anger is inappropriate against those who stumble in the dark, are deaf, are children forgetful of their responsibilities, or are elderly or sick. "The bulk of their limbs" appears also in Cyprian, *Ad Dona.* 7 (CCL 3A.7).

49. Cicero, *Senec.* 19.69, observes that nothing is lengthy if it comes to an end. Gen 5:5 records Adam dying at the age of 930; 5:8 records Seth dying at the age of 912; and 5:11 records Enoch dying at 905 years of age. *Macrobii*, once attributed to Lucian, lists some Greeks who lived long lives, but only a couple of them beyond 100. Pliny, *NH* 7.48–49, discussed various opinions about the normal length of life. Lucretius, *Nat.* 5.925–30, accepted that people long ago lived longer than his own day because conditions were hardier.

50. Was Cyprian referring to progeria? Cyprian was asking not only whether Christians could be blamed for the natural effects of old age, but also for the unnatural effects of premature aging. The last was a risky path to follow, since, given the ancient view of premature aging as a form of monstrosity, it could well be believed by many that such a rare condition was indeed a punishment for Christians not being dealt with properly. On the Greco-Roman attitude, although without reference to Cyprian or Christians in general, see D. Felton, "Monstrosity or Disability? Ancient Accounts of Accelerated Ageing," *Folklore* 123 (2012): 355–61. The younger Seneca, *Epp.* 13.17 and 23.11, warned Lucilius of the folly of old men embarking on fresh careers. The idea is repeated by Seneca in *De brev.* 4.5.

51. Wis 5:13. One presumes the allusion would have been lost on Demetrian, except to the extent that it echoed Stoic idea as mentioned above, yet, by introducing it, Cyprian was attempted to divert blame from the Christians for the existence of this genetic disorder; it was a result of the aging world itself.

52. Cicero, *Senec.* 19.66–68, observed that death is a natural accompaniment to old age and further, that death can come to a person at any age. Such an idea would support Cyprian's argument that Christians were not to blame, although a good opponent could counter that Christians could be responsible for hastening that inevitable death. Seneca, *Ep.* 26.3, argued that no one had any right to complain when something that ought to finish did finish.

53. *Morbis*: Cicero, *Tusc.* 4.13.28, defined *morbus* ("disease") as the breakdown of the whole body, distinct from *aegrotatio* ("sickness"), which happened when weakness accompanied disease.

54. This sentence includes a partial repetition of some points made in section 2 above.

55. *In novissimis temporibus*: Brent, *On the Church*, 73, translates this to indicate that the predictions have been made recently. Instead, it is clear that the predictions have been made about the last days. Here Cyprian begins the

second argument of his *confirmatio* (5–22) in shifting the blame for the world's disasters. Not only was the world coming to a natural conclusion, but non-Christians were to blame because their failure to worship the one, true God has seen God's judgment visited upon the world in the last days. Fredouille, *Cyprien,* 55, sees the two arguments to shift the blame as one section (3–6).

56. The allusion is to Mark 13:7–8; Matt 24:6–7; and Luke 21:9–11, especially the last, which has mention of disease. Cyprian doubled the reference, including both *morbus* and *lues,* and omitted the reference to earthquakes from the scriptural text. He used the Lukan passage in *De mort.* 2 (CCL 3A.17). The scriptural passages stressed that these signs did not mean that the end of the world was as imminent as many thought, an idea that Cyprian left to one side here. Even though reference to disease made these scriptural verses appropriate, they also coincide, I would suggest, with the reality of the pestilence being the occasion for this writing but not being so dominant a feature of life that it was the only thing worth mentioning.

57. See Cyprian, *Ep.* 11.2.1 (CCL 3B.58).

58. *Plagas*: *plaga* can describe an act of violence against someone ("stroke" or "blow") as well as the result of that act ("wound" or "injury"). The question whenever Cyprian uses the word in this pamphlet (as in sections 7, 9, and 22) is whether he was thinking in general terms or specifically about this pestilence.

59. While Lunn-Rockliffe, "Cyprian on the Senescence of the World," 267–76, made the valid point that God's sentence against the world was passed at the time of the expulsion of Adam and Eve from paradise, but she has not considered why the sentence was only now being executed in Cyprian's time. Of course, the question has to be asked as to why Cyprian would mention God's punishment in a pamphlet to a non-Christian if we presume that Demetrian would not find it persuasive. Either Cyprian did not mind arguing from a starting point the other side would not accept or the pamphlet really had a Christian readership in mind. It could, of course, be a combination of both.

60. Cyprian repeats exactly the accusation against the Christians mentioned in section 3 above.

61. The same argument is found in Tertullian, *Apol.* 40.10–15 (CCL 1.155); and Tertullian, *Ad Scap.* 3 (CCL 2.1129–30).

62. *Ipse*: translated in a gender-neutral fashion.

63. See Cyprian, *De domi.* 1 (CCL 3A.90), where there is mention of "the Lord, the leader and director" (*duce et rectore domino*).

64. *Eius*: translated in a gender-neutral fashion.

65. See Lam 3:37. Fahey, *Cyprian and the Bible,* 42, does not include this allusion. On the operation of the divine will, see Cyprian, *De laps.* 21 (CCL 3.233).

66. God's anger raises questions about anthropomorphism and the attribution of human characteristics, including feelings, to the divine.

Tertullian, *Adv. Marc.* 2.16.1–7 (CCL 1.492–94), saw anger as part of a totally legitimate divine justice, as did Cyprian, thereby distinguishing it from blind rage. See Joseph M. Hallman, "The Mutability of God: Tertullian to Lactantius," *TS* 42 (1981): 374–86; and Susan Wessel, "A Comparative Study of Anger in Antiquity and Christian Thought," *Journal of Ethics in Antiquity and Christianity* 2 (2020): 40–49. According to Tertullian, *De praescr.* 9–10 (CCL 1.195–96), God need only be sought by the nonbeliever; once found, God was to be believed, thus rendering Matt 7:7 irrelevant to the Christian. The fear of God is biblical (Deut 10:12; Prov 9:10; Luke 23:40; 2 Cor 7:1; and Rev 14:7). The scriptural passages gathered in Cyprian, *Ad Quir.* 3.20 (CCL 3.114–18), were designed to show that fear was the foundation of hope and faith. *Meritis*: can refer both to a service that deserves recompense (reward or punishment) and the recompense itself. Here Cyprian uses it in its negative sense.

67. See n. 13 above.

68. *Superstitiones*: Cicero, *Nat. d.* 2.28.71–72, distinguished *religio*, which was approved, from *superstitio*, which was censured. While Pliny, *Ep.* 10.96(97).8, called Christianity a depraved cult, Cyprian was turning that around and accusing Roman practices regarding the gods as being cultic. In this he was following Tertullian, *Apol.* 6.8 (CCL 1.98) (agreeing with the Romans that Egyptian religion was cultic); 12.6 (CCL 1.110); 21.29 (CCL 1.126); 38.4 (CCL 1.149); and 46.4 (CCL 1.160), not to mention other instances in other pamphlets. See n. 13 above, as well as L. F. Janssen, "'Superstitio' and the Persecution of the Christians," *VC* 33 (1979): 131–59; Maijastina Kahlos, *Debate and Dialogue: Christian and Pagan Cultures* c. *360–430*, Ashgate New Critical Thinking in Religion, Theology and Biblical Studies Series (Farnham: Ashgate, 2007), 93–112; Richard Gordon, "*Superstitio*, Superstition and Religious Repression in the Late Roman Republic and Principate (100 BCE–300 CE)," *Past & Present* 199 supp. 3 (2008): 72–94; and Jörg Rüpke, *Religious Deviance in the Roman World: Superstition or Individuality?* trans. David M. B. Richardson (Cambridge: Cambridge University Press, 2016), 1–11.

69. Fredouille, *Cyprien*, 147, sees this as the third part of the argument (the first starting at the beginning of 3 and the second at the start of 5). Instead, I see this as an extension or development of the second, in which scriptural proofs are offered for the claims made in the previous section. In fact, I see 6–22 as part of the overall theme begun in section 5. It will continue, starting in 7, with Cyprian attempting to demonstrate how that scriptural prophesies had been fulfilled.

70. *Ipsum*: translated in a gender-neutral fashion.

71. *Inquit*: translated in a gender-neutral fashion.

72. Deut 6:13. The verse is quoted in Matt 4:10. The verse is used also by Cyprian in *De laps.* 7 (CCL 3.224); *Ad Fort.* 2 (CCL 3.188); and *Ad Quir.* 3.10 (CCL 3.98). In the last instance the passage is identified explicitly as coming from Deut, while in *Ad Fort.* the three passages that follow are identified as coming from Deut, but not the first. One may note that *Ad Fort.* agrees with

Ad Deme. in using *ipsi*, while *Ad Quir.* and *De laps.* use *illi.* The Vulgate would go on to use *adorabis* in the Matthean version but *timebis* for the version in Deuteronomy. See Fahey, *Cyprian and the Bible*, 90–91, who simply regards them as coming from Deut.

73. Deut 5:7. The verse appears also in Exod 20:3 and Ps 80:9 (LXX). The verse is used also by Cyprian in *Ad Fort.* 2 (CCL 3.188), where it is identified explicitly as coming from Deut. See Fahey, *Cyprian and the Bible*, 89–90. Wallis, "The Treatises of Cyprian," 459, takes the verse as coming from Exod, but mistakenly stated it was 29:3 instead of 20:3.

74. Jer 25:6. The verse is used also by Cyprian in *Ad Quir.* 1.2 (CCL 3.7), with the addition of *et non audistis me* from verse 7; and *Ad Fort.* 3 (CCL 3.189–90). See Fahey, *Cyprian and the Bible*, 226. Brent, *On the Church*, 74, mistakenly conflates this passage with the previous one, identifying them both as Deut 5:7.

75. Hag 1:9b–11. See Fahey, *Cyprian and the Bible*, 253, who notes that this was the only occasion Cyprian used this minor prophet, discounting what appears in *Ad Quir.* 3.20 (CCL 3.118).

76. Amos 4:7–8. See Fahey, *Cyprian and the Bible*, 246–47. Again, one wonders what advantage there would have been for Cyprian to quote passages of Scripture to Demetrian, who would not have recognized their authority or standing in a forensic debate as admissible evidence. Of course, Cyprian was not shy to promote his faith to his non-Christian acquaintances and to impress Christian readers with his debating skills, giving them material to ponder themselves or use in their own encounters with the non-Christians of Carthage who sought to blame them for the pandemic.

77. In *Epp.* 4.3.2 (CCL 3B.21); 59.12.2 (CCL 3C.356); 65.1.2 (CCL 3C.427); 73.19.1 (CCL 3C.552); *De unit.* 18 (CCL 3.262); *Ad Quir.* 2.6 (CCL 3.36); and *Ad Fort.* 5 (CCL 3.192), Cyprian employed the two words or combined them in other ways.

78. *Eum*: translated in a gender-neutral fashion. In *De laps.* 7 (CCL 3.224), where Cyprian had also employed Deut 6:13 (see n. 72 above), there is also mention of divine wrath. One may note that, while in this pamphlet Cyprian wanted to stress to non-Christians that God's justice is and will result in divine punishment, he could also stress, for a Christian readership, the divine patience and lack of punishment in the hope of enticing reconciliation, as in *De bono* 4 (CCL 3A.119–20). Fredouille, *Cyprien*, 55, sees 7 as the start of a part that runs to the end of 11, in which Cyprian showed that non-Christians did not understand the meaning of these evil events. I think instead that Cyprian was demonstrating the fulfilment of the scriptural passages he had assembled in the previous section.

79. Pliny, *Ep.* 10.96(97).3, had called the Christians stubborn. It would suit Cyprian's rhetorical purpose of deflecting blame from the Christians onto someone else to use the term used against Christians now against non-Christians.

80. *Situ*: Wallis, "The Treatises of Cyprian," 459, and Roy J. Deferrari, *Saint Cyprian: Treatises*, Fathers of the Church 36 (Washington, DC: Catholic University of America Press, 1958), 172, translate this as "neglect" and link it with earth, as does Gallicet, *Cipriano*, 85, who translates it as "la squallida campagna" ("bleak countryside"), and Fredouille, *Cyprien*, 83, who translates it as "terre en friche" ("wasteland"). See Seneca, *Phaed.* 471. However, following Antonella Cerretini, *Cipriano: Trattati*, CTP 175 (Rome: Città Nuova, 2004), 89, who offers "se la terra è ricoperta di uno strato di polvere" ("if the earth is covered with a layer of dust"), I have taken the ablative *situ* as linked with the genitive *pulveris* in the sense of a "geographic layout." As geometricians drew their figures in dust (Cicero, *Nat. d.* 2.18.48), this example of divine punishment might not have seemed that bad to Demetrian. However, dust was also seen as part of the grind of life (Quintilian, *Inst.* 10.1.33; and Cicero, *Nat. d.* 2.57.145) or human fate after death (Cicero, *Tusc.* 3.25, quoting Euripides, *Hyp.*). Fronto's *Laud. fumi et pulv.* was on a topic he knew to be disdainful and trifling.

81. *Ieiunas et pallidas*: Grass turns yellow for a number of reasons, particularly a lack of nutrients, especially nitrogen and iron, in the soil. One is reminded of Caesar's comment in Plutarch, *Ant.* 11.3, of being wary of τοὺς ὠχροὺς καὶ λεπτοὺς ("the pale and lean") Brutus and Cassius, which became in Shakespeare, *Julius Caesar* 1.2, a reference to the "lean and hungry" Cassius.

82. Hail was a regular worry to farmers. See Pliny, *Ep.* 4.6. See Minucius Felix, *Oct.* 5.13 (CSEL 2.9).

83. See nn. 24 and 133 of the translation of *De mort.*

84. *Pestilens*: The idea is that the stench carries contagion in the air.

85. In *De laps.* 16 (CCL 3.230), Cyprian had employed a similar list. See n. 133 of the translation of *De mort.* With the last two examples Cyprian returns to the cause of this particular outburst of antagonism against the Christians of Carthage, viz., the outbreak of the deadly pestilence.

86. Brent, *On the Church*, 75, adds "your" to "sins." This is reasonable given that part of Cyprian's argument was to turn the tables; Christians were not responsible for bad things happening, non-Christians were.

87. *Talia et tanta*: This is a common expression in Cyprian. See *Epp.* 37.3.2 (CCL 3B.181); 59.5.1 (CCL 3C.344); and *De bono* 8 (CCL 3A.123). As God's punishment is proven to be taking place, Cyprian noted that non-Christians complained, which exacerbated the punishment. This will be contrasted with the Christian response (17).

88. See n. 42 above.

89. *Malorum*: Deferrari, *Saint Cyprian*, 173, translates this as "devil" but the plural would indicate that people were meant.

90. Jer 2:30. See Fahey, *Cyprian and the Bible*, 220.

91. *Dicatus*: Brent, *On the Church*, 75, must have taken the verb here as *dicere* rather than *dicare* in order to translate this as "under his dictation." See Cyprian, *Ad Fort.* incip.1 (CCL 3.183).

92. Jer 5:3. See Fahey, *Cyprian and the Bible*, 220.

93. Gallicet, *Cipriano*, 190, punctuates these two sentences differently, making with the first being the one-word question "what?" and the second a lengthy conditional statement.

94. *Obsequium*: while the meaning is clear—the world is being less cooperative with human wants—the word Cyprian chose here indicates not only that the world was being less useful but also less pliable to human demands. It is this notion of obedience that leads Cyprian to employ the metaphor of slavery.

95. The classical cosmology of four elements (earth, air, water, and fire) lies behind Cyprian's comments here, although he mentions water twice and omits fire.

96. We find much the same idea expressed a couple of generations later in Arnobius, *Adv. nat.* 1.9 (CSEL 4.9), which is a strong indication of the later apologist's knowledge of Cyprian.

97. Cyprian's comments seem particularly biting here. If Demetrian were among the upper echelons of local Carthaginian society, it would have been galling to be called a slave and it would have been just as galling to be criticized for the way he chose to treat his slaves. Cyprian's words are also ironic in that Demetrian would have rejected Cyprian's assertion in this sentence that he served the Christian God. On slavery in the Roman world, see Keith Bradley, *Slavery and Society at Rome* (Cambridge: Cambridge University Press, 1994); William Fitzgerald, *Slavery and the Roman Literary Imagination* (Cambridge: Cambridge University Press, 2000); Sandra R. Joshel, *Slavery in the Roman World* (Cambridge: Cambridge University Press, 2010); Kyle Harper, *Slavery in the Late Roman World, AD 275–425* (Cambridge: Cambridge University Press, 2011); Jerry Toner, *Roman Guide to Slave Management: A Treatise by Nobleman Marcus Sidonius Falx* (New York: Abrams, 2016); and Kostas Vlassopoulos, *Historicising Ancient Slavery*, Edinburgh Studies in Ancient Slavery (Edinburgh: Edinburgh University Press, 2021). The compassion of slave owners is mentioned in Cyprian, *De mort.* 16 (CCL 3A.25) and the slave-like stubbornness of those who want to cling to this life in *De mort.* 18 (CCL 3A.26).

98. The idea that all people, Christian and non-Christian, slave and free, shared or possessed the same human nature is found regularly in Cyprian: *Ad Deme.* 19 (CCL 3A.46); *De mort.* 8 (CCL 3A.20–21); and *De oper.* 25 (CCL 3A.71). It is found also in Minucius Felix, *Oct.* 37.10 (CSEL 2.53), and the Stoics, like Seneca, *Ben.* 3.18; 3.28.1; Seneca, *Otio* 4.1; Seneca, *Ira* 2.22.1; and Seneca, *Ep.* 47.10.

99. Demetrian would have been very familiar with the Latin expression *memento mori* ("remember, you will die"). The point is that it applied to all people without exception.

100. Since the comparison is with "body," *anima* here is best translated as "soul." Cf. Cyprian, *De mort.* 5 (CCL 3A.19).

101. Brent, *Cyprian and Roman Carthage*, 102–3, notes Cyprian's idea of natural equality as being derived from the Stoic ideas found in Cicero and Seneca. See also Gallicet, *Cipriano*, 193–96.

102. There is much attention in early Christian scholarship on the question of free will, particularly with regard to Augustine, whose *De libero arbitrio* was written some 150 years after Cyprian's time. Radu Bandol, "*Voluntas as liberum arbitrium* at Saint Augustine and Three Meanings of the *servum arbitrium* at Martin Luther," *Philobiblon* 17 (2012): 402–20, distinguishes *arbitrium* as the faculty of judgment from *voluntas* as a disposition or inclination. Cyprian was probably using the terms synonymously and interchangeably rather than as terms with discrete meanings. See Richard Sorabji, *Perception, Conscience and Will in Ancient Philosophy*, Variorum Collected Studies (London: Routledge, 2013).

103. For Lucretius, *Nat.* 5.339–50, proof that the world would come to an end was to be found in previous disasters and diseases. All that was needed was something stronger to bring the world to an end. At the end of this section he wrote about disease being a natural sign of mortality and said nothing about it being a divine punishment.

104. Matt 5:22 mentions hell of fire, while Matt 18:8 refers to eternal fire and the equivalent passage in Mark 9:43 refers to the unquenchable fire of hell. In Matt 25:41, the parable of the sheep and the goats, those represented by the goats are sent to the eternal fire prepared for the devil and the evil angels. In the interpretation of the parable of the wheat and the weeds in Matt 13:42, those represented by the weeds will, at the last judgment, be thrown into the furnace of fire where they will weep and gnash their teeth. In the parable of the rich man and Lazarus, the rich man ends up in Hades in torment (Luke 16:23) in flames (Luke 16:24). The idea that not only are the fires eternal but that one will be there for eternity is in Luke 16:26 about the chasm between the bosom of Abraham and Hades. See Scott G. Bruce, ed., *The Penguin Book of Hell*, Penguin Classics (London: Penguin, 2018). Tertullian, *Apol.* 40.13 (CCL 1.155), while stating that people deserved and experienced punishment from God for sin, wanted to stress that such punishment was reducing because of Christians, rather than increasing with the approaching end of the world in Cyprian. See Cyprian, *De mort.* 14 (CCL 3A.24); and Cyprian, *Ep.* 58.10.1 (CCL 3C.333–34).

105. *Rogantium*: rogation days began to appear in Christian liturgy from the fifth century in Gaul through prayer and fasting in preparation for the celebration of the Ascension with litanies and processions asking God for blessings upon crops and for protection against earthquakes. See Daniel T. Reff, *Plagues, Priests, and Demons: Sacred Narratives and the Rise of Christianity in the Old World and the New* (Cambridge: Cambridge University Press, 2005), 100. Of course, here Cyprian was stating that those entreating God after they had died had left it too late.

106. *Filii*: translated in a gender-neutral fashion.

107. Hos 4:1–4. See Fahey, *Cyprian and the Bible*, 242. The passage is cited by Cyprian in *Ad Quir.* 3.47 (CCL 3.136), where he attempted to show that Christians did not receive God's help because of their sins, while in our pamphlet God's words are used as a response to non-Christian failures. The Latin is identical in the two extracts. Again, one wonders how effective it would have been in a debate with a non-Christian to base an argument on an appeal to documentary evidence (the Bible) that the opponent would not have considered admissible or probative.

108. *Se*: translated in a gender-neutral fashion.

109. See Cyprian, *De unit.* 19 (CCL 3.263).

110. *Anima*: the reference here is not so much to the intellect as it is to the very soul or spirit of a person being unable to breathe because of choking presence of evil.

111. Brent, *On the Church*, 77, translates this as first person rather than second.

112. See Matt 7:1–5; Luke 6:37; Rom 2:1, 21; 14:4, 10, 13. The idea of self-examination is not exclusively Christian. See Seneca, *Ep.* 80.10. Nor is it something applicable only to non-Christians. See Cyprian, *De laps.* 21 and 26–27 (CCL 3.233 and 235–36).

113. The alliteration here is to capture the rhetorical polish Cyprian created in this list of the unacknowledged wrongdoing in people like Demetrian. Cyprian frequently listed groups of sins: *Ad Dona.* 3 (CCL A.4); *De mort.* 4 (CCL 3A.19); *De laps.* 6 (CCL 3.223–24); *De unit.* 16 (CCL 3.261); *De zelo* 6 (CCL 3A.78).

114. Gallicet, *Cipriano*, 206 prefers to read *plagas* rather than *poenas*.

115. Tertullian, *Apol.* 42–43 (CCL 1.156–58), concentrated on the complaints of the non-Christians about the social and, more importantly, economic consequences of Christians not participating in the society in which they lived. Cyprian has them complain more about the consequences of changes in the natural environment.

116. *Togas*: the toga was the outer garment draped around the body, worn by Roman citizens and forbidden to foreigners, freedmen, and slaves, the wearing of which had decreased in popularity by the time of Cyprian except for formal occasions among the Roman elite. Brent, *On the Church*, 78, translated this as referring to generals in triumph, although I think that the reference was intended to be applied more broadly than that. See Seneca, *Ira* 2.8.2, for such a broader context.

117. Cyprian, *Ep.* 62 (CCL 3C.385–88), wrote of the need to ransom captive Christians. The barbarians who took them would have been indigenous people in the southern area of North Africa.

118. *Annonarum*: The *annona* was the food, principally grain but other produce as well, supplied to feed the population of Rome. First introduced under C. Sempronius Gracchus in 123 BCE, managing the collection (from Egypt, Africa, Sicily, and Sardinia primarily as tax payments) and distribution

of the *annona*, exercised through a *praefectus annonae* was a principal determinant of an emperor's public regard. Delays in the arrival of the grain ships would see product hoarding and consequent skyrocketing prices, which led to starvation and urban unrest. By regulating supply, the imperial machinery of government was able to regulate inflation and provide the free allocation of grain to those who qualified. One of the effects of the pestilence during Cyprian's time was a smaller grain harvest, which resulted in significant economic and social pressures not only in Rome but in North Africa as well. See G. E. Rickman, "The Grain Trade under the Roman Empire," *Memoirs of the American Academy in Rome* 36 (1980): 261–75; Garnsey, *Famine and Food Supply*; Paul Erdkamp, *The Grain Market in the Roman Empire: A Social, Political and Economic Study* (Cambridge: Cambridge University Press, 2005); and Philip Kay, *Rome's Economic Revolution* (Oxford: Oxford University Press, 2014). The problem was mentioned in Prov. 11:26, which Cyprian cited in *Ad Quir.* 3.61 (CCL 3.151). See Fahey, *Cyprian and the Bible*, 163.

119. See Cyprian, *De mort.* 8 and 16 (CCL 3A.21 and 25). See Cicero, *Har. resp.*

120. Cyprian returns to the issue of climate change, which had been mentioned earlier in sections 2 and 3. Again, Cyprian was complaining about supply manipulation in that the wealthy were not making their grain reserves available during a drought, thereby keeping prices high and starving those who could not afford to buy food. See also the parable in Luke 12:16–21.

121. *Pestem et luem*: Cyprian uses the same phrase in *De mort.* 16 (CCL 3A.25). The words can refer to disease and illness themselves, but I have chosen to translate them more with a sense of the impact of such disease and illness, particularly given that Cyprian used a wide range of other terms to refer to such things in themselves. On *crimen*, see n. 21 above.

122. *Pietatis*: On the importance of this virtue of respect and duty for the Roman world, see Gertrude Emilie, "Cicero and the Roman *Pietas*," *CJ* 39 (1944): 536–42; Gerald Malsbary, "Pietas and the Origins of Western Culture," *Logos* 4 (2001): 93–116; and Rodney Stark, "Religious Competition and Roman Piety," *Interdisciplinary Journal of Research on Religion* 2 (2006) (www.religjournal.com/articles/article_view.php?id=18).

123. Given the use of the present participle, I think Cyprian is not referring to the funeral rites of the dead, as Brent, *On the Church*, 78, offers.

124. See n. 42 above.

125. Cyprian observes that unscrupulous people, such as Demetrian, took advantage of other people's misfortunes (and those that did not were generally thought to miss out badly), all of which Cyprian rejects.

126. Cicero, *Verr.* 5.171, shows that such a place is as far away from normal life as a Roman could imagine.

127. Cyprian, *Ep.* 59.11.2 (CCL 3C.), argued that lies, like those told in Rome on behalf of Fortunatus, a rival bishop set up in Carthage against Cyprian by the laxists, about how much support he had in Africa, would be

exposed, just as day replaced night. See Geoffrey D. Dunn, "Cyprian's Rival Bishops and Their Communities," *Aug* 45 (2005): 73–87.

128. *Falsarii*: literally "forgers."

129. Cicero, *Cat.* 2.4.7, blamed Catiline for being behind every poisoning, gladiatorial uprisings, robbery, assassination, parricide, forgery of wills, cheating, gluttony, adultery, prostitution, and youth corruption happening in Rome at the time.

130. Was Cyprian arguing that everyone was just as guilty as anyone else or that victims were so intimidated that they were unwilling to come forward? I am inclined to think the latter, as the following sentences make clear.

131. Hartel's 1868 edition in CSEL read *iudice*, which Simonetti changed to *indice* in his 1976 CCL edition. Gallicet, *Cipriano*, 92, and Fredouille, *Cyprien*, 94, also maintained *iudice*. The idea of someone like Demetrian acting with impunity is even stronger if the person for whom he had no respect was the judge not just a witness.

132. Isa 59:1–2. The verses are used also in Cyprian, *De laps.* 21 (CCL 3233); and Cyprian, *Ad Quir.* 3.47 (CCL 3.136)—with the addition of verses 3 and 4 in the latter—with exactly the same wording in the first and only *peccata* instead of *delicta* in the second. See Fahey, *Cyprian and the Bible*, 213–14. Fredouille, *Cyprien*, 159, points out that Cyprian was the first Latin-writing Christian to use these verses.

133. Cyprian, *Ad Dona.* 12 (CCL 3A.10).

134. Although Simonetti presents this as a question in his edition, I follow Gallicet, *Cipriano*, 211, in translating this as a statement. This begins a subsection about non-Christian responsibility for the world's woes: they are being punished for persecuting Christians (12–13).

135. *Feralium.* See Cyprian, *De laps.* 10 (CCL 3.226); Cyprian, *De mort.* 16 (CCL 3A.25); and Cyprian, *Epp.* 55.9.2 (CCL 3B.267); 55.14.2 (CCL 3B.272); and 58.9.2 (CCL 3C.333). When linked with edicts, Clarke translates it as "savage."

136. See n. 68 above.

137. This had been stated already above in section 5 (CCL 3A.37). See n. 13 above for comment on *religio.*

138. Fredouille, *Cyprien*, 162, prefers *fatigatis* ("accabliez"—"overwhelm" or "tire") to *flagitatis* on the basis that this verb is found in 18.2 (CCL 3A.46); and Cyprian, *De laps.* 13 (CCL 3.227).

139. *Eius*: translated in a gender-neutral fashion.

140. See Tertullian, *Apol.* 24.2 (CCL 1.133).

141. See Tertullian, *Apol.* 12.2 (CCL 1.109–10).

142. *Portenta quaedam et monstra*: the Latin here could be translated as "portents and omens," but translations generally take the phrase in a more specific sense, as specific signs of something sinister. See Cyprian, *Quod idola* 4 (CSEL 3/1.21); and Minucius Felix, *Oct.* 25.9 (CSEL 2.36), with reference

to Egypt. In Minucius Felix, *Oct.* 10.5 (CSEL 2.14), non-Christians are said to claim that the Christian God is a monstrous invention.

143. On sacrifice in Roman religion, see C. A. Faraone and F. S. Naiden, eds., *Greek and Roman Animal Sacrifice* (Cambridge: Cambridge University Press, 2012); G. S. Aldrete, "Hammers, Axes, Bulls, and Blood: Some Practical Aspects of Roman Animal Sacrifice," *JRS* 104 (2014): 28–50; and Celia E. Schultz, "Roman Sacrifice, Inside and Out," *JRS* 106 (2016): 58–76, who argues that ritual slaughter of animals was not the central part of Roman sacrifice, arguing for other parts of the ritual being central and for other things besides animals being more frequently the object of sacrifice. Cyprian here was not so much concerned with the slaughter as with the end result of the holocaust of the sacrificed animals as a sign of their (unjustifiable) popularity. See Tertullian, *Apol.* 23.14 (CCL 1.132). Of course, there was no point in Cyprian reminding Demetrian that as a result of Decius's edict many Christians had joined in such sacrifices and had created a real crisis for Christian membership, as he did to his fellow Christians in *De laps.* 8 (CCL 3.225).

144. Cyprian has not taken this information from Tertullian, who only mentions in passing non-Christian divinization of animals (*Apol.* 16.5 [CCL 1.115]). Minucius Felix, *Oct.* 28.8 (CSEL 2.42), mentions snakes and crocodiles being worshipped as gods by the Egyptians. Given the mention of crocodiles and baboons it would seem that Cyprian had Egypt in mind, where the worship of Sobek (the crocodile god), was popular. See Michal Molcho, "Crocodile Breeding in the Crocodile Cults of the Graeco-Roman Fayum," *Journal of Egyptian Archaeology* 100 (2014): 181–93. The hamadryas baboon (*papio hamadryas*) was sacred to the Egyptians, as shown in some depictions of Thoth (who otherwise is ibis-headed) and Babi (the deified baboon who would devour the souls of the sinful after a negative judgment from Maat after a person's death), although the yellow baboon (*papio cynocephalus*) that lives in south central Africa has been given the designation "dog-headed," employing the Latin term used here by Cyprian. Nehebkau, a serpent god, was also associated with funerary practices in Egypt. See Richard Wilkinson, *The Complete Gods and Goddesses of Ancient Egypt* (London: Thames and Hudson, 2017). During the reign of Elagabalus (218–22), the baetyl (sacred stone) of the Syrian sun god Elgabal was housed in the Elagabalium, a temple on the Palatine facing the Colosseum. Brent, *Cyprian and Roman Carthage*, 32–41, sees Cyprian taking serpents as chthonian gods in the Carthaginian tradition, as exemplified in Virgil, *Aen.* 6, with Aeneas's journey through the underworld and as depicted on a panel of the Carthaginian version of the Ara Pacis (now in the Louvre) and on a panel of the *gens Augusta* altar from Carthage dedicated by Hedulus (now in the Bardo). See Barbette Stanley Spaeth, "The Goddess Ceres in the Ara Pacis Augustae and the Carthage Relief," *American Journal of Archaeology* 98 (1994): 65–100; and Megan Goldman-Petri, "The Altar of P. Perelius Hedulus in Carthage and Social Aspects of Provincial Image-Making,"

in *The Social Dynamics of Roman Imperial Imagery*, ed. Amy Russell and Monica Hellström (Cambridge: Cambridge University Press, 2020), 180–214.

145. Tertullian, *Apol.* 10–28 (CCL 1.105–40), had dealt with the charge of Christians not worshipping the gods by asserting that the gods were nonexistent. See n. 28 above. In 14.1 (CCL 1.112), he criticized the Romans for destroying (*mactatis*) only the inedible parts as an offering to the gods.

146. Seneca, *Ep.* 14.5, mentioned a very similar list as a form of evil.

147. Fredouille, *Cyprien*, 160–64, shows a gradation in what non-Christians demand against Christians throughout this section.

148. At first sight this appears contradictory; Christians were indeed put to death for their Christianity. However, it would seem that the aim of Roman authorities was not to punish Christians but to secure their participation in the mandated cultic practices. Thus, the person who admitted their Christianity was not killed but tortured in order to deny or renounce their faith and participate in sacrifice. Only when that failed was execution considered. The person who denied their faith was unmolested. Tertullian, *Apol.* 2.10–17 (CCL 1.89–90), had pointed out how perverse this was: normally someone who denied the charged was tortured to confess it rather than the person who admitted the charge being tortured in order to deny it. In Cyprian's own time those who admitted their Christianity in response to the religious revival instigated by Decius were imprisoned and tortured or banished rather than killed. On the tortures see Cyprian, *De laps.* 13–14 (CCL 3.227–228). Gallicet, *Cipriano*, 218–21, sees the difference between Tertullian and Cyprian here as the former presenting a somewhat more juridical argument and the latter a more moral and psychological one. However, this rests on the mistaken assumption that Tertullian had specialist legal training. Both Tertullian and Cyprian had the standard rhetorical training as orators (with Cyprian being a teacher of oratory), which was sufficient for anyone to practice as an advocate in a legal setting.

149. *Prius* here is not suggesting that one no longer is what one had been before but is used in a simple chronological fashion to indicate what one has been up to (and continued to be) the point of encounter.

150. The lie would be to say, "I am not a Christian," hiding the fact that he is a Christian and that he does not worship the gods.

151. The crime here is probably more the concealment of one's Christianity than simply being a Christian, which Cyprian did not hold as being a crime even though the provincial authorities did.

152. *In abditis et secretis locis*: the same expression is used in Cyprian, *De domi.* 4 (CCL 3A.91), although one should note that a significant number of manuscripts read *semotis* rather than *secretis* in that work. It comes from Matt 6:6. In writing to Demetrian, Cyprian was not rejecting Jesus's teaching on prayer but affirming, for Christian readers who picked up on the scriptural reference, that, while prayer was personal, confession of faith was public.

153. *Praesidibus*: while Africa Proconsularis was governed by a proconsul as it was a prestigious senatorial province, *praeses* had become a generic term for a governor. Under the provincial reforms of Diocletian late in the third century, it was the title applied to governors of most of the new, smaller provinces he created, although Africa Proconsularis remained under the governorship of one of the three proconsuls. See Cyprian, *Ep.* 80.1.3 (CCL 3C.627).

154. I take this to be a reference to the lies about the existence of the gods; such lies ought to be more hated because they have been disproved all the more through Christian proclamation.

155. Gallicet, *Cipriano*, 224, includes *vince* only once and so the English translation would read "demolish the faith by debate, conquer by reason if you can." For similar use see Cyprian, *Ep.* 71.3.1 (CCL 3C.519) and 73.13.1 (CCL 3C.543).

156. Here begins the second subsection (14–22) about why non-Christians are being punished by God and thus responsible for the problems the world faced: their idolatry. The first part of this subsection (14–15) considers non-Christian failure to worship God as the reason for the bad things happening in the world. Cyprian wanted to demonstrate the impotency of these non-Christian gods.

157. On the significance of idolatry for Cyprian, see *Ad Fort.* 1–5 (CCL 3.187–93) and on the impotence of idols, see *Quod idola* 7 (CSEL 3/1.24–25). The authorship of that latter work has long been challenged and Sage, *Cyprian*, 373–75, is more than disinclined to accept it as being by Cyprian. However, the fact that it is listed among Cyprian's works in Augustine's *Serm.* 313C.2 (Morin, *Miscellanea Agostiniana* 1.531), would be a strong argument in favor of its authenticity, unless the reference were actually to Cyprian's *Ad Fort.*

158. *Tutela* was the concept in Roman law of the protection offered to minors and women who were, for whatever reason, not under the responsibility of a *paterfamilias*. In religion the gods were meant to offer protection to people. Cyprian's point here is that because of a role reversal, the gods were shown to be impotent.

159. *Clausus* is the passive participle of both *claudeo* and *claudo*, so Brent, *On the Church*, 83, is correct that this could be translated as "retarded" (or "defective" or "enfeebled") from *claudeo*. Gallicet, *Cipriano*, 101, offers "custodite rinchiusi" and Fredouille, *Cyprien*, 101, suggests "enferme," both from *claudo* and I follow them here. The principal verb *pereo*, has the sense of "vanish," "perish," "be destroyed," or "be ruined" and could be used with either verb. Given that temples frequently stored valuables meant that they were locked at night, and the obvious meaning would be to the cult statues of the gods, along with their valuables, thus protected. Indeed, there could be the suggestion that the power of a non-Christian gods, if they existed, did not stretch beyond their temples, while the Christian God was omnipresent.

However, both meanings of the participle could have been intended by Cyprian taking advantage of its homonymous form.

160. Cyprian here provides reference to exorcism. See also Cyprian, *Ad Dona.* 5 (CCL 3A.6); Cyprian, *Quod idola* 7 (CSEL 3/1.25); and Cyprian, *Ep.* 69.15.1 (CCL 3C.493). This rite was used in imitation of the activity of Jesus, described in the gospels, of healing people by driving out the demons that possessed them. It was ritualized further by being celebrated as part of the process of instruction during the catechumenate and in the immediate preparation of catechumens during the scrutinies to receive initiation in the weeks leading up to the Easter vigil. To which of the two was Cyprian referring? Everett Ferguson, *Baptism in the Early Church: History, Theology, and Liturgy in the First Five Centuries* (Grand Rapids: Eerdmans, 2009), 351 n. 4, sees the reference here as a general one to exorcism. Given that Cyprian mentions the shrieking of those being driven out it would seem that he was thinking of non-Christian gods manifesting themselves as demons in real possessions rather than simply of the liturgical expression in ritual of such renunciation of one's non-Christian background, without ruling the latter out. See Maxwell E. Johnson, *The Rites of Christian Initiation: The Evolution and Interpretation* (Collegeville, MN: Liturgical Press, 1999); Graham H. Twelftree, *In the Name of Jesus: Exorcism among Early Christians* (Grand Rapids: Baker Academic, 2007); Andrew Daunton-Fear, *Healing in the Early Church: The Church's Ministry of Healing and Exorcism from the First to the Fifth Century* (Eugene, OR: Wipf and Stock, 2009); Daniel G. Van Slyke, "The Human Agents of Exorcism in the Early Christian Period: All Christians, Any Christians, or a Select Few Christians?," *Antiphon* 16 (2012): 179–223; Frances Young, *A History of Exorcism in Catholic Christianity*, Palgrave Historical Studies in Witchcraft and Magic (London: Palgrave Macmillan, 2016); and Mikael Tellbe and Tommy Wasserman with Ludvig Nyman, *Healing and Exorcism in Second Temple Judaism and Early Christianity*, WUNT 2. Reihe 511 (Tübingen: Mohr Siebeck, 2019). Tertullian, *Apol.* 22–23 (CCL 1.128–33), had discussed demons, but more about their nature and activity than impotence before Christian exorcism, which is mentioned in 23.8 (CCL 1.131); and in *De idol.* 11.7 (CCL 2.1111). See also Minucius Felix, *Oct.* 27.5–7 (CSEL 2.40).

161. See n. 204 in the translation of *De mort.*

162. The translation of the preposition *de* creates some interesting possibilities for the meaning of this sentence. Wallis, "The Treatises of Cyprian," 462, and Deferrari, *Saint Cyprian*, 180, translate it as indicating the subject of the gods' thoughts ("the gods will speak about you"), Brent, *On the Church*, 84, ignores the preposition and turns the third-person *loquetur* into a second-person verb when he translates this as "while you are speaking these words." Gallicet, *Cipriano*, 101, and Fredouille, *Cyprien*, 103, take it as a preposition of means when they translate this as "parlerà con la tua stessa voce" and "il parlera par ta bouche." This would be a possibility ("it will speak from within you yourself"). I have followed Gallicet and Fredouille here.

163. In the opening lines of the pamphlet, Cyprian had labelled what Demetrian had said as the "frenzy of the deranged." This section (16) is a deliberative call to non-Christians to stop worshipping their impotent, so-called gods and to worship the true God.

164. The metaphor of darkness to light for conversion and the coming to faith is scriptural: Isa 9:1 (Matt 4:16); Luke 1:79; John 8:12; Acts 26:18; 2 Cor 6:14; Eph 1:18; 5:8–14; Col 1:12–13; 1 Thess 5:5; and 1 Pet 2:9. Cyprian, *Ad Dona.* 3 (CCL 3A.4), described his own conversion, in part, as a movement from darkness to light.

165. *Laqueis*: In *De mort.* 7 and 26 (CCL 3A.20 and 31); *De zelo* 3, 10 and 14 (CCL 3A.76, 80, and 82); *De unit.* 23 (CCL 3.266); *De domi.* 20 (CCL 3A.103); and *Ep.* 4.2.2 (CCL 3B.19), Cyprian employed the same word to reference those things that prevent one from being saved.

166. Exod 22:20. The text is used also in Cyprian, *De laps.* 7 (CCL 3.224); Cyprian, *Ad Fort.* 3 (CCL 3.189); Cyprian, *Epp.* 59.12.2 (CCL 3C.356); and 65.1.3 (CCL 3C.427), in exactly the same version. See Fahey, *Cyprian and the Bible*, 76–77. Fredouille, *Cyprien*, 170, noted that this was the first use of this verse and the following passage by a Latin-writing Christian. One may note that another passage used in *Ad Fort.* 3 (from Jer 25) had been used already in this pamphlet (see n. 74 above).

167. Isa 2:8–9. The text is used also in Cyprian, *De laps.* 7 (CCL 3.); Cyprian, *Ad Fort.* 3 (CCL 3.189); and Cyprian, *Ep.* 65.1.3 (CCL 3C.427), in the same version. See Fahey, *Cyprian and the Bible*, 190–191. One may note that in Cyprian when this passage is used (it is not used in *Ep.* 59) it always follows the one from Exod 22:20, except in *De laps.* where it precedes it. One may note that the question applies to the whole statement and is not part of the quotation from Isaiah.

168. Following Simonetti's reading of *ad Dominum suum* rather than Hartel's *ad Dominum susum.*

169. See the similarity with Minucius Felix, *Oct.* 17.2 and 11 (CSEL 2.21 and 23), which some have seen as an indication of direct dependence by Cyprian. However, the importance of the upright stance (*status rectus*) of humans and their superiority over the rest of creation was part of Greek philosophy. See Plato, *Tim.* 90a; and Cicero, *Tusc.* 1.28.69.

170. Was Cyprian contrasting earthly and heavenly spheres or what is below the earth (the realm of the dead or even hell) with what is above the earth?

171. See Cyprian, *De zelo* 14 (CCL 3A.83).

172. *Lapsus* here recalls not only those who had fallen from their faith during the religious renewal program of Decius, but also the slithering motion of a snake. Cyprian here seems to be referring not to any particular snake deity but to the devil of Gen 3. This seems confirmed by the next question that Cyprian posed. Yet, as Brent, *Cyprian and Roman Carthage*, 41, suggests,

there would have been an obvious connection between the chthonian deities, so important in Carthaginian religious identity, and the devil.

173. The concept of original sin was not a concern to Cyprian in the middle of the third century, or at least not a topic he wished to get distracted by with Demetrian.

174. See n. 110 above.

175. The maxim was found inscribed in the temple of Apollo at Delphi according to Pausanias (10.24.1). Aeschylus quoted it in *PV* 309. Plato, *Phdr.* 229E; Plato, *Chrm.* 164D; Plato, *Prt.* 343B; Plato, *Phlb.* 48C; Plato; *Alc.* 124A; Plato, *Leg.* 2.923A; and Xenophon, *Mem.* 4.2.24, saw it as central to Socrates's search for meaning. For Cyprian, true knowledge of self led to true knowledge of God.

176. Brent, *On the Church*, 85, omits this sentence in his translation.

177. *Vivificandis ac reparandis*: Gallicet, *Cipriano*, 235, sees the first term as particularly Christian and the second one used also by non-Christians.

178. While Christians must have been only a tiny fraction of the empire's total population in the middle of the third century, it could suit Christian apologetical argument at times to exaggerate that percentage. See Tertullian, *Apol.* 37.4 and 42.2–3 (CCL 1.148 and 157); and Tertullian, *Ad Scap.* 5.2 (CCL 2.1132).

179. In the first part (17–22) of this subsection, Cyprian points out to Demetrian that punishment for non-Christian idolatry must come from God since it cannot come from Christians, who are nonretaliatory and submissive. Fredouille, *Cyprien*, 56, sees this section as the start of the second major part of the pamphlet (17–22). I see it more connected with 14–16 than he does.

180. Gallicet, *Cipriano*, 237, notes a similar sense of assurance in the Stoicism of Seneca.

181. Tertullian, *Ad nat.* 1.10 (CCL 1.12); and Tertullian, *Apol.* 37 (CCL 1.138–139), had mentioned Christian nonretaliation. He also mentioned that if Christians were to retaliate, they were so numerous as to inflict severe retribution and that the non-Christians had no one to help them resist. The more positive Christian command of loving enemies (Matt 5:44; Luke 6:27–28) is mentioned at the start of Tertullian, *Ad Scap.* (1.3 [CCL 2.1127]). The idea of divine retribution, which features in these sentences of Cyprian, was not a feature of Tertullian's *Ad nat.* or *Apol.* but is found in *Ad Scap.* 3.5 (CCL 2.1129). Cyprian also dealt with retaliation in *De bono* 21–24 (CCL 3A.130–33). On Christian nonretaliation in Tertullian and Cyprian, see Geoffrey D. Dunn, "Turn the Other Cheek: Patience and Non-retaliation in the Early Christian African Tradition," in *Cristianesimo e violenza: gli autori cristiani di fronte a testi biblici "Scomodi."* XLIV Incontro di studiosi dell'antichità cristiana, Rome 5–7 May 2016, SEAug 151 (Rome: Institutum Patristicum Augustinianum, 2018), 323–40.

182. That is, the Christian group.

183. See Tertullian, *Ad Scap.* 3 (CCL 2.1129–30).

184. Eberhard Heck, *MH ΘEOMAXEIN oder: Die Bestrafung des Gottesverächters. Untersuchungen zu Bekämpfung und Aneigung römischer religio bei Tertullian, Cyprian und Laktanz*, Studien zur klassischen Philologie 24 (Frankfurt am Main: Peter Lang, 1987), 174–80, takes this as a reference to Decius, as have many others. See n. 57 in the introduction. The fact that Cyprian was referring to divine retribution would make the death of Decius the most obvious point of reference.

185. Rom 12:19, referring to Deut 32:35. It is used also in Cyprian, *Ad Quir.* 3.106 (CCL 3.173). See Fahey, *Cyprian and the Bible*, 436–37.

186. Prov 20:22. It is also used in Cyprian, *Ad Quir.* 3.106 (CCL 3.173). One may note that while both this and the previous passage are both used in both works, they are reversed. See Fahey, *Cyprian and the Bible*, 166.

187. Gallicet, *Cipriano*, 242, states that in sections 18–21, Cyprian was inspired by Minucius Felix, *Oct.* 12 (CSEL 2.16–17), in dealing with the non-Christian objection that the Christian God did not protect Christians. Tertullian, *Apol.* 41.2–4 (CCL 1.155–56), had also briefly responded to this objection, so it is not surprising that Cyprian worked it into his argument that God was punishing non-Christians for their idolatry. Cyprian would also use the argument in *De mort.* 8 (CCL 3A.20 21). In *De bono* 11 (CCL 3A.124), Cyprian explained to a Christian readership that all people struggled in this life as a consequence of the sin of Adam. In 17 (CCL 3A.128), he repeated the point that the unjust person complains in the face of the same adversities that the just person bears with patience as a test. This ultimately was Cyprian's explanation of the pestilence: a test for Christians and a condemnation of non-Christians.

188. Christian *gloria* is not in this life but the next according to Cyprian: *De bono* 13 (CCL 3A.125–26); *De laps.* 4 and 20 (CCL 3.222 and 233); *Epp.* 6.2.1 and 6.4 (CCL 3B.31 and 36); and 10.4.3 (CCL 3B.52).

189. Cyprian, *De mort.* 2 (CCL 3A.17–18), also discussed those whose sense of purpose and fulfillment is to be found only in this life.

190. There is much in this attitude that matches the Stoic sense of equilibrium. It is found also in *De mort.* 11 (CCL 3A.22), where Cyprian attributed it to a scriptural injunction.

191. In Rom 8:12–17 and Gal 5:17–23, Paul discussed the difference between those led by the spirit and those led by the flesh. It was a topic of some interest to Cyprian since he raised it in *De domi.* 16 (CCL 3A.99–100); *Ad Quir.* 3.64 (CCL 3.154–55); *De zelo* 14 (CCL 3A.82–83); and *Ep.* 56.2.1–2 (CCL 3B.297–98).

192. *Anima*: the comparison with body suggests "soul" as the appropriate translation here.

193. See n. 13 above. The same phrase, *religiosa patientia*, is found in Cyprian, *Ep.* 19.1 (CCL 3B.103), which Clarke, *Letters*, 1.99, translates simply as "religious patience."

194. *Mitis et lenis*: Cyprian, *De bono* 5 (CCL 3A.120), used the same terms to describe the patience of a Christian.

195. *Stabilis*: see its use in Cyprian, *De mort.* 1 (CCL 3A.17), where it was applied to the rock that resists the challenge of the pestilence. See n. 6 there.

196. See n. 24 of the translation of *De mort.*

197. See n. 66 of the translation of *De mort.*

198. The idea of being able to remain calm when surrounded by a chaotic world was shared with Platonism and Stoicism, using similar imagery of waves crashing against the cliffs or a person being tossed about on life's waves. See Cicero, *Tusc.* 5.2.5; Seneca, *Ira* 3.25.3; Seneca, *Constant.* 3.5; and Seneca, *Vita* 27.3.

199. Brent, *On the Church*, 88, translated *condicio communis* as "covenant." In section 21 below he translates it as "shared agreement." While the Latin can certainly mean this, the context suggests it is not appropriate here. The condition into which Christians and non-Christians are born is not the result of any shared agreement; it is simply a given of there being one human nature. The idea of human nature shared by both Christian and non-Christian alike appears also in Cyprian, *De mort.* 8 (CCL 3A.20–21); and Cyprian, *De bono* 11 (CCL 3A.124), as well as in Seneca, *Ben.* 4.28.1.

200. See section 8 above.

201. One is reminded of the parables of the wheat and weeds of Matt 13:24–30, and of the net in Matt 13:47–50. See Dunn, "Ecclesiology in Early North African Christianity," 371–401. When Cyprian referred explicitly to these parables, he applied it to relations between heretics/schismatics and other Christians and he reached a very different conclusion, given that the sin of schismatics was public and well known. Here the situation concerned Christians and non-Christians and the parables are not referenced. It is also a Stoic idea found in Cicero, *Nat. d.* 2.90; Seneca, *Ben.* 7.1.7; and Seneca, *Ep.* 90.42.

202. The reference is to the distinction of fate in the afterlife between Christian and non-Christian.

203. Faith and hope frequently are linked together in Cyprian: *De bono* 1 and 13 (CCL 3A.118 and 125); *De domi.* 1 (CCL 3A.90); *Ep.* 71.3.2 (CCL 3C.521); and *Ad Quir.* 3.20 (CCL 3.114–18).

204. *Inmobilis*: Cyprian, *Ad Fort.* 13 (CCL 3.215), applied this notion of unshakability to the *animus* ("intellect" or "spirit" or "character"), while in *De laps.* 13 (CCL 3.227), he applied it to the *anima*, while also mentioning the *mens stabilis* ("steadfast mind") (see nn. 194 and 195 above) and *fides fortis* ("strong faith")—while we find *fortis...patientia* ("strong patience") in the previous section. In *De unit.* 2 (CCL 3.249–50), Cyprian called those "strong and steadfast" being able to withstand the swirling tempests (see n. 24 of the translation of *De mort.*) as fixed.

205. See nn. 100, 110, and 192 above.

206. Simonetti, following Hartel, reads *salutari*, while Gallicet, *Cipriano*, 253, opts for *salvatore*.

207. Hab 3:17–18. This is the only time Cyprian used this passage. See Fahey, *Cyprian and the Bible*, 250–51. Fredouille, *Cyprien*, 182, observes that Cyprian was the first Christian writer to refer to these verses.

208. Similar images are found in Virgil, *Georg.* 1.107.

209. For Cyprian, *Ep.* 66.7.3 (CCL 3C.441), paradise is the kingdom of heaven.

210. See Cyprian, *De domi.* 17 (CCL 3C.101). The earthly birth was what Christians and non-Christians shared, but the Christians' spiritual birth gave them a completely different destiny.

211. *Recreati et renati*: these words refer to Christian initiation without distinguishing various aspects of the theological understanding of forgiveness and adoption. See Cyprian, *De domi.* 36 (CCL 3A.113), for the same employment of both terms.

212. Cyprian writes about Christian initiation. The question of initiation celebrated by a schismatic/heretical minister was one that would occupy the last few years of his episcopate in the years after the laxist (and rigorist) controversy had been resolved, as those whose only form of initiation was into a laxist or rigorist schismatic/heretical community. Unlike those who had been Christian before entering such a community, who needed only a form of reconciliation to be accepted back when they changed their minds, Cyprian regarded the first group as never having been validly initiated and it could never be a question of them rejoining the church because, as he argued, they had never been part of it. Cyprian's view on the invalidity of sacraments celebrated in schismatic/heretical communities contrasted with that held by Stephen I, bishop of Rome, and later by Augustine of Hippo; the latter view of sacraments not depending upon the status of the minister but operating *ex opere operato* became official Christian teaching. *Ad Deme.* was written before what has been inaccurately called the rebaptism controversy emerged. On the overlap in the meaning of heresy and schism for Cyprian, see Geoffrey D. Dunn, "Heresy and Schism According to Cyprian of Carthage," *JTS* n.s. 55 (2004): 551–74. On the so-called rebaptism controversy in Cyprian, see Geoffrey D. Dunn, *Cyprian and the Bishops of Rome: Questions of Papal Primacy in the Early Church*, ECS 11 (Strathfield, NSW: St Pauls Publications, 2006), 134–80.

213. Christians were commanded by Jesus to pray for their persecutors in Matt 5:44 and Luke 6:27. See Tertullian, *Ad Scap.* 1.3 (CCL 2.1127). In Christian apology it also served the practical purpose of holding back the anger of God from punishing non-Christians. See Tertullian, *Apol.* 30–32 (CCL 1.141–43). There is a weakness in Cyprian's argument, however, since he inserted it into his *senectus mundi* and God punishing non-Christian sin position. Either Christian prayer prevented the punishment from happening, which was not the thrust of the argument, or Christian prayer was ineffective

at stopping the disasters, which, as the pamphlet seems to acknowledge, were not stopping. This is an example where Cyprian's borrowing from Tertullian is less than successful.

214. Cyprian sometimes presented flesh and body together, possibly as synonyms: *De habi.* 6 (CCL 3F.292); and *De mort.* 13 (CCL 3A.23). They are used as synonyms in Tertullian, *Adv. Marc.* 5.10.4 (CCL 1.692); and Tertullian, *De res.* 37.8 (CCL 970).

215. *Profanus*: we find the word used in Cyprian, *Epp.* 55.8.5 (CCL 3.266); and 69.2.1 (CCL 3C.472); and Cyprian, *De unit.* 6 (CCL 3.253). We find it also in Tertullian, *Apol.* 18.3; 21.5; 41.2–3; and 48.13 (CCL 1.118, 123, 156, and 1168). See Pier Franco Beatrice, "On the Meaning of 'Profane' in the Pagan-Christian Conflict of Late Antiquity: The Fathers, Firmicus Maternus and Porphyry before the Orphic 'Prorrhesis' (OF 245.1 Kern)," *Illinois Classical Studies* 30 (2005): 137–65; and Matthew Recla, "*Homo profanes*: The Christian Martyr and the Violence of Meaning-Making," *Critical Research on Religion* 2 (2014): 147–64. As Gallicet, *Cipriano*, 257, observes, by the use of this term Cyprian could refer to both non-Christians and former Christians (schismatics and heretics).

216. *Ipsius* translated in a gender-neutral fashion.

217. In Cyprian's contribution to the September 256 episcopal synod in Carthage, the final of the eighty-seven bishops to speak, he spoke of evangelical and apostolic testimony (*Sent. episc.* 87 [CCL 3E.107). On this synod, see Joseph A. Fischer, "Das Konzil zu Karthago in Spätsommer 256," *AHC* 16 (1984): 1–39; Geoffrey D. Dunn, "*Nam quae foris exercentur nullum habent salutis effectum*: Cyprian and the Synod of September 256," in *Pagani e Cristiani alla ricerca della Salvezza (I–III sec.).* XXXIV Incontro di studiosi dell'antichità cristiana, Rome 5–7 May 2005, SEAug 96 (Rome: Institutum Patristicum Augustinianum, 2006), 513–24; and Dunn, *Cyprian and the Bishops of Rome*, 174–76.

218. See Tertullian, *Ad Scap.* 3.3 (CCL 2.1129).

219. See Cyprian, *Ep.* 65.4.1 (CCL 3C.431), which Clarke, *The Letters of St. Cyprian*, 3.115, translates as "incurable." See Seneca, *Ira* 3.40.5. Here the reference is to the day of the Lord rather than to insanity or anger and so "unstoppable" seems more appropriate.

220. Isa 13:6 and 9. This is the only occasion when Cyprian used these two verses. See Fahey, *Cyprian and the Bible*, 199. Fredouille, *Cyprien*, 187, notes that Cyprian is the first recorded Latin Christian writer to use these verses.

221. *Alienigenae*: literally "foreigners" or "aliens." In this instances Cyprian was interpreting the passage as referring to non-Christians.

222. Mal 3:19. The verse is used in Cyprian, *Ad Quir.* 2.28 (CCL 3.66); and Cyprian, *De bono* 22 (CCL 3A.131), in exactly the same wording. Not only will God come as judge, but that judgment will be in repayment for all the miseries suffered by God's people at the hands of nonbelievers. See Fahey, *Cyprian and the Bible*, 257.

223. *Filios*: translated in a gender-neutral fashion.

224. Fredouille, *Cyprien*, 190–91, states that here Cyprian distinguished between spiritual renewal in baptism and the signing with the sign of Christ in the postbaptismal anointing. Since these were both parts of the same ritual, Cyprian might not have been trying to distinguish the various elements of initiation as much as stressing the unity of a ritual composed of different parts. See Johnson, *The Rites of Christian Initiation*, 66–71; and Ferguson, *Baptism in the Early Church*, 351–61.

225. *In ultimo*: it seems obvious that Cyprian was referring to the actions of the last day than simply stating that God was saying finally or ultimately or more seriously than previously, as some of the other translations have read it.

226. *Caedo* is found in Hos 4:2 in section 9 above, where I have translated it as murder. The difference would appear to be that of motivation in that the action is unlawful and is condemned in that passage while here the same action is divinely commanded.

227. Ezek 9:5–6. This, in a slightly longer version, and the following passage are used, in reverse order, in Cyprian, *Ad Quir.* 2.22 (CCL 3.60–61). See Fahey, *Cyprian and the Bible*, 228–29. Tertullian, *Adv. Iud.* 9.6 (CCL 2.1382), had used a longer version of this passage. See Dunn, *Tertullian's* Aduersus Iudaeos, for the authenticity of this as a pamphlet by Tertullian.

228. Ezek 9:4. See n. 149 above.

229. See n. 46 above.

230. Exod 12:13. This passage is found in *Ad Quir.* 2.22 (CCL 3.61) after the two extracts from Ezek. See Fahey, *Cyprian and the Bible*, 71. Of course, the afflictions that tormented Egypt were a series of so-called plagues of Egypt, the fifth and sixth of which (Exod 9:1–7 and 8–12) were some kind of pestilence or disease. This reference to Exod might be an instance of Cyprian trying to demonstrate to Demetrian an ancient prophesy that it was not God's followers who were responsible for contagion and pandemics, but those who were opposed to God, like Demetrian himself, who were to blame.

231. *In imagine*: the term appears most famously in Gen 1:26; 5:1; and 9:6, where the Latin translates the Greek as *imago Dei*. The term also appears in such New Testament passages as Rom 8:29; 1 Cor 11:7; 2 Cor 3:18; 4:4; Col 1:15; 3:10; and Heb 1:3. What it means for the human person to be the "image" or "likeness" of God has long been debated. See J. Richard Middleton, *The Liberating Image: The* Imago Dei *in Genesis 1* (Grand Rapids: Brazos Press, 2005). Here Cyprian was not interested in that particular issue but contrasted the guise (the slain lamb at Passover) with the reality (the slain Christ on the cross) or, to use the later language developed by Augustine, where the first is the sacrament of the second. Cyprian could also use *figura* or *typus* for much the same purpose. On the Passover lamb and Christ, see also Cyprian, *De unit.* 8 (CCL 3.255); Cyprian, *Ad Quir.* 2.15 (CCL 3.49–50); and Cyprian, *Ep.* 69.4.1 (CCL 3C.474).

232. On figures and events from the Hebrew scriptures being a prefiguring of Christ, see Cyprian, *De bono* 10 (CCL 3A.123); and *Ep.* 63.4.3 (CCL 3C.394).

233. The *peroratio* of the pamphlet begins with a deliberative call to the non-Christians to recognize that the evils in the world were occurring because of their failure to worship the one God and they should start believing in this God so that they would not be recipients of divine punishment. Fredouille, *Cyprien*, 193, sees the final section of the pamphlet starting here, all of which he regards as a deliberative exhortation to conversion. On the urgency for action see Cyprian, *De laps.* 29 (CCL 3.237); and Cyprian, *De oper.* 24 (CCL 3A.71).

234. See Luke 21:31.

235. See Virgil, *Georg.* 1.154. One thinks also of Matt 13:24–30, the parable of the wheat and the weeds, although the parable does not contain a sense of one plant dominating the other. See n. 137 above. The wild oat (*avena fatua*) is an invasive weed and lowers the quality of the yield of a crop of wheat, barley, or cultivated/domesticated oats (*avena sativa*) dramatically if unchecked. While it can be used to graze animals while young or later cut for hay, it depletes soil and encourages pests and disease.

236. Amos 5:6. See Fahey, *Cyprian and the Bible*, 247, who identifies the passage instead as actually from Ps 68:33 (LXX), attributing Cyprian's attribution to the prophet as the result of faulty memory.

237. The linking of *docere* and *dicere* creates a word play.

238. John 17:3. The verse is used (sometimes in an extended quotation) elsewhere in Cyprian: *Ad Quir.* 2.1 (CCL 3.30); *De domi.* 28 (CCL 3A.108); *Ad Fort.* 2 (CCL 3.189); and *Ep.* 73.17.1 (CCL 3C.549). On each occasion the verse is employed for a different purpose. See Fahey, *Cyprian and the Bible*, 399–400.

239. See n. 32 of the translation of *De mort.*

240. Gehenna was the valley of Hinnon in Jerusalem where child sacrifice at the Tophet seems to have been performed (2 Kgs 23:10; Jer 7:31; 19:2–6). Under rabbinic Judaism it was seen as a place of punishment of the wicked. Cyprian used the term in *De mort.* 14 (CCL 3A.24); *De oper.* 2 (CCL 3A.55); *Epp.* 6.3.1 (CCL 3B.35); and 59.18.3 (CCL 3C.371). One may note the use of rhetorical epanaphora in the last few sentences.

241. See Cyprian, *Ep.* 28.1.1 (CCL 3B.133).

242. One may note the rhetorical antithesis here.

243. For a similar idea, see Minucius Felix, *Oct.* 35.3 (CSEL 2.50).

244. Isa 66:24. This is the only time this verse was used by Cyprian. See Fahey, *Cyprian and the Bible*, 216–17.

245. *Paenitentia*: in the Christian context the word means more than "regret." For his translation of Tertullian's pamphlet *De paen.*, William P. Le Saint, *Tertullian: Treatises on Penance: On Penitence and On Purity*, ACW 28 (New York: Newman Press, 1959), 132, n. 10, preferred "penitence" to either

"repentance" or "penance" as the more appropriate translation for the entire process of the human restoration of the relationship with God. On all four occasions in this work (in sections 25 and 26) when Cyprian employed this word it is used with regard to non-Christians who realize too late the mistakes of their lives in persecuting Christians. In this particular context, "regret" is the appropriate translation.

246. Wis 5:1–9. The passage is used in Cyprian, *Ad Fort.* 12 (CCL 3.212); and Cyprian, *Ad Quir.* 3.16 (CCL 3.107–108), in the context of the punishment of persecutors of Christians, and verses 8–9 are used in Cyprian, *De habi.* 10 (CCL 3F.297–8), to remind wealthy virgins that their wealth was not something about which to boast. See Fahey, *Cyprian and the Bible*, 173–75.

247. For Cyprian, punishment was not an end in itself but was designed to lead to repentance. However, in the final punishment, it was too late for repentance.

248. The allusion is to such scriptural passages as Matt 5:39; Luke 6:27–29; Rom 12:17; 1 Thess 5:15; and 1 Pet 3:9.

249. *Satisfacere*: "Satisfaction" or "making amends" is seen as the result of the penitential process in Cyprian, *De laps.* 29 (CCL 3.237); and Cyprian, *Ep.* 43.3.2 (CCL 3B.203). Clarke, *The Letters of St. Cyprian*, 2.218, n. 13, notes how Cyprian insisted on the episcopal role in reconciliation. The question of the priority of human repentance or a divine willingness to forgive was not addressed by Cyprian.

250. See n. 12 above.

251. See n. 54 above.

252. Speaking about benefits or advantages is what one would expect in a deliberative piece of oratory, which Cyprian has inserted at several points in this otherwise forensic argument.

253. Tacitus, *Ann.* 15.44.4, stated that Christians were targeted under Nero because of their hatred of the human race (*odium humani generis*). Cyprian seems to turn that back against Demetrian, stating that the eternal punishment of persecuting non-Christians would be because of their hatred of Christians. For recent evaluations of the reliability of Tacitus, see Paul Keresztes, "Nero, the Christians and the Jews in Tacitus and Clement of Rome," *Lat* 43 (1984): 404–13; Richard Carrier, "The Prospect of a Christian Interpolation in Tacitus, *Annals* 15.44," *VC* 68 (2014): 264–83; Brent D. Shaw, "The Myth of the Neronian Persecution," *JRS* 105 (2015): 73–100; Christopher P. Jones, "The Historicity of the Neronian Persecution: A Response to Brent Shaw," *NTS* 63 (2017): 146–52; Birgit van der Lans and Jan N. Bremmer, "Tacitus and the Persecution of the Christians: An Invention of Tradition?," *Eirene* 53 (2017): 299–331; and Ivan Prchlík, "*Auctor nominis eius Christus.* Tacitus' Knowledge of the Origins of Christianity," *Acta Universitatis Carolinae Philologica* 2 (2017): 95–110.

254. See Acts 16:17.

255. See Ezek 18:32.

256. See n. 160 above. Whatever Cyprian might or might not have made of a later concept such as purgatory, which those who look to his allusion to Matt 5:25–26 and Luke 12:58–59 in *Ep.* 55.20.3 (CCL 3B.279) sometimes detect, here it is quite clear that he rejected the notion that after death one could *begin* the reconciliation process.

257. See n. 160 above.

258. *Indulgentiam*: See Cyprian, *De bono* 8 (CCL 3A.123); and Cyprian, *De domi.* 14 (CCL 3A.98).

259. *Eius* translated in a gender-neutral fashion.

260. *Redimendo*: One aspect or perspective on the work of Christ in making the believer, mired in sin, righteous with God came from the commercial world through the use of the verb *redere*: "to pay back," "to return," "to recover," "to be restored," or "to ransom." It would become the English word *redeem*. In Christian theology it was a Pauline and pseudo-Pauline concept (Rom 3:24; 8:23; 1 Cor 1:30; 6:20; 7:23; Gal 3:13; 4:6; Eph 1:7, 14; 4:30; Col 1:14; 1 Tim 2:6; Tit 2:14). In Cyprian, the verb also occurs in *De laps.* 35 (CCL 3.241); *De oper.* 1, 2, 5, 17, 18, and 22 (CCL 3A.55, 56, 58, 66, and 69); *De habi.* 2 and 11 (CCL 3F.286 and 300); *De domi.* 30 and 34 (CCL 3A.108 and 112); *De mort.* 24 (CCL 3A.30); *Ad Fort.* incip.3 (CCL 3.184) and 6 and 10 (CCL 3.193 and 199); *Ad Quir.* 2.7 and 15 (using the verb *emere*) (CCL 3.39, 50); and *Epp.* 2.2.2 (CCL 3B.8); 55.19.2 and 22.1 (CCL 3B.278 and 281); 62.1.2; 2.2; and 3.1 (CCL 3B.386 and 387); 63.2.2 (CCL 3C.391); and 76.2.1 (CCL 3C.608).

261. Fredouille, *Cyprien*, 207, calls this final section of the pamphlet a hymn to eternal life.

262. *Sacramentum*.

263. Cyprian was not suggesting two destinations (the earthly paradise of Genesis and heaven) but treating the terms as synonymous.

THE DEADLY PESTILENCE

1. In the introduction I noted that Cyprian's distinction between "many" and "some" might have been somewhat exaggerated in order to gain as much goodwill from his community as possible, as well as to minimize the extent of the problem and not sound alarmist. Antonella Cerretini, *Cipriano: Trattati*, CTP 175 (Rome: Città Nuova, 2004), 62 n. 2, accepts Cyprian's numbers at face value.

2. M. G. E. Conway, *Thasci Caecili Cypriani: De bono patientiae*, CUAPS 92 (Washington, DC: Catholic University of America Press, 1957), 95–96, suggested that *dilectissimi*, the word employed here, was used in addressing laity and *carissimi* when addressing clergy. Charles A. Bobertz, "The Historical Context of Cyprian's *De Unitate*," *JTS* n.s. 41 (1990): 111, claims that in his treatises Cyprian addressed the laity in Carthage as *fratres dilectissimi* while he addressed those in Rome as *fratres carissimi*. Yet Geoffrey D. Dunn, *Cyprian and the Bishops of Rome: Questions of Papal Primacy in the Early Church*, ECS 11

(Strathfield, NSW: St Pauls Publications, 2006), 80–81, points to any number of references in Cyprian's writings where he used *carissimi* for those in Carthage as well as Rome and observes that *dilectissimi* is fairly rare in Cyprian's letters: see *Epp.* 39.1.1 (CCL 3B.186); 58.1.1 (CCL 3C.319); 75.1.1 (CCL 3C.582); and 76.1.1 (CCL 3C.605)—not counting repetitions within a letter. To that should be added 15.4 (CCL 3B.89); 28.incip. (CCL 3B.133); 43.7.1 (CCL 3B.209); and 59.20.1 (CCCL 3C.372). We may note that CCL 3C.447 for *Ep.* 67 has changed *carissimi* (in CSEL 3/2.735) to *dilectissimi.* Lucianus of Carthage addressed Celerinus, then in Rome, as *frater dilectissimus* in *Ep.* 22.1 (3B.116). The Roman clergy called their Carthaginian counterparts *fratres dilectissimi* in *Ep.* 8.2.1 (CCL 3B.41). Cyprian himself is addressed as *dilectissimus* in *Epp.* 77.1.1 (CL 3C.618) and 78.2.2 (CCL 3C.623). One may note that Clarke has not attempted to make any distinction between the two terms in his English translation of Cyprian's letters. Mary Bridget O'Brien, *Titles of Address in Christian Latin Epistolography to 543 A.D.*, CUAPS 21 (Washington, DC: Catholic University of America Press, 1930), 95, stated that *carissimus* was used to address bishops, other clergy, and lay people, and (100) that *dilectissimus* was used by bishops to other bishops as well as to clergy and lay people. I would regard the terms as interchangeable. Translating *fratres* as "brethren" rather than "brothers" is in an attempt to minimize gender-specific language.

3. *Mens solida* was used also by Horace, *Carm.* 3.3.4, in much the same sense. Except for a few sentences later in this section I have translated *mens* as "resolve" to highlight that sense of the exercise of the will that Cyprian suggested.

4. *Anima devota*: G. W. Clarke, *The Letters of St. Cyprian of Carthage*, 3: *Letters 55–66*, ACW 46 (New York: Newman Press, 1986), 1.231, n. 7, observes how in *Ep.* 10.1.1 (CCL 3B.47) Cyprian used *devotio* in the military sense of committing oneself in return for victory.

5. Mary Louise Hannan, *Thasci Caecili Cypriani—De Mortalitate: A Commentary, with an Introduction and Translation*, CUAPS 36 (Washington, DC: Catholic University of America Press, 1933), 48, noted that in the few instances in which *mortalitas* occurs in classical Latin it means death. We may refer to Tacitus, *Ann.* 16.13.3 (where, interestingly, the fact that all ranks of people without discrimination were dying, which meant, ironically, that the wealthy and elite were able to avoid Nero's bloodthirstiness, was the result of disease [*pestilientia*]) and Pliny, *Ep.* 10.41(50).4. Beyond Hannan's definition, we may note also that the word was employed to refer to the mortal or perishable condition of humanity as a class (Cicero, *Nat. d.* 1.26; Seneca, *Dial.* 2.8.2; Pliny, *HN* 2.22; 35.139; 36.166; Tacitus, *Ann.* 6.50; Pliny, *Ep.* 2.1.10; and Suetonius, *Claud.* 46.1). It is with this idea to the fore that Cerretini, *Cipriano: Trattati*, 62, translates the title of the work, when translated into a gender-neutral English, as "The Human Mortal Condition." In many of the uses of the word in this pamphlet it is equivalent to pestilence, but in the opening section it refers to the rate or extent of death caused by pestilence. The terms

death and *pestilence* are interchangeable to the extent that the thinking was, even though somewhat exaggerated, that everyone who caught the disease died from it soon after in a most horrible way. I have adopted the solution of translating *mortalitas* as "deadly pestilence" in an effort to capture both shades of meaning.

6. *Fortis et stabilis*: Cyprian used the same terms in *Epp.* 10.1.1 (CCL 3B.47); 11.8 (CCL 3B.66); 28.2.1 (CCL 3B.134); 59.2.3 (CCL 3C.338); *De laps.* 13 (CCL 3.227); *De unit.* 2 (CCL 3.249); *Ad Fort.* 13 (CCL 3.215). The analogy of faith or God or Christ as a rock (*petra*) is present in the Bible (Exod 17:6; Deut 32:4, 18; 1 Sam 2:2; Ps 18:2, 31, 46; 28:1; 62:2; 71:3; 89:26; 95:1; 144:1 (LXX); Isa 51:1; Matt 16:18; 1 Cor 10:4; 1 Pet 2:4). The image of a rock standing firm against crashing waves comes most directly from Matt 7:24–25 = Luke 6:48. The passage is cited in Cyprian, *Ad Quir.* 3.96 (CCL 3.169), to show that actions speak louder than words. In Cyprian, *De unit.* 2 (CCL 3.250), the passage is applied to those who remained strong against the actions of Decius. Michael A. Fahey, *Cyprian and the Bible: A Study in Third-Century Exegesis* (Tübingen: Eberhard-Karls Universität, 1971), 289, does not notice the allusion to the passage in *De mort.* The authorship of *Ad Quir.* has been subject to recent reexamination with Charles A. Bobertz, "An Analysis of *Vita Cypriani* 3.6–10 and the Attribution of *Ad Quirinum* to Cyprian of Carthage," *VC* 46 (1992): 112–28, who argues that Cyprian made extensive use of the material in *Ad Quir.*, which had been written by someone else. This is followed by Andy Alexis-Baker, "*Ad Quirinum* Book Three and Cyprian's Catechumenate," *JECS* 17 (2009): 357–80. Against that, Edwina Murphy, "'As Far as My Poor Memory Suggested': Cyprian's Compilation of *Ad Quirinum*," *VC* 68 (2014): 533–50, has defended Cyprian's authorship.

7. See n. 26 of the translation of *Ad Deme.* Hannan, *Thasci Caecili Cypriani*, 49, noted Cyprian's characteristic alliteration, which I have attempted to capture through use of the words *shatter* and *swells.*

8. *Vinco* and *probo* are coupled later in *De mort.* 10 (CCL 3A.21). *Probo* is used throughout this pamphlet not in the sense simply of "testing" but of "proving something through testing."

9. *Temptatio*: While "temptation" conveys the idea of being induced to do wrong, "testing" has more the broader idea of being investigated to see whether one would do either right or wrong. This sentence, as divided here in this translation, forms the *exordium* of the pamphlet in which Cyprian briefly sets out the context that gave rise to the concerns he had about the attitude of his community.

10. The use of *etsi* ("although") and *tamen* ("nevertheless") make all of section 1 of the pamphlet one long sentence, which I have broken into two by ignoring *etsi.*

11. *Inbecillitate animi*: the same term is used in Caesar, *B.Gall.* 7.77; and Cicero, *Tusc.* 4.28.60.

12. This is the only occasion Cyprian used the noun *mollities* in his pamphlets. Although the term could be applied to men, as in Velleius 2.88.2; Martial, *Epig.* 5.37.2; Horace, *Epod.* 1.9–10; and Juvenal, *Sat.*, Cyprian here meant women. Tertullian, *De cult.* 2.13.3 (CCL 1.369), stated that softness and fragility (*fluxus*) render the strength (or manliness) of faith effeminate, indicating that women (the words would be applicable equally to pampered men) absorbed by luxury would have a hard time welcoming persecution and martyrdom. See Catharine Edwards, *The Politics of Immorality in Ancient Rome* (Cambridge: Cambridge University Press, 1993), 68; Craig A. Williams, *Roman Homosexuality: Ideologies of Masculinity in Classical Antiquity* (Oxford: Oxford University Press, 1999), 175; and Carly Daniel-Hughes, *The Salvation of the Flesh in Tertullian of Carthage: Dressing for the Resurrection* (New York: Palgrave Macmillan, 2011), 76–77. In contrast, in *Ad Fort.* 11 (CCL 3.208), Cyprian mentioned the mother of Maccabees as overcoming the *sexus infirmitate* (see 2 Macc 7:21) to encourage her sons to accept martyrdom (2 Macc 7:27–29). See Fahey, *Cyprian and the Bible,* 116–17. On Cyprian's attitudes toward women, see Geoffrey D. Dunn, "Infected Sheep and Diseased Cattle, or the Pure and Holy Flock: Cyprian's Pastoral Care of Virgins," *JECS* 11 (2003): 1–20; Geoffrey D. Dunn, "Widows and Other Women in the Pastoral Ministry of Cyprian of Carthage," *Aug* 45 (2005): 295–307; Geoffrey D. Dunn, "Cyprian and Women in a Time of Persecution," *JEH* 57 (2006): 205–25 (especially 212 and 214–15, for Cyprian's comments about women overcoming their natural weakness); and Edwina Murphy, "Widows, Welfare and the Wayward: 1 Timothy 5 in Cyprian's *Ad Quirinum,*" in *SP* 94, ed. Markus Vinzent, papers presented at the Seventeenth International Conference on Patristic Studies, Oxford 2015 (Leuven: Peeters, 2017), 67–74.

13. *Veritatis errore*: A similar term is found in Tacitus, *Hist.* 2.72. *Error* has shades of meaning in Latin. Hannan, *Thasci Caecili Cypriani,* 21, translated the phrase as "wandering from the truth." The notion of "wandering" or "uncertainty" suggests personal culpability, while notion of "deception" places less blame on the individual. As we shall see throughout the pamphlet, Cyprian does lay the blame on the individuals concerned. Cyprian argues that, of all the reasons that had caused the anxiety and despair among members of his community, the most significant reason was the doubt they held. The purpose of the pamphlet, then, was to remind them of the promises found in the scriptures, which God had made.

14. *Nostra mediocritas*: Mary Bridget O'Brien, *Titles of Address in Christian Latin Epistolography to 543 A.D.*, CUAPS 21 (Washington, DC: Catholic University of America Press, 1930), 74–75, noted the use of the term in Aulus Gellius and Velleius and its Christian use when addressing both superiors and inferiors. It is common in Cyprian: *Ad Quir.* 3.incip. (CCL 3.73); *Ad Fort.* incip.1 (CCL 3.183); *Epp.* 20.1.2 (CCL 3B.107); 20.2.1 (CL 3B.107); 58.1.1 (CCL 3C.319) (a letter of some significance for *De mort.*); and 69.17 (CCL 3C.496). On the humility *topos,* particularly in later centuries, see Philippe

Bruggisser, *Symmaque ou le rituel épisolaire de l'amitié littéraire. Recherches sur le premier livre de la correspondance,* Paradosis 35 (Freiburg: Éditions universitaires, 1993), 20; David Konstan, "Problems in the History of Christian Friendship," *JECS* 4 (1996): 97–106; and Andrew Cain, "In Ambrosiaster's Shadow: A Critical Re-evaluation of the Last Surviving Letter Exchange between Pope Damasus and Jerome," *REAug* 51 (2005): 260. Rhetorically, it was common for orators to exaggerate their limited abilities in order to boost their *ethos,* their trustworthy and relatable character, one of the three means of persuasion, and make them more appealing and reliable to their audience. See Plato, *Apol.* 1; Quintilian, *Inst.* 6.2; and William W. Fortenbaugh, "Quintilian 6.2.8–9: *Ethos* and *Pathos* and the Ancient Tradition," in *Peripatetic Rhetoric after Aristotle,* ed. William W. Fortenbaugh and David C. Mirhady, Rutgers University Studies in Classical Humanities 6 (New Brunswick, NJ: Transaction Publishers, 1994), 183–91.

15. *Delicatae mentis*: The parallel with Seneca, *De brev.* 12.6 (*delicati animi languor solvuntur*), suggests Cyprian's familiarity with his writings.

16. Even though Cyprian used the word *sermo* at this point I have not translated it as "sermon" or "homily."

17. *Dominica lectione*: Cyprian used these words, although not necessarily forming this phrase, in *Ep.* 27.1.1 (CCL 3B. 127); *Ad Fort.* incip.3 (CCL 3.184); and *De zelo* 16 (CCL 3A.84).

18. *Homo Dei*: Cyprian used the term in *Ad Deme.* 20 (CCL 3A.47); and *De domi.* 21 (CCL 3A.103). Hannan, *Thasci Caecili Cypriani,* 52, noted that the addition of *et Christi* is only found here.

19. This paragraph constitutes the *partitio* of the pamphlet, in which Cyprian set out the point he wished to prove through this example of deliberative oratory, which was to change the thinking and behavior of his fellow Christians in Carthage who were complaining about the impact of the pestilence. He wanted Christians not to doubt that death by disease was the will of God for Christians as much as for nonbelievers since all such trials and tribulations had been predicted in the scriptures, that dying in the pandemic with the right attitude was just as beneficial as martyrdom, and that the fate of dead Christians should not be lamented but celebrated by the fellow Christians since this was the goal of faith. These points would be demonstrated in the main body of the pamphlet, in the *confirmatio* (2–7) and *refutatio* (8–24).

20. Here begins the *confirmatio* of the pamphlet. J. H. D. Scourfield, "The *De mortalitate* of Cyprian: Consolation and Context," *VC* 50 (1996), 15, sees these sections being about "the attitude of his audience to their own deaths." I think it is more than this; Cyprian was seeking to persuade his readers not to be surprised that the pandemic has occurred because predictions of it are contained in the scriptures. The idea of the soldier of Christ derives from Eph 6:14–17 and 2 Tim 2:3. Cyprian cited the first passage in *Ad Quir.* 3.117 (CCL 3.177), under the heading of being brave in order to fight the devil. The soldier of God or of Christ is mentioned frequently in Cyprian: *De laps.*

2 and 36 (CCL 3.221 and 241); *Ad Fort.* incip.1–2 and 13 (CCL 3.183 and 215); and *Epp.* 10.1.2 (CCL 3B.47); 10.2.3 (CCL 3B.49); 10.5.2 (CCL 3B.55); 15.1.1 (CCL 3B.85); 28.2.4 (CCL 3B.136); 31.5.2 (CCL 3B.156); 37.1.1 (CCL 3B.177); 38.1.2 (CCL 3B.183–84); 39.2.1 (CCL 3B.187); 39.3.1 (CCL 3B.189); 46.2.1 (CCL 3B.225); 51.2.2 (CCL 3B.242); 54.2.2 (CCL 3B.254); 57.1.2 (CCL 3B.302); 57.4.2–3 (CCL 3B.306); 57.5.1–2 (CCL 3B.308–10); 58.1.2 (CCL 3C.320); 58.3.1 (CCL 3C.323); 58.4.2 (CCL 3C.325); 58.10.3 (CCL 3C.335); 59.16.3 (CCL 3C.367); 73.10.1 (CCL 3C.540); 74.9.1 (CCL 3C.575); 76.6.1 (CCL 3C.614); 77.2.1 (CCL 3C.619); and 80.2 (CCL 3C.628). Besides these explicit references to Christians as soldiers, there are numerous other references to Christians engaged in fighting with the enemy. The fighting was nonviolent and was performed by confessing the faith before persecutors, and victory was achieved by accepting imprisonment and martyrdom. Here the deadly pestilence is another sort of enemy in the face of which one had to maintain one's faith perspective. One may note the frequent appearance of this image in *Epp.* 57 and 58, letters often linked with *De mort.* G. W. Clarke, *The Letters of St. Cyprian of Carthage,* 1: *Letters 1–27,* ACW 43 (New York: Newman Press, 1984), 232 n. 16 (referring to *Ep.* 10.2.3), notes that soldiers take their oath of loyalty (*sacramentum*). Courage in the face of the enemy was part of that loyalty.

21. *Spirat*: CSEL 3/1.297 reads *sperat.* Although Cerretini, *Cipriano: Trattati,* 41, claimed to be following the CCL text, her translation as "speranze" indicates that she chose to follow CSEL.

22. See n. 2 above.

23. *Trepidatio nulla...nulla turbatio*: I have translated as "no terror" and "no turmoil" to keep the alliteration.

24. One could just as easily translate *turbo* as "sandstorm" in keeping with its North African situation or as "whirlwind" or, more dramatically to capture the sense of the severity of the situation, as "tornado," "cyclone," or "hurricane." The point Cyprian seems to be making is that the assault is coming from every direction at once. Here I have chosen "tempest" (qualified by swirling to keep that sense) so as to be able to use its adjectival form to translate *turbidos* in section 1 and to link *turbatio* ("turmoil") a few words earlier with *turbo* ("tempest"). Cyprian used *post procellas et turbines* in *Ep.* 11.8 (CCL 3B.66), which Clarke translates simply as "wild storms." In *Ep.* 58.4.2 (CCL 3C.325), the letter to the people of Thibaris that is strongly linked to *De mort.* in scholarship and that was probably written shortly after this pamphlet, we find *tempestas ac procella* (note the reverse order), which Clarke translates as "storm and tempest." The context is not the house on the rock but a ship at sea. In *De unit.* 2 (CCL 3.249), Cyprian coupled *tempestates et turbines* as having no effect on the rock of faith, the former term being used in our work only in sections 12 and 25. In Cyprian, *De habi.* 2 (CCL 3F.285), we find *ad procellas et turbines saeculi* instead of *ad procellas et turbines mundi,* again with reference to the battering of the house built on solid rock. We find *procellas mundi* on

its own in Cyprian, *De bono* 12 (CCL 3A.125). In Cyprian, *Ad Deme.* 19 (CCL 3A.46), there is reference to Christians withstanding *omnes fluctuantis mundi turbines.* See n. 196 there. In Cyprian, *Ad Dona.* 14 (CCL 3A.11), we find "from the swirling tempests of the troubling present age" (*inquietans saeculi turbinus*). The fact that the image occurs frequently enough in Cyprian means that it is unlikely to be of any use in trying to sequence these two texts.

25. Hannan, *Thasci Caecili Cypriani,* 53, commented on the polysyndeton here with the repetition of the conjunctions. On the different rhetorical effects of polysyndeton and asyndeton, see Aristotle, *Rh.* 3.12.4 (1413b). See Elizabeth Blettner, "One Made Many and Many Made One: The Role of Asyndeton in Aristotle's Rhetoric," *Ph & Rh* 16 (1983): 49–54.

26. See Luke 21:10–11. Fahey, *Cyprian and the Bible,* 323, claims that Cyprian was alluding to Matt 24:7, to which he added *pestilentias,* which I have translated here as "pandemics" (the only occasion of this word in the pamphlet; it does not occur at all in Cyprian, *Ad Deme.*). What Fahey does not recognize is that Luke 21:11 already has this included, indicating that Cyprian was relying upon a Lukan rather than Matthean text at this point.

27. One may note Cyprian's use of rhetorical synonymy (*interpretatio*), on which see *Rhet. Her.* 4.28.38, through the variety of verb choices he made: *praedixerit, praenuntiavit, cecinit,* and *praemonuit* ("foretold," "foreshadowed," "predicted," and "forewarned").

28. *Novus*: Cerretini, *Cipriano: Trattati,* 63, translates this as "folle" ("crazy" or "mad").

29. See Mark 13:9–27; Matt 10:17–22 and 24:9–31; and Luke 17:23–24 and 21:12–28. Allen Brent, *Cyprian and Roman Carthage* (Cambridge: Cambridge University Press, 2010), 97 and 106–8, places *De mort.* within the eschatological framework of apocalyptic expectation.

30. Luke 21:31. Fahey, *Cyprian and the Bible,* 365, correctly identifies that Cyprian used the Lukan version rather than the other Synoptic alternatives (Mark 13:29; Matt 24:33). This is further proof for me that throughout this section of *De mort.* Cyprian was using a Lukan rather than Matthean text. Matt 24:4–31 is cited in full in Cyprian, *Ad Fort.* 11 (CCL 3.202–203).

31. See n. 2 above.

32. *Praemium*: Cerretini, *Cipriano: Trattati,* 63, translates this as "ricompensa" ("reward"), as does Roy J. Deferrari, *Saint Cyprian: Treatises,* FC 36 (Washington, DC: Catholic University of America Press, 1958), 200. Since the Latin can also mean "gift," we have to decide whether Cyprian's language would support a later Pelagian interpretation or not. Certainly, the use of the word in Cyprian, *De oper.* 26 (CCL 3A.72), in connection with the white crown of almsgiving and the crimson crown of martyrdom suggests that he saw it as a reward. See Geoffrey D. Dunn, "The White Crown of Works: Cyprian's Early Pastoral Ministry of Almsgiving in Carthage," *CH* 73 (2004): 716. Since the Pelagian question of whether salvation was merited or gifted had not

confronted the church in the middle of the third century, it would be unfair to judge Cyprian by later standards.

33. *Nuper.* It is a stretch of the imagination to say that paradise was lost "recently." Cerretini, *Cipriano: Trattati*, 63, says that it was "tempo fa" ("long ago"), which does not respect that Latin. I have translated it as "in our time" to suggest that Cyprian was not thinking chronologically but regarded all of human history as a single epoch.

34. The idea of the end of the world and humanity living in the last days is found also in Cyprian, *Ad Deme.* 3 (CCL 3A.36); 5 (CCL 3A.37); 23 (CCL 3A.48); and Cyprian, *Ep.* 58.1.2 (CCL 3C.320). See Clarke, *The Letters of St. Cyprian*, 3.228–29 n. 5; and n. 30 in the translation of *Ad Deme.*

35. I translated *desum* as "abandon" rather than "lack" as being a little kinder to his target readers. They had faith at one time but seem to have lost it once it was tested. While Cyprian would certainly believe that faith was only proved through testing, the purpose of the work was not to condemn the doubtful but to reinvigorate their faith, so indicating that they had faith to recover rather than never had any faith would seem preferable.

36. See 2 Tim 2:12. Cyprian cites the passage in *Ad Fort.* 5 (CCL 3.193), focusing on the negative half of the verse in a section on why idolaters or those who persuade others to idolatry deserved death. See Fahey, *Cyprian and the Bible*, 512, who does not note the allusion to the positive half of the verse in our passage under consideration.

37. Rom 1:17 referring to Hab 2:4. Fahey, *Cyprian and the Bible*, 422, points out that Cyprian has the present infinitive *vivere* here rather than a future indicative, perhaps suggesting that he sees the verse as not having simply a future reference but a present one. While the Greek and the Vulgate have Paul explicitly quoting Habakkuk directly, in Cyprian it has been turned into an indirect quotation by use of the infinitive and subject accusative (*iustum*). I take this to be a direct quotation from Paul, although without treating Habakkuk as a direct quotation. CCL itself and other translations of the pamphlet refer to this as a passage from Romans, but do not include *scriptum est* as part of the quotation, even though that is found in Paul. On Cyprian using an African, fixed Latin version of the New Testament, rather than translating himself, see H. A. G. Houghton, *The Latin New Testament: A Guide to Its Early History, Texts, and Manuscripts* (Oxford: Oxford University Press, 2016), 9–14. On this verse of Romans in the *Vetus Latina*, see H. A. G. Houghton, C. M. Kreinecker, R. F. MacLachlan, and C. J. Smith, *The Principal Pauline Epistles: A Collation of Old Latin Witnesses*, New Testament Tools, Studies and Documents 59 (Leiden: Brill, 2019), 38. On other uses of the Habakkuk passage as used by Cyprian, see *Ad Quir.* 1.5 (CCL 310–11); and 3.42 (CCL 3.134). See Fahey, *Cyprian and the Bible*, 249. In Cyprian, *Ep.* 59.5.3 (CCL 3C.345), we find reference to not having the faith by which we live. Clarke, *The Letters of St. Cyprian*, 3.243, n. 22, is unsure whether Cyprian has taken this from Hab or Rom. I am inclined to the former. On Cyprian using Paul, see

Edwina Murphy, "Divine Ordinances and Life-Giving Remedies: Galatians in the Writings of Cyprian of Carthage," *JTI* 8 (2014): 81–101; Edwina Murphy, "Cyprian's Use of Philippians: To Live Is Christ and to Die Is Gain," *Aug* 56 (2016): 35–56; and Edwina Murphy, *The Bishop and the Apostle: Cyprian's Pastoral Exegesis of Paul*, Studies of the Bible and Its Reception 13 (Berlin: De Gruyter, 2018).

38. Luke 2:25–30. Edwina Murphy, "Death, Decay and Delight in Cyprian of Carthage," *Scr* 15 (2019): 85, also comments on Simeon's old age when she observes: "Simeon may have already been old, but his response is a model for all those facing death, no matter what their age."

39. This is only one of eleven occasions in all of Cyprian's writings in which there is reference to Mary, most of which were simple citations of scriptural passages. See Geoffrey D. Dunn, "References to Mary in the Writings of Cyprian of Carthage," *SP* 42, ed. F. Young, M. Edwards, and P. Parivs, papers presented to the Fourteenth International Patristics Conference, Oxford 2003 (Leuven: Peeters, 2006), 369–78.

40. *Arcessitio*: Hannan, *Thasci Caecili Cypriani*, 57–58, noted that Cyprian was the first to use this word to mean death and that he used it on a couple of occasions: *Ad Fort.* 13 (CCL 3.216), discussing those who died without being able to be martyred not being disadvantaged, an important point in our pamphlet too; *Ep.* 22.5 (CCL 3B.117), where it is used by the martyred Paulus and repeated by Lucianus, making Cyprian not the first to use the word in this sense (see Clarke, *The Letters of St. Cyprian*, 1.334, n. 11); as well as being used several more times in this pamphlet: 18, 19, 20, and 24 (CCL 3A.26, 27 and 30), the first of which was not noted by Hannan.

41. Luke 2:29–30. Cyprian used Luke 2:29–30 in *Ad Quir.* 3.58 (CCL 3.146) in the same context. See Fahey, *Cyprian and the Bible*, 339. One may note that of the thirteen scriptural references in *Ad Quir.* 3.58 (CCL 3.143–46) about the fact that no one should be sad because of death since living is peril and death is peace (Gen 3:17–19; 5:24; Isa 40:6b–7a, 8b; Ezek 37:11b–12, 14; Wis 4:11 and 14; Ps 83:2–3 (LXX); 1 Thess 4:13–14; 1 Cor 15:36, 41–44, 53–55; John 17:24; Luke 2:29–30; and John 14:28), eight are used in this pamphlet: Gen 5:24 in *De mort.* 23 (CCL 3A.29); Wis 4:11 and 14 in *De mort.* 23 (CCL 3A.29); Ps 83:2–3 (LXX) in *De mort.* 23 (CCL 3A.29); 1 Thess 4:13–14 in *De mort.* 21 (CCL 3A.28); 1 Cor 15:53–55 in *De mort.* 8 (CCL 3A.20); John 17:24 in *De mort.* 22 (CCL 3A.29); Luke 2:29–30 in *De mort.* 3 (CCL 3A.18); and John 14:28 in *De mort.* 7 (CCL 3A.20). See Scourfield, "The *De mortalitate* of Cyprian," 30.

42. See n. 24 above.

43. *Quando expuncta hac morte*: Cerretini, *Cipriano: Trattati*, 64, translates this in the sense of overcoming death ("dopo aver vinto questa morte"), which suggests she was reading the verb as *expugno* instead of *expungo*. While Hannan, *Thasci Caecili Cypriani*, 59, followed by Deferrari, *Saint Cyprian*, 201, took this in the sense of "execute" or "accomplish," I prefer the more regular

sense of the verb as "sting," with the possibility of Cyprian alluding to 1 Cor 15:56, although the Pauline use was to emphasize sin as what gave death power whereas here Cyprian was not interested in sin.

44. Using the passage from Luke, Cyprian has been able to argue for his position from both perspectives of it being beneficial to leave the world behind and to advance to the next world.

45. Who are the rest? It is obviously the opposite of the just who live by faith of Hab 2:4 (Rom 1:17). Here Cyprian indicates those who, unlike Simeon, have not yet been released from the cares and troubles of the world. This would comprise Christians of wavering faith and non-Christians. It is to Cyprian's advantage not to be too clear about who belongs to which group for the success of this pamphlet, which depends upon people believing that it was possible to cross from doubt to faith. Cyprian's use of the first person rather than the second in the following sentences would be a rhetorical ploy to assure doubtful Christians that they were not alone in their struggles.

46. Christian life as a struggle or war against the devil takes inspiration from the Synoptic accounts of the temptation of Jesus (Mark 1:12–13 = Matt 4:1–11 = Luke 4:1–13). It is a common metaphor for Cyprian, matching well with the image of the Christian as a soldier of Christ: *Ep.* 13.2.1 (CCL 3B.72); 19.2.3 (CCL 3B.104); *De bono* 12 (CCL 3A.125); *Ad Fort.* incip.2 (CCL 3.183); and *De zelo* 2 (CCL 3A.75–76).

47. *Iacula eius et tela*: The usual difference between a javelin and a spear is that the former, being lighter, is used for throwing and the latter, being longer and heavier, used for thrusting. The idea of the devil having a spear comes from Eph 6:16, where the shield, as part of the armor of God, protects one from the spears of the wicked. Cyprian quotes from Eph in *Ep.* 58.8.2 (CCL 3C.331–32), with reference to an impending struggle involving martyrdom. See also Wis 5:17–20; and Rom 13:12–14. Tertullian used the idea of struggle (*conflictatio*) frequently. For example, in *De res.* 48.13 (CCL 2.989), he wrote about the "struggle of the flesh" (*carnis conflictationem*); and in *De pat.* 14.3 (CCL 1.315), a work Cyprian knew well, about the "struggles of the body" (*corporis...conflictationibus*) in relation to the "javelins of temptations" (*iaculis temptationum*) in 14.6 (CCL 1.315).

48. See n. 7 above.

49. The verb *infesto* indicates not only something spreading widely, but also aggressively and with damage.

50. One may note the range of terminology Cyprian employed to refer to the engagement with the devil: *pugna, geritur, conflictationibus, dimicatur, congressio, luctatio, obsessa, infestatio, vallata, occurrit, resistit* ("fight," "waged," "struggles," "contested," "battle," "conflict," "assailed," "damage," "hemmed in," "put up a fight," and "resists"). Such an expansive vocabulary gives weight to the concept and a pleasantness to the style.

51. Hannan, *Thasci Caecili Cypriani*, 25, and Deferrari, *Saint Cyprian*, 202, translate *invidia* as "envy" and Cerretini, *Cipriano: Trattati*, 65, translates it

as "invidia" ("envy"). Since Cyprian's regular word for envy was *livor* (as in the title of the pamphlet), I have decided to offer another shade of meaning of the Latin word.

52. We could take this as Cyprian's version of the deadly sins; greed, lust, anger, pride, and jealousy all appear. Intoxication could be taken as a form of gluttony. Cyprian added ambition, which can be paralleled with pride, and spite, which can be paralleled with anger or jealousy. All that is missing is sloth, and Cyprian has no reference to *inertia, pigritia, segnitia, desidia,* or the like here. This kind of list comes well before those devised by Evagrius Ponticus and Cassian and determined by Gregory the Great, *Mor.* 31.45 (CCL 143B.x). See S. Schimmel, *The Seven Deadly Sins: Jewish, Christian and Classical Reflections on Human Psychology* (Oxford: Oxford University Press, 1997); Angela Tilby, "From Evil Thoughts to Deadly Sins: Evagrius of Pontus's Psychology of Sin," in *Wilderness: Essays in Honour of Frances Young,* ed. R. S. Sugirtharajah (London: T & T Clark, 2005), 143–52; and Angela Tilby, *The Seven Deadly Sins: Their Origin in the Spiritual Teaching of Evagrius the Hermit* (London: SPCK, 2009). Morton W. Bloomfield, *The Seven Deadly Sins: An Introduction to the History of a Religious Concept, with Special Reference to Medieval English Literature* (East Lansing: Michigan State University Press, 1952), 51, refers to this passage of Cyprian but claims that it was not influential on later Christian thinking. The idea of one sin leading to another, which Cyprian presents through asyndeton and which here may be taken as an illustrative sequence but not a fixed one, is endorsed by Gregory. While Cyprian might not have been influential, one could presume that he was influenced by ideas on vice found in classical and religious texts, e.g., Horace, *Ep.* 1.1.33–40. Cyprian addressed a number of these vices in his pamphlets. *De oper.* can be seen as dealing with greed. See Dunn, "The White Crown of Works," 715–40; Geoffrey D. Dunn, "Cyprian's Care for the Poor: The Evidence of *de Opere et Eleemosynis,*" in *SP* 42, ed. F. Young, M. Edwards, and P. Parvis, papers presented to the Fourteenth International Conference on Patristic Studies, Oxford 2003 (Leuven: Peeters, 2006), 363–68; Edwina Murphy, "Cyprian, Paul, and Care for the Poor and Captive; Offering Sacrifices and Ransoming Temples," *ZAC* 20 (2016): 418–36; and Edwina Murphy, "Sell Your Possessions: Cyprian, Luke, and Wealth." *Colloquium* 49 (2017): 11–23. Cyprian, *De habi.*, can be seen as dealing with pride. See Dunn, "Infected Sheep and Diseased Cattle," 5–12. Cyprian, *De zelo,* can be seen as dealing with jealousy. See Edwina Murphy, "Imitating the Devil: Cyprian on Jealousy and Envy," *Scr* 14 (2018): 75–91.

53. Exod 22:27; Lev 24:15–16; Num 15:30; 1 Sam 3:13; Tob 1:18; Isa 37:6; Matt 27:29; Mark 15:29; Luke 22:65; 23:39; Acts 26:11; 1 Tim 1:13: and Jas 2:7 prohibit cursing and blaspheming God and Christ, making it a punishable offense. We can understand blasphemy as the slander of God and cursing God as one particular form of blasphemy (as opposed *merely* to insulting God). Pliny, *Ep.* 10.96(97).5, wrote of a twofold process to establish an accused's innocence with regard to being Christian (given that those who professed

their guilt—that is, they proclaimed their Christian identity—were led away to execution). The first was to get them to swear their allegiance to the gods and the emperor and the second was to revile the name of Christ (*male dicerent Christo*). On this trial process, see Candida R. Moss, *Ancient Christian Martyrdom: Diverse Practices, Theologies, and Traditions*, Anchor Yale Bible Reference Library (New Haven: Yale University Press, 2012), 10–12 and 49–50. In a pamphlet addressed to Christians, the sense of "blaspheme" is appropriate. In Cyprian, *Ad Deme.* 2 (CCL 3A.36), the adjective is better translated, as addressed to a non-Christian, simply as "slanderous." See n. 23 of the translation of that pamphlet.

54. We should not understand *iurare* as swear in the sense of utter profanities, but in the sense of swearing an oath. On this basis one could suggest that these last two sentences refer to the policy of traditional religious revival instituted by the emperor Decius at the end of 249. Allen Brent, *The Imperial Cult and the Development of Church Order: Concepts and Images of Authority in Paganism and Early Christianity before the Age of Cyprian*, Supplements to *Vigiliae Christianae* 45 (Leiden: Brill, 1999), 2–4, sees this in terms of a clash between the imperial and Christian cults. I agree with Rives, "The Decree of Decius," 135–54, that the emperor's intention was not specifically against Christians but was for a reversal in the empire's fortunes through a renewal of traditional cultic practices designed to protect the empire. Some Christians, like Cyprian, fled in order to avoid the edict's demands, others who refused to obey it were punished for their lack of civic patriotism, while many complied with the demands either through offering incense, participating in sacrifice, or obtaining a certificate stating that they had fulfilled the requirements in some way. This group (the *thurificati, sacrificati,* and *libellatici*), collectively known as *lapsi,* occasioned a deep division within Christian communities that lasted more than a year. Their denial of their faith excluded them from the church, yet opinions differed as to the possibility of them being reconciled. In Africa, the decision was reached at the post-Easter synod of bishops in 251 to readmit penitent *libellatici* to communion. Cyprian's reference here then, in the light of those recent catastrophic events, would be to the cursing of the Christian God and the vowing of allegiance to the state-endorsed pantheon of polytheistic divinities entailed in fulfilling the edict. In light of the pestilence there was every possibility that Decius's policy could have been resuscitated. *Cogo* and *conpello* are present tense, which I have translated as present simple. Although Cyprian's words were addressed to the community who was starting to face the renewed challenge to their faith (the threatened persecution of Gallus or, more probably, a local version thereof)—without implying that the local edict had been already issued by the time Cyprian wrote this pamphlet—it seems more than likely that he had the events of recent years under Decius very much in mind and, in an exaggerated way, was suggesting that being targeted by the imperial administration was an unending reality for Christians, hence my use of the present simple. See also Cyprian, *De bono*

16 (CCL 3A.127). In other words, I do not find in his comments here precise information to help with the issue of dating the pamphlet.

55. *Animus* admits of several shades of meaning, from "mind" and "intellect" to "soul" and "spirit." Since Cyprian is going to discuss the beliefs and feelings of Christians throughout the next sections, it would seem appropriate to choose "intellect" here.

56. Here Cyprian is referring to the persecution by the devil on a moral level rather than any persecution by imperial authority or popular agitation on a physical level, although linking the persecutions by the state with the persecutions by the devil, one of which was to try to produce doubt or hesitancy about God's promise, was one of Cyprian's aims. All the persecutions are a test of faith.

57. See n. 7 above.

58. John 16:20. This version is found also in Cyprian, *Ad Fort.* 11 (CCL 3.201), one of many passages cited to illustrate that it was predicted that the world would hate Christians and that the good always would be tormented by the unjust. See Fahey, *Cyprian and the Bible*, 397–98, where he claims that Cyprian uses this passage to console Christians "recoiling at death under persecution." This is a mistaken impression since Cyprian was referring to the moral persecutions of the devil more than to physical persecutions by non-Christians. The last sentence of section 5 does refer to a wider context, but this should not be taken as revealing that when he wrote this work a new round of persecution like that under Decius was foreseen. Hannan, *Thasci Caecili Cypriani*, 61–62, noted that while the *Vetus Latina* used *flebitis et lugebitis*, Cyprian used *plorabitis et plangetis* and that Cyprian used *saeculum* rather than *mundus*, as is found in the *Vetus Latina*. There are similarities between Cyprian and Tertullian, *De spect.* 28.2 (CCL 1.250). With this verse from John's Gospel, Cyprian's argument turns from the idea of how good it is to leave the world to the idea of how good it is to enter the next.

59. John 16:22. See Fahey, *Cyprian and the Bible*, 398.

60. See 2 Cor 5:6 for a similar Pauline sentiment. Fahey, *Cyprian and the Bible*, 465–66, does not list this as a passage ever used by Cyprian.

61. Cyprian linked blindness (*caecitas*, or its adjective *caeca*) with madness (*dementia*) in *Ad Deme.* 16 (CCL 3A.44); and *De unit.* 23 (CCL 3.266).

62. See n. 2 above.

63. We can read this not in the sense that God's word is any different from those who do not believe, but for them God's word is not true because they have chosen to reject it.

64. Gravity or seriousness (*gravus*) was an indication of someone's importance in the Roman world.

65. In *De bono* 6 (CCL 3A.121), Cyprian used *verbo* instead of *sermo* and *factum* instead of *actus*, but the meaning is the same. It is not that actions speak louder than words, but that words and deeds together reveal a person's true character.

66. English lacks a single word as closely related as *fluctus* and *fluctuo* in Latin. I have had to make do with "waves" and "tossed about on the waves." See Cyprian, *Ad Dona.* 3 (CCL 3A.4); Cyprian, *Ep.* 11.3.2 (CCL 3B.60); and Cyprian, *Ad Deme.* 19 (CCL 3A.46); and n. 197 of the translation of the last text. Note the number of words repeated from section 1 (*firmus, mens,* and *fluctus/fluctuo*) here in section 6.

67. In *De oper.* 9 (CCL 3A.61), Cyprian also used *perfidus* and *incredulus.* I have taken *perfidus* here not simply as "faithless" as other translations do, but in the stronger sense of the Latin for the person whose belief not only is wrong but would be harmful to others.

68. The use of *recedo* is not in marked contrast with Cyprian's use of *excedo* (see n. 117 below). The difference seems to be a matter of perspective. The former is used when Cyprian commented about what is left behind (hence the word is frequently linked with *saeculum,* see n. 7 above), while the latter is used when he saw things from the perspective of where the dead were heading.

69. Note the use of epanaphora (*repetitio*) (*Rhet. Her.* 4.13.19), the figure of speech where successive sentences are introduced by the same word/s (here, *hoc est*).

70. *Exire.* While the verb has the regular meaning of "depart" and "die," as it does at the start of this section with regard to Jesus leaving the world, in the context Cyprian was addressing it would seem that he wanted to emphasize the sense of "escape" in his choice here. One who died was getting away from a bad situation to a better one. However, the *confirmatio* finishes with Cyprian talking less about the world one is escaping and more about the world Jesus promised where Christians could join him.

71. See n. 7 above.

72. I have translated *contristo* as a stronger form than *tristor,* particularly given its possible meaning of afflicting.

73. John 14:28. This passage is found also in *Ad Quir.* 3.58 (CCL 3.146) in the same context. See Fahey, *Cyprian and the Bible,* 394–95. See n. 41 above. Hannan, *Thasci Caecili Cypriani,* 64, noted that the form of *diligo* used by Cyprian in these two passages (pluperfect) differed from the form found in the *Vetus Latina,* also used in the later Vulgate (imperfect).

74. See n. 70 above.

75. Phil 1:21. See Fahey, *Cyprian and the Bible,* 496; and Murphy, "Cyprian's Use of Philippians," 53.

76. One of the dangers of believing that the present age is bad and that happiness will only be found in the age to come is the temptation to neglect conditions in the world or even to hasten departure from it. Cyprian was certainly not encouraging Christians to get themselves deliberately infected with the pestilence. He makes it clear here that it is Christ who decides when someone's time in the present age comes to an end, not that someone themselves.

77. Here begins the *refutatio* of the pamphlet with the first argument, which runs from 8–16, responding to those who complain that as Christians God should not be targeting them in this pandemic. One may note again Cyprian wanting to paint those who hold these points of view as being a minority. While this major section of the pamphlet starts with an attempt to persuade Christians to accept the idea that it is good to escape from the bad things of this world, the focus is not so much on that as on trying to prove that God has not promised those who believe in him that they would avoid all the bad things in the world in equal measure with their non-Christian neighbors. This negative form of argumentation continues until the end of this first section of the *refutatio* at the end of section 16.

78. Cyprian's use of the subjunctive following *quod* indicates that he is reporting the claims of others without agreeing with their interpretation. One may note here the use of *valitudo* ("illness").

79. *Gentilis*, when used in contrast with Christians, is to be understood not as "Gentile" (a term of contrast with Jew) but as "non-Christian other." As "heathen" in modern English has overtones of being uncivilized or irreligious, which was not the point Cyprian was making in the pamphlet, "pagan" could be a better alternative, although Cyprian was not focusing on their polytheistic identity or their rural backwardness (for which he could have chosen *paganus* as his term), but only on the fact that they were not Christian. I have chosen to use "nonbeliever" to emphasize their identity, from a Christian perspective, simply as being other than Christian. As I. L. S. Balfour, "Tertullian's Description of the Heathen," in *SP*, vol. 17/2, ed. Elizabeth A. Livingstone, papers presented at the Eighth International Conference on Patristic Studies, Oxford 1979 (Oxford: Pergamon, 1982), 785–89, observed, Tertullian, in the preceding generation, had preferred *gentilis* early in his literary career, *natio* in the middle, and *ethnicus* in his Montanist phase. Furthermore, *gentilis* was not Tertullian's word to contrast Gentile with Jew, for which he tended to use *natio*. See Alan Cameron, *The Last Pagans of Rome* (Oxford: Oxford University Press, 2011), 14–32. With Tertullian's supersessionism, the word the Jews could use for non-Jews became the appropriate word for Christians to use for non-Christians.

80. *Immunis a contactu*: Cyprian's point is not that some Christians believe that God will provide them with happiness in this life "free from contact" with the pestilence (that is, God will not let it come near them) but that some believe that God will keep them "immune from infection" when they are exposed to the pestilence. The same could be argued for Cyprian, *De habi.* 11 (CCL 3F.298–300). Just as the true Christian could not avoid the trials of the state (2 Tim 3:12), the true Christian could not avoid the trials of the flesh.

81. See n. 7 above.

82. See Cyprian, *Ad Deme.* 19 (CCL 3A.46). The first birth in the flesh is common to all people, and thus diseases of the flesh are common to all. The

second birth in the Spirit is unique to Christians and cannot be destroyed by disease, although it may be undermined by the lack of trust in God's promises.

83. *Coniungimur*: The sense here is not only that Christians are "joined" with non-Christians but, as far as the flesh is concerned, are "combined" with them to form an inseparable reality (perhaps in the same way that marriage makes a new reality out of two individuals). Of course, where they are distinct is with regard to the spirit.

84. *Genere humano*: Here Cyprian takes "human race" as the non-Christian believers. See Cyprian, *Ad Deme.* 22 (CCL 3A.48), where, from a spiritual perspective, Christians form a divine race.

85. See 1 Cor 15:54. 1 Cor 15:53–55 is used in Cyprian, *Ad Quir.* 3.58 (CCL 3.145). See Fahey, *Cyprian and the Bible*, 463. See n. 41 above. Hannan, *Thasci Caecili Cypriani*, 67, observed that Cyprian's use of *corruptiuum* and *incorruptionem* was influenced by the *Vetus Latina*.

86. On being led by the Spirit, see not only the references to Jesus being led by the Spirit into the wilderness to face temptation (Mark 1:12; Matt 4:1; Luke 4:1), but those referring to Christians being led as well (John 16:13; Rom 8:14; Gal 5:18, 25).

87. See Cyprian, *Ad Deme.* 7 and 10 (CCL 3A.38 and 40).

88. *Nubila serena*: While dark clouds indicate rain, bright ones indicate fair weather. Other translations read this as "clear skies."

89. See Cyprian *Ad Deme.* 2 and 10 (CCL 3A.35 and 40).

90. *Scopulosa saxa confringunt*: In *Ep.* 4.2.2 (CCL 3B.19), Cyprian employed the terms as coordinated substantives (*inter scopulos et saxa frangatur*), which Clark, *Letters* 1.58, translates as "smashed among the reefs and rocks." The image reminds one of the opening of this pamphlet, except there the rock was steadfast, here it is treacherous.

91. See n. 7 above.

92. There is no reason to believe that Cyprian was referring only to males at this point, so, although the Latin has the singular *Christianus*, it has been translated as plural here in order to be gender neutral.

93. See n. 7 above.

94. See Cyprian, *De habi.* 14 (CCL 3F.304); Cyprian, *Ad Deme.* 10 (CCL 3A.40); and Cyprian, *Ep.* 43.1.2 (CCL 3B.201).

95. Sir 2:1. Hannan, *Thasci Caecili Cypriani*, 67, claimed that Cyprian's version of the passage is not different from the *Vetus Latina* or the LXX. However, Fahey, *Cyprian and the Bible*, 178, notes that Cyprian's version departs from the LXX. The inclusion of the admonition to stand firm in justice and fear is not in the LXX. Linking the assault of the devil with standing firm in faith are passages such as Gal 5:1; Eph 6:11–13; and 1 Pet 5:9.

96. Sir 2:4–5. See Fahey, *Cyprian and the Bible*, 178. The identical passage is used in Cyprian, *De bono* 17 (CCL 3A.128).

97. See section 1. Scourfield, "The *De mortalitate* of Cyprian," 16, sees more of a division between sections 9 and 10 than I do.

98. Job 1:21. Job 1:21–22 is used in Cyprian, *Ad Quir.* 3.6 (CCL 3.94) in the same context. See Fahey, *Cyprian and the Bible*, 119–20. One may note that of the twelve scriptural references in *Ad Quir.* 3.6 (CCL 3.94–96) about the fact that good people suffer and need to endure (Sir 27:5; Ps 50:19 (LXX); 33:19, 20 (LXX); Job 1:21–22; Matt 5:4; John 16:33; 2 Cor 12:7–9; Rom 5:2–5; Matt 7:13–14; Tob 2:14; Prov 28:28), five are used in this pamphlet: Sir 27:5 in *De mort.* 13 (CCL 3A.23–24); Ps 50:19 (LXX) in *De mort.* 11 (CCL 3A.22); Job 1:21–22 in *De mort.* 10 (CCL 3A.21); 2 Cor 12:7–9 in *De mort.* 13 (CCL 3A.23); and Tob 2:14 in *De mort.* 10 (CCL 3A.22).

99. While most translations take the wife as the subject of the participle *inpatiens* ("impatient"), Ernest Wallis, "The Treatises of Cyprian," in *The Ante-Nicene Fathers*, vol. 5: *Hippolytus, Cyprian, Caius, Novatian*, Appendix, ed. Alexander Roberts and James Donaldson, rev. A. Cleveland Coxe (Buffalo, NY: Christian Literature Co., 1886), 471, made Job himself the subject of the participle.

100. Job 2:10. The last sentence is the author of Job's comment on what Job said rather than part of Job's response to his wife. Job 2:9–10 is used in Cyprian, *Ad Quir.* 3.14 (CCL 3.105) in the same context. See Fahey, *Cyprian and the Bible*, 119. One may note that of the six scriptural references in *Ad Quir.* 3.14 (CCL 3.105–106), about the fact that we must not murmur but must bless God for all that happens (Job 2:9–10; 1:8; Ps 33:2 [LXX]; Num 17:25; Acts 16:25; Phil 2:14–15), three are used in this pamphlet: Job 2:9–10 in *De mort.* 10 (CCL 3A.21); Job 1:8 in *De mort.* 10 (CCL 3A.21); and Num 17:25 in *De mort.* 11 (CCL 3A.22).

101. Job 1:8. This verse, with a further clause at the end, is found in *Ad Quir.* 3.14 (CCL 3.105) in the same context. See Fahey, *Cyprian and the Bible*, 119. See n. 100 above. Bobertz, "An Analysis of *Vita Cypriani* 3.6–10," 113–14, argues that the presence of the word "witness" (*testimonium*) used to introduce the quotation here (repeated by Pontius, *V. Cyp.* 3 [CSEL 3/1. xciv]) indicates that not only was it taken from *Ad Quir.* but that *Ad Quir.* Was a preexisting source used by Cyprian rather than written by him. I was not entirely convinced.

102. Tob 2:14. This verse is also used in Cyprian, *Ad Quir.* 3.6 (CCL 3.95) in the same context. See Fahey, *Cyprian and the Bible*, 111–12. See n. 98 above. Cyprian certainly regarded Tobit as scriptural, even though it was not part of the Masoretic text, making it, in later tradition, apocrypha (in the Protestant sense) or deuterocanonical (in the Catholic and Orthodox sense). In the context of the story, the blind Tobit is not being tempted by his wife, Anna, to show impatience to God but is being accused and chastised by his wife for not showing her the patience and understanding for which he was famous, when he mistakenly insisted that she return the goat he heard in the house since he thought it could have been stolen and did not believe her that it was a bonus payment for the cloth she had woven for sale. The author of Tobit, however, sympathizes with Tobit rather than Anna, for in 3:7, he juxtaposes Rachael,

Tobit's relative, as another who suffered abuse at the hands of someone. Tobit's response to the castigation from his wife is his prayer for forgiveness and death (3:1–6), which is hardly a demonstration of patience. On Tobit in Cyprian and other early Christian writers, see Chris L. de Wet, "The Book of Tobit in Early Christianity: Greek and Latin Interpretations from the 2nd to the 5th Century CE," *HTS Theological Studies* 76 (2020): 1–13, who, while noting this passage in Cyprian, observes only that Cyprian employed it to demonstrate the steadfastness of Tobit. In the same vein is Murphy, "Death, Decay and Delight," 87.

103. One may note the echo of Cyprian's affirmation of some in the community who had not fallen victim to the doubt brought about by the plague in the opening lines of the pamphlet.

104. Hannan, *Thasci Caecili Cypriani,* 29, and Deferrari, *Saint Cyprian,* 207, mistakenly translate *tu* as "I."

105. While Tob 1:16–18 does show Tobit burying not only his own relatives but any Israelite whom the neo-Assyrian king Shalmaneser V (727–22 BC) had killed, Pontius, *V. Cyp.* 19 (CSEL 3/1.ci), noted that, in contrast with Tobit who only buried people of his own race, Cyprian during the pestilence buried Christian and non-Christian alike. In contrast with *sepelisi* ("buried") in the *Vetus Latina,* Cyprian used *condisti,* which has more of the sense of preparing a body for burial through embalming.

106. Rafael is named in Tobit and in 1 Enoch 40, a noncanonical (pseudepigrapha in the Protestant and apocryphal in the Catholic and Orthodox sense) Hebrew text written in the Hellenistic age.

107. Tob 12:11–15. These verses are used in Cyprian, *De domi.* 33 (CCL 3A.110), with reference to the speed at which prayers ascend to God; while Cyprian, *Ad Quir.* 1.20 (CCL 3.20), refers to Tobit and Raphael with regard to the significance of the number seven. See Fahey, *Cyprian and the Bible,* 111–12.

108. *Mussitare:* Here the negative sense of "murmur" prevails. See Cyprian, *Ad Deme.* 18 (CCL 3A.45), not section 5, as Hannan, *Thasci Caecili Cypriani,* 71, stated; and Cyprian, *Ad Fort.* 7 (CCL 3.194), with reference to Exod 14:11–14.

109. See n. 7 above.

110. Num 17:25. This verse is found in Cyprian, *Ad Quir.* 3.14 (CCL 3.105). See Fahey, *Cyprian and the Bible,* 85–86. See n. 100 above.

111. See n. 2 above.

112. Ps 50:19 (LXX). The verse is used in a similar context in Cyprian, *Ad Quir.* 3.6 (CCL 3.94). See Fahey, *Cyprian and the Bible,* 141–42. See n. 98 above.

113. Deut 8:2. Fahey, *Cyprian and the Bible,* 91, states that Cyprian used the two passages from Deut to illustrate that Christians are to bear persecutions with patience. In fact, Cyprian was not discussing persecution but pestilence.

114. Deut 13:4. See Cyprian, *Ad Fort.* 9 (CCL 3.197–98); and Cyprian, *Ad Quir.* 3.15 (CCL 3.106), where, in the first, the context does refer to persecutions and afflictions. See Fahey, *Cyprian and the Bible,* 91.

115. See Gen 22:1–18. Fahey, *Cyprian and the Bible*, does not refer to any allusion to these verses in *De mort.*

116. See n. 49 above.

117. The use of *excedo* in this pamphlet is an affirmation of Cyprian's Christian belief. Clarke, *The Letters of St. Cyprian*, 1.357, n. 4, notes that in *Ep.* 27.1.2 (CCL 3B.128), Cyprian refrained from calling Paulus a martyr, something he had been prepared to do in *Ep.* 22.2.1 (CCL 3B.117), simply observing instead that he had "passed over." One may observe that in the several instances in which the word appears in this pamphlet, it has no negative implication. On whether Christians pass over to immediate afterlife or a period of sleep before the final resurrection, see David C. Sim, "Death after Life or Life after Death?," *Scr* 11 (2015): 143–59.

118. The impact of the deadly pestilence, either physically on oneself or emotionally from its physical impact on others, is best understood as an opportunity to struggle with and defeat the devil rather than some sign of God's indifference or nonpreferential treatment of believers.

119. Of course, *virtus* may have a wider meaning than just courage, as in "strength," "virtue," or "good character." Pliny, *Ep.* 9.26.4, used *virtus* with reference to the helmsman example, where the sense of the word is "courage." On the several occasions in this work where Cyprian used the word *virtus*, "courage" has seemed the best translation. In these particular circumstances, courage seemed to be the highest virtue for him.

120. One may note that in sections 1 and 2 Cyprian employed the metaphors of violent weather and waves and of soldiers, much as here. Ovid, *Tr.* 4.3.77–84, also, in addition to observing that adversity may bring out someone's best and a crisis should be taken as an opportunity, noted that this was not possible in times of prosperity. He used the example of Tiphys, the helmsman of the Argo. The proverb was common, as we find it in Pliny, *Ep.* 9.26.4; Seneca, *Prov.* 4.5 (a combination of the examples of the helmsman and the soldier as found here in *De mort.* in words so similar that this must be Cyprian's direct source); Seneca, *Marc.* 5.5; 6.3; Seneca, *Epp.* 30.3 (more a statement about what a helmsman can do even with a damaged ship); and 85.33–34.

121. Virgil, *Georg.* 2.291–95, presents the same image of a tree with deep roots withstanding wind and rain. Cyprian used the image of the sturdy root (*radix fundata*) elsewhere in his writings: *De unit.* 5 (CCL 3.253); and 10 (CCL 3.256), in the latter instance with the same sense that the deep-rooted tree is not blown over by storms. In *De bono* 10 (CCL 3A.123), he used both words in their noun form and in *Ep.* 37.4.2 (CCL 3B.181–82), as participles, as found in Eph 3:17. In *Ep.* 37 the root is founded upon the rock, a change to the idea of the house built on the rock. See Clarke, *The Letters of St. Cyprian*, 2.177.

122. Seneca, *Ep.* 30.2, in his consolatory letter about the failing health of Aufius Bassus, noted that his physical condition was like a ship that had sprung too many leaks to stay afloat. Seneca, *Nat.* 7.9.4, spoke of *terrae solida*

fortisque compages. Cyprian, *Ep.* 63.13.4 (CCL 3C.408), spoke of wheat grains and water fused *conpage solidatum* into one bread.

123. See Isa 41:16; Matt 3:12; and Luke 3:17. In the earlier *De unit.* 10 (CCL 3.256), Cyprian had used the images of the deep-rooted tree together with that of the grain remaining after the wind blows away the husks. In *Ep.* 37.2.2 (CCL 3B.179), he referred to the Decian religious revival as having separated grain from husk, yet later warning in *Epp.* 54.3.2 (CCL 3B.254) and 55.25 (CCL 3B.287–8) that the separation was the Lord's work alone. There are other allusions in *Epp.* 58.10.1 (CCL 3C.333); and 66.8 (CCL 3C.442). See Fahey, *Cyprian and the Bible,* 266–67; and Geoffrey D. Dunn, "Ecclesiology in Early North African Christianity: The Parable of the Wheat and the Weeds," *Aug* 57 (2017): 380–89, for the importance that this and other passages on the last judgment would have in the later Donatist controversy.

124. See Acts 27:9–44.

125. See 2 Cor 6:5.

126. See 2 Cor 4:8–12.

127. See n. 119 above.

128. 2 Cor 12:7–9. These verses are used also in Cyprian, *Ad Quir.* 3.6 (CCL 3.95) in the same context. Fahey, *Cyprian and the Bible,* 470, claims that Cyprian was referring to trials and suffering in persecution, but neither text is that specific. See n. 98 above.

129. See Cyprian *Epp.* 58.7.1 (CCL 3C.329), one of the letters most associated with this pamphlet; 59.11.2 (CCL 3C.355); Cyprian, *Ad Dona.* 5 (CCL 3A.6); 11 (CCL 3A.10); Cyprian, *De unit.* 1 (CCL 3.249); and Cyprian, *Ad Deme.* 10 (CCL 3C.40).

130. Sir 27:5. This verse is used also in Cyprian, *Ad Fort.* 9 (CCL 3.198) (not *Ad Fort.* 8 as noted in the index of CCL 3.277); and Cyprian, *Ad Quir.* 3.6 (CCL 3.94). Only in *Ad Fort.* is there specific reference to persecution. See Fahey, *Cyprian and the Bible,* 183. See n. 98 above.

131. *Exaestuat:* In *De laps.* 26 (CCL 3.235), Cyprian employed the same verb to describe the spasms a young woman endured as punishment for sin for having lapsed during the religious revival of Decius and then taking communion. I do not think that Cyprian was making any parallel between the two, however.

132. *Inardescunt:* In *De zelo* (CCL 3A.79), Cyprian wrote of the jealous burning with envy.

133. *Morbidae:* One may note how Cyprian had used the imagery of contagion in his earlier *De habi.* 17 (CCL 3F.309) to refer to female virgins (and other women) who defaced themselves with cosmetics as "infected sheep and sickly cattle." See Dunn, "Infected Sheep and Diseased Cattle," 1–20. In *De laps.* 16 (CCL 3.230), Cyprian described the lapsed who sought too quick a reconciliation with the church as damaging their salvation like hail to the crops, like a swirling tempest (*turbo*) to trees, like noxious devastation (*pestilens vastitas*) to cattle, like violent weather (*tempestas*) to ships, with their

sickly (*morbido*) word and their deadly infection (*contagio*) they dash ships against jagged rocks (*scopulus*). One may observe how all these words and images would be reused here in *De mort.* See also *Ad Deme.* 7 (CCL 3A.38), where Cyprian offered a similar series of examples as in *De laps.*, including a reference to sickly illness (*morbida valitudo*); and *Ep.* 59.15.2 (CCL 3C.364), where Cyprian referred to sinners as "sickly and infected sheep" (*morbidas et contactas oves*).

134. *Languore*: This word appears in Cyprian, *Ep.* 57.4.3 (CCL 3B.306). Cyprian wrote of someone who might die "from fever and weakness" (*in febribus et in languor*). See also *Ep.* 69.12.1 (CCL 3C.487); and 69.13.3 (CCL 3B.491).

135. This passage, with its vivid description of symptoms, resulted in this outbreak of the pestilence involved being named after Cyprian. One can imagine that Cyprian's graphic description served to let his community know that he knew all about the effects of this disease and had seen it first-hand and was not remote from its devastation in some episcopal isolation (as he had been during the religious revival under Decius).

136. *Inconcussis*: See Cyprian, *De laps.* 3 (CCL 3.222); Cyprian, *De unit.* 2 (CCL 3.250), where the rock that is battered by the swirling tempests and violent weather (see nn. 24 and 120 above) is unshaken; and Cyprian, *Epp.* 28.1.1 (CCL 3B.133); and 59.2.3 (CCL 3C.338) (see n. 6 above).

137. See n. 120 above.

138. In *Ep.* 63.13.2 (CCL 3C.407), Cyprian referred to the people who persevered in their faith as *fideliter et firmiter*.

139. See Matt 7:13; and Luke 13:24.

140. See n. 32 above.

141. See John 20:31; Rom 5:15–17; 6:23; Eph 2:8–9; and 1 John 5:11–12.

142. See John 3:5. See also Cyprian, *De domi.* 17 (CCL 3A.101). This verse would be important in the context of the "rebaptism" controversy several years later to establish that one cannot be washed clean without at the same time also receiving the Spirit. See Fahey, *Cyprian and the Bible*, 374–76. See also Cyprian, *Epp.* 72.1.2 (CCL 3C.524); 73.21.3 (CCL 3C.556); and also *Sent. Episc.* 5 (CCL 3E.17). Cf. *De rebapt.* 3 (CCL 3F.551–52). One should note the placement of the Johannine apodosis before protasis in this anonymous treatise. Cyprian characterized the belief that one could separate ritual washing from conferring the Spirit through the laying-on of hands as the erroneous view of his opponents. Their argument was (or was presented as) that while schismatics or heretics could free the baptized from sin in the sacrament, they could not confer the Spirit, which would need to happen if such a person sought admission to a nonschismatic church. Cyprian argued that such schismatic ministers could impart nothing at all to an initiate and that such a person would need the sacrament of initiation to be administered validly if they wished to become Christian (that is, it was a repeat of the ceremony but could not be called rebaptism because the

first ceremony had been devoid of any efficacy). While some scholars take Cyprian as referring mistakenly to Stephen of Rome's view on this matter (was Stephen's laying-on of hands for people in this situation initiatory or reconciliatory?) and then try to explain whether Cyprian misunderstood or misrepresented him (Maurice Bévenot, "Cyprian's Platform in the Rebaptism Controversy," *HJ* 19 [1978]: 130–31; Sage, *Cyprian*, 323; S. G. Hall, "Stephen I of Rome and the One Baptism," in *SP*, vol. 17/2, ed. Elizabeth A. Livingstone, papers presented at the Eighth International Conference on Patristic Studies, Oxford 1979 [Oxford: Pergamon Press, 1982], 797; and Brent, *Cyprian and the Roman Church*, 294–327), I have pointed to the fact that there was an opposing view to Cyprian, different from Stephen's, represented in *De rebapt.* 1 (CCL 3F.547–50), which was therefore likely to be an African document, in Dunn, *Cyprian and the Bishops of Rome*, 165–68. One should note that in *Ep.* 74.5.1–4 (CCL 3C.569–70), Cyprian did not pay attention to what Stephen wrote (insofar as we can construct that from the brief extract Cyprian repeated). On *De rebapt.*, see Paul Mattei, "Tradition et notions connexes dans la querelle baptismale. Le cas du Ps.-Cyprien, *De rebaptismate*," in *La Tradizione: forme e modi.* XVIII Incontro di studiosi dell'antichità Cristiana, Rome 7–9 May 1989, SEAug 31 (Rome: Institutum Patristicum Augustinianum, 1990): 325–39; Paul Mattei, "'Extra ecclesiam nulla salus' et puissance du nom de Jésus. Tensions et fractures dans la théologie du *De rebaptismate*," in *SP*, vol. 24, ed. Elizabeth A. Livingstone, papers presented at the Eleventh International Conference on Patristic Studies, Oxford 1991 (Leuven: Peeters, 1993), 300–5; and Paul Mattei, "Remarques sur la tradition textuelle (manuscrite et imprimée) du *De rebaptismate*," in *SP*, vol. 36, ed. M. F. Wiles and E. J. Yarnold with P. M. Parvis, papers presented at the Thirteenth International Conference on Patristic Studies, Oxford 1999 (Leuven: Peeters, 2001), 35–45.

143. See n. 240 of the translation of *Ad Deme.*

144. Given that the original idea of *torqueo* was to twist or spin on an axis, from which derived the notion of extracting evidence by the use of a rack, a device that twisted the body, one could be tempted here to translate it as "spit-roasted" because of its association with the idea of flame. When it comes to dissuading people, the grislier and more graphic the consequences to be avoided the better.

145. See nn. 7 and 68 above.

146. One may note another instance of ephanaphora (*repetitio*) here.

147. See n. 7 above.

148. This is Cyprian's only use of *gens* in this treatise. See n. 79 above. In Geoffrey D. Dunn, *Tertullian*, The Early Church Fathers (London: Routledge, 2004), 166, n. 4, I adopted either "clan" (when unspecified) or "Gentile" or "foreigner" (when the contrast was with the Jews) to translate it, a practice I have adopted here. Modern English terms such as "nation" and particularly "race" do not reflect ancient classifications of peoples, despite Denise Kimber Buell, *Why This New Race: Ethnic Reasoning in Early Christianity* (New York:

Columbia University Press, 2005), who attempts to invest such modern terms as "race" and "ethnicity" with an ancient meaning. For someone like Cyprian, a person's identity was not genetic but could change and so the modern term "race," which to the modern mind is a biologically fixed reality, is best avoided. From a Christian perspective religious affiliation had much to do with what today we may term one's ethnic identity, a concept Buell does not believe is sufficiently distinguished or distinguishable from race.

149. See n. 117 above.

150. See Wis 4:7; and Luke 16:22–23. See Cyprian, *Epp.* 6.3.1 (CCL 3B.34); 30.7.2 (CCL 3B.149); and 59.3.3 (CCL 3C.342). See Johannes Quasten, "'Vetus superstitio et nova religio': The Problem of *Refrigerium* in the Ancient Church of North Africa," *HTR* 33 (1940): 253–66; and Clarke, *The Letters of St. Cyprian*, 1.195–96, n. 26.

151. See n. 2 above.

152. See n. 117 above.

153. See Cyprian, *De habi.* 12 (CCL 3F.300–301); and Cyprian, *Ep.* 62.2.3 (CCL 3C.387).

154. CSEL 3/1.306 read *venientes* instead of *venientis.*

155. On Cyprian's reference to the antichrist see *Ad Fort.* incip.1 (CCL 3.183); *Epp.* 58.1.2 (CCL 3C.320); 58.7.1 (CCL 3C.329); 59.13.4 (CCL 3C.360); 59.18.2 (CCL 3C.369); and 67.7 (CCL 3C.458). See Clarke, *The Letters of St. Cyprian*, 3.228, n. 5.

156. See Cyprian, *Ep.* 4.2.1 (CCL 3B.19).

157. See n. 32 above.

158. *Delicata* was used also in sections 1 and 12 in a more negative fashion (hence translated as "frivolous"). Here, though, the wife is spoken of approvingly, as are the virgins and boys. Despite her refinement, her courage in the face of the pestilence puts to shame those grumbling about the disease's lack of discrimination.

159. This is one of the few references in this work (the other being the more opaque statements at the end of section 4) to the other factor besides the pandemic that persuaded the forty-two African bishops at the synod described in *Ep.* 57 to make changes to the policy established at the 251 synod concerning the treatment of those who had lapsed. That other factor was the fear of renewed persecution. See n. 54 above and the introduction.

160. I presume Cyprian meant that they were prevented from becoming even more lax in their adherence to Christianity.

161. Cyprian used *desertor* in *Ad Dona.* 11 (CCL 3A.10), but not in the context of the Decian religious revival. Andrew Cain, "Tertullian, Cyprian, and Lactantius in Jerome's *Commentary on Galatians,*" *REAug* 55 (2009): 44, sees an influence of this passage in *Ad Dona.* on Jerome. It seems to have been an accusation against Cyprian himself for going into hiding during the Decian religious revival. See Cyprian, *Epp.* 8.2.2 (CCL 3B.41); and 31.6.1 (CCL 3B.157).

162. *Gentiles*. See n. 79 above.

163. As noted in the introduction, many commentators take these words at the end of section 15 as an indication that Cyprian was aware of a new imperial decree having been issued. The great army that was being gathered could well be a reference to an impending imperial or provincial persecution or even a more remotely imagined one. It could even refer to the resolve of Christians prepared to face the pandemic and die resolutely. Indeed, if Cyprian were to have pushed the idea of a new round of imperial persecution too enthusiastically, his argument to follow shortly (17–19) that dying from disease was not a second-rate option would have been weakened. Inadvertently, he would have been encouraging Christians to avoid the pandemic and wait for the coming persecution. Yet, he stated that having been steeled through the pandemic they would be prepared for what came next. At most, I would think that Cyprian had some vague notion about possible persecution in mind rather than any clear sense that one was coming or likely to come soon.

164. See n. 2 above.

165. While *pestis* and *lues* can both have a literal meaning of "pestilence," I have taken them here in a more abstract, transferred sense. For the use of the same terms coupled together, see Cyprian, *Ad Deme.* 10 (CCL 3A.40); and Cyprian, *De unit.* 10 (CCL 3.257).

166. See n. 135 of the translation of *Ad Deme.*

167. While Hannan, *Thasci Caecili Cypriani*, 81, correctly noted the similarity of this expression to Cyprian, *De laps.* 22 (CCL 3.233), the idea of the proud being stiff-necked is found in Deut 9:6, 13; 10:16; 31:27; 2 Kgs 17:14; 2 Chron 30:8; 36:13; Neh 9:16–17, 29; Ps 75:5 (LXX); Prov 29:1; Jer 7:26; 17:23; 19:15 (plus many other references to those who have been humbled by having a yoke placed on their necks, which forces them to bow their heads in submission). The beating of slaves is mentioned also in Cyprian, *Ad Deme.* 8 (CCL 3A.39).

168. One is reminded of Cyprian's primitive version of the seven deadly sins in section 4 through an employment of something vaguely akin to the seven capital virtues (diligence, charity, chastity, patience, humility, gratitude, and temperance). One could equate looking after the sick with diligence, masters showing compassion to slaves with patience, the quenching of avarice with charity, the proud bending the neck with humility, and the rich helping others with charity.

169. The fact that death from disease prevents Christians from embracing martyrdom in practice is the topic to be addressed in following sections of this pamphlet.

170. On the crowns to be received by Christians, see n. 32 above.

171. See n. 120 above.

172. Here begins the second part of the *refutatio*. The lapsist controversy of 249–50 had involved those who had been too afraid to confess or acknowledge their faith before magistrates of the Roman state because they feared the

penalties for failure to comply with the imperial edict to participate in traditional Roman religious sacrificial practices. Their failures had seen them excluded from active membership of the church with long penance imposed on them before the possibility of reconciliation. Those who had refused the demands of the imperial edict suffered the consequences, including imprisonment, which made them confessors, or death (either directly or as a result of imprisonment), which made them martyrs. Even while imprisoned, many considered the confessors to be living martyrs, so a clear-cut distinction between confessors and martyrs was not observed, although Cyprian did so in general. In Carthage, the confessors had assumed leadership of the church in the absence of Cyprian, who had gone into hiding, in making determinations about who could be reconciled and when. It is not clear, but the way the objection in this pamphlet is framed could suggest that the theoretical person making the objection is only now prepared to confess their faith, that is, they could have been a *lapsus* previously. Their argument rested on the presumption that there was going to be a fresh round of imperial activity that would confront Christians. On whether there was a new campaign by Gallus or merely something local, and its timing with regard to the pestilence, see Clarke, *The Letters of St. Cyprian*, 3.4–17, and the introduction to this volume.

173. *Dignatio* indicates that it is God who decides who is worthy of the honor of martyrdom. See Cyprian, *Ep.* 28.1.1; 28.2.3 and 4 (CCL 3B.133–36), where it is used three times.

174. *Renes* are the kidneys, which, in the ancient mind, was understood to be the seat of the affections while the heart was the seat of knowledge and memory. The word can also refer to the loins or pelvic area (as in "fruit of the loins" or "girding the loins") in that the sexual urge is a strong emotive drive. Yet, since the kidneys were thought to control all emotions (not just the sexual ones), I consider loins to be too restrictive a translation of those scriptural instances where the reference is to something more general than the pelvic region. See Ps 7:10; 26:2 (LXX); Jer 20:12; 17:10; and Rev 2:23. Cyprian used the same expression in *Ep.* 10.5.1 (CCL 3B.54), which Clarke, *The Letters of St. Cyprian*, 1, translates as "hearts and minds." See also *Ep.* 55.26.1 (CCL 3B.288). To modern readers the heart is the seat of feelings rather than of thinking, so the ancient idea that the phrase referred to both intellect and will (the rational and affective parts of the soul) is confused in that *cor* figuratively means "mind" for the ancient but "heart" for the modern reader and that *renes* meant "heart" for the ancient, but any connection to "mind" for the modern reader seems quite inexplicable.

175. See Dan 13:42. This is not alluded to in Fahey, *Cyprian and the Bible*.

176. In *Ep.* 10.5.1 (CCL 3B.54), Cyprian had employed the same argument already in much the same words that would be repeated in our pamphlet, that those who were prepared to die and had demonstrated that in their confession but did not die were in no way inferior to those who did. In *Ep.* 12.1.2 (CL 3B.68–69), he had also indicated that those who had died in

prison, where they had been held because of their confession of faith, were no less martyrs even if their death was not the result of torture. Here Cyprian was extending that circumstance to cover those who died because of the disease. The only difference was that their resolve to endure martyrdom had not been demonstrated as it had been for those imprisoned because of Decius. Here, then, Cyprian had to emphasize the fact that the condition of their will and intellect was known already to God.

177. Gen 4:3–8. See Fahey, *Cyprian and the Bible*, 562.

178. Cyprian used the word *parricidium*, but in the more general sense of killing a relative rather than the specific sense of killing one's father.

179. In *De domi.* 24 (CCL 3A.105), Cyprian stated that God could distinguish the offerings of Cain and Abel on the basis not of their gifts but what was in their hearts. Only in *De mort.* did he spell out what God was discerning in Cain's heart. In *De bono* 19 (CCL 3A.129) and *De zelo* 18 (CCL 3A.85), Cyprian attributed impatience and jealousy as Cain's motives, but without reference to God's insight or foresight into those motives. As Murphy, "Imitating the Devil," 79–83, observes, although omitting this passage in *De mort.*, Cyprian often referred to Cain and Able, the former as an imitator of the devil. For further on Cyprian's use of Cain, see Jack P. Lewis, "The Offering of Abel (Gen 4:4): A History of Interpretation," *JETS* 37 (1994): 487; and Lee Blackburn, "Razing Cain: Two North African Christians on the Forgiveness of Debts," *Leaven* 19 (2011): 88.

180. Cyprian contrasted a lack of willingness to endure martyrdom with a lack of opportunity. The fact that in the second statement the reference is to a past time (*defuisse*) could suggest that Cyprian was thinking of the Decian religious revival a couple of years previously and not to a renewed persecution of Christians in the light of the plague. I would contend that such a scenario, as envisaged in *Epp.* 57 and 58, was not yet in Cyprian's mind. One may note the presence of reciprocal change (*commutatio*), on which see *Rhet. Her.* 4.28.39. See Cyprian, *Ep.* 12.1.2 (CCL 3B.68).

181. Rev 2:23. See Cyprian, *Ad Quir.* 3.56 (CCL 3.142); Cyprian, *De laps.* 27 (CCL 3.236); and Cyprian, *De domi.* 4 (CCL 3A.91). See Fahey, *Cyprian and the Bible*, 540–41.

182. The image of heaven as a banquet is common in the gospel parables. The idea of sharing that banquet with the patriarchs is found in Matt 8:11 (slightly different in Luke 13:28–29). Fahey, *Cyprian and the Bible*, 290–91, did not notice this allusion in *De mort.* when he considered this Matthean verse.

183. Cyprian discusses Matt 6:10b in *De domi.* 14–16 (CCL 3A.98–100). In these sections Cyprian focused on the fact that human will is weak and that we need to do the will of the Father, as the Son did, to reach eternal happiness, on what the will of God entails, and on the correlation between heaven and earth and spirit and flesh. None of this helps determine which work was composed first. The traditional order, if Pontius, *V. Cyp.* 7 (CSEL 3/1.xcvii–xcviii), refers to Cyprian's works in chronological order, is that *De domi.* came before *Ad*

Deme. and *De mort.* See Alistair Stewart-Sykes, *Tertullian, Cyprian and Origen: On the Lord's Prayer,* Popular Patristics Series (Crestwood, NY: St. Vladimir's Press, 2004), for a recent English translation and brief introduction to this work of Cyprian.

184. Enthusiasm for martyrdom was a common feature of early Christian rhetoric, especially in North Africa. As the Decian religious revival revealed, however, it was not an ideal many Christians wanted to actualize when the opportunity arose. Cyprian's comments here, though, are not specific to martyrdom but can be related simply to death in general.

185. Although in section 7 I translated *exire* as "escape," here the same verb, given the differing attitude toward death that Cyprian was criticizing, is better translated as "depart."

186. That Cyprian found a slave simile a useful thing to include in his pamphlet would suggest that the Christians of Carthage were familiar with the harsh treatment of slaves, either because many of them were former slaves or were slave owners or it was just so well-known a literary trope. On slavery in the Roman world, see n. 97 of *Ad Deme.* On the translation of *voluntas* as "inclination" see n. 102 of *Ad Deme.*

187. See n. 32 above.

188. *Votum* can range in meaning from a wish to a vow. Given the force of Cyprian's overall argument I think the stronger translation is warranted here, even though it is doubled with *desideria,* which is a word at the more optative end of the spectrum.

189. In *De laps.* 35 (CCL 3.240), Cyprian instructed the penitent *lapsi* that they needed to engage in constant prayer and entreaty and, following the advice of Tob 12:8–10, almsgiving for the expunging of their sins. Given that penitent *libellatici* were readmitted to full communion after the African synod of 251 (Cyprian, *Ep.* 55.17.3—55.18.1 [CCL 3B.276–77]) and the penitent *sacrificati* were to be readmitted after the 253 synod (Cyprian, *Ep.* 57.2.1–2 [CCL 3C.302–303])—a change to the 251 policy of readmitting penitent *sacrificati* to communion just before their death (Cyprian, *Epp.* 55.17.3 [CCL 3B.276]; and 57.1.1 [CCL 3C.301])—one should take Cyprian's comments here as being addressed to a community that included some who once had proved their reluctance to die for the faith by lapsing. While the *stantes,* those who resisted Decius's edict and confessed their faith, thereby enduring some form of punishment including prison and torture, or who had been overlooked during the whole episode, probably because their poverty made them insignificant, had shown a willingness to heed the Lord's summons, perhaps Cyprian's words were still applicable to them in other spheres of their lives, such as their attachment to possessions or the pleasures offered in this life. See the comments in the introduction to this work for dating the synod referred to in *Ep.* 57 to 253. On reigning with Christ, see 2 Tim 2:12; and Rev 20:4. The pseudo-Pauline verses appear in *Ad Fort.* 5 (CCL 3.193) and those

from Rev in *Ad Fort.* 12 (CCL 3.214). Fahey, *Cyprian and the Bible,* 512 and 552, did not see an allusion to *De mort.* when he considered these verses.

190. Here *collegea* and *consacerdos* are used in typical pleonastic fashion by Cyprian. *Consacerdos* was also used in *Epp.* 55.7.3 (CCL 3B.263) and 60.1.1 (CCL 3C.374). See Richard Seagraves, *Pascentes cum disciplina: A Lexical Study of the Clergy in the Cyprianic Correspondence,* Paradosis 37 (Fribourg: Editions Universitaires, 1993). Whenever Cyprian referred to *sacerdos* or *sacerdotium* he meant the episcopate and not the presbyterate. See Cyprian, *Epp.* 1.1.1 (CCL 3B.1); 40.1.2 (CCL 3B.194); 43.2.2 (CCL 3B.202); and 67.4.3 (CCL 3C.453). Clarke, *The Letters of St. Cyprian,* 2.198–99, n. 6, believes that even though it appears that in *Ep.* 40 he referred to presbyters as *sacerdoti,* Cyprian was being "designedly honorific and proleptic." Clarke, *The Letters of St. Cyprian,* 4.148, n. 13, explains that in *Ep.* 67 Cyprian might not have been referring to *episcopi, sacerdoti,* and *diaconi* as the three highest clerical grades, but might have been using *episcopus* and *sacerdos* as synonyms and was only contrasting two of those three grades (bishops and deacons) with each other.

191. *Commeatum*: Militarily, the term was used for a leave of absence. Elsewhere Cyprian used the term to speak of a delay in martyrdom: *Epp.* 10.5.2 (CCL 3B.55)—a letter where very similar arguments to those proposed here are to be found, see n. 174 above; 39.1.1 (CCL 3B.186); and 55.13.1 (CCL 3B.270). See Clarke, *The Letters of St. Cyprian,* 1.236, n. 33. Such a reprieve was not held to be a bad thing. The point Cyprian wants to make to his objector in this pamphlet is that martyrdom is not the only way to be pleasing to God. One should not try to avoid the pestilence in order to save oneself for martyrdom, but to embrace whatever the will of God demanded of one.

192. See n. 7 above.

193. The unbearable brightness of the young man indicates his angelic or divine nature.

194. *Sollicitus*: The normal translation as "anxious," as employed by Hannan, *Thasci Caecili Cypriani,* 39, and Deferrari, *Saint Cyprian,* 215, does not make sense here, nor does the normal sense of *preoccupato* as used by Cerretini, *Cipriano: Trattati,* 76. The angelic youth, the one whose voice was rebuking the reluctant bishop, ought not to be anxious about persecution. The voice ought to be "concerned" (not in the sense of troubled but involved in or attentive to promoting persecution). The alternative, offered by Wallis, "The Treatises of Cyprian," 474, was to make the anxiety and indifference refer to those addressed by the voice, but here being indifferent or untroubled by the summons does not match being anxious about persecution.

195. The bishop's approaching death was attributed to sickness (*infirmitas*) and not persecution. This makes him the exact match with Cyprian's idealized interlocutor. Perhaps the bishop was simply afraid of death or perhaps he did not want to die from disease but rather from some future persecution. The point of Cyprian giving the example is that the bishop was

rebuked by the angelic youth, just as the interlocutor needs to be. Death, as an expression of the divine will, needs to be embraced not shirked.

196. *Sacerdos.*

197. See n. 173 above.

198. See n. 2 above.

199. See n. 7 above.

200. For a similar thought, see *Ad Dona.* 14 (CCL 3A.12).

201. See n. 68 above.

202. See John R. Levison, "The Roman Character of Funerals in the Writings of Josephus," *JSJ* 33 (2002): 245–77; Valerie M. Hope and Janet Huskinson, eds., *Memory and Mourning: Studies on Roman Death* (Oxford: Oxbow, 2011); Aerynn Dighton, "*Mutatio vestis*: Clothing and Political Protest in the Late Roman Republic," *Phoenix* 71 (2017): 345–69; and Diana Gorostidi Pi, "'Too Young to Die': Grief and Mourning in Ancient Rome," *Thersites* 9 (2019): 71–88. Black as a color for mourning is mentioned, for example, in Ovid, *Met.* 6.568 and 8.448; Tacitus, *Hist.* 3.67; and Cicero, *Vat.* 13. On white for those in heaven, see Dan 7:9; Rev 3:4–5; 4:4; 6:11; 7:9, 13; and 19:14. For other information provided about mourning, see Cyprian, *De laps.* 30 (CCL 3.237–38).

203. *Gentilibus.* See n. 79 above.

204. If Cyprian was being consistent with his earlier usage of heart and kidneys in section 17, he was referring here not to an emotional but a rational testimony, with *cor* and *pectus* being used as synonyms. Yet, Cyprian appears to be contrasting word with action, so "heart and breast" would make best sense as referring to courage in action.

205. A third topic in the *refutatio* begins here. Rather than countering arguments concerning survivors of the epidemic, Cyprian turned his attention to the fate of those who had died as well as the correct attitude to be held by those who survived concerning their dead friends and family. They were not to be mourned. This was to counter potential arguments from nonbelievers that Christians were not putting into practice what they proclaimed about the afterlife and the resurrection of the dead. Scourfield, "The *De mortalitate* of Cyprian," 17, says that it is only in this section that Cyprian confronted the question of the grief of the living at the losses they have suffered. I would disagree somewhat, to the extent that the whole pamphlet has been an attempt to persuade his readers that grief is the reaction of the nonbeliever. While Cyprian may seem unfeeling to a modern reader, his attitude of zeal and total commitment to his Christianity is typical of the rigorous and severe way in which North African Christianity, so characteristic of Tertullian and then of the later Donatists, expressed itself. In order to prove to his readers that dead Christians were not to be mourned, Cyprian needed to demonstrate convincingly that the fate of believers who died far outweighed any benefits from continuing to live in the present life. Thus, this whole section is about the promises of the world to come.

206. The translation misses the alliteration in this last sentence with *verbis, virtutem,* and *veritatem.*

207. *Denique* was used in section 19 to mark the final point in the second part of the *refutatio.* It will be used in that same sense in section 23. Here, however, rather than being the last in a list, it introduces an illustration of the point made in the previous section.

208. See n. 117 above.

209. See n. 2 above.

210. 1 Thess 4:13–14. This passage is found also in Cyprian, *Ad Quir.* 3.58 (CCL 3.145), in the same context. See Fahey, *Cyprian and the Bible,* 50; and Murphy, "Death, Decay and Delight," 85. See n. 41 above.

211. See n. 117 above.

212. See nn. 7 and 68 above.

213. See n. 68 above.

214. John 11:25–26. There is an allusion to the passage in Cyprian, *De domi.* 13 (CCL 3A.97). See Fahey, *Cyprian and the Bible,* 391. In both instances, Cyprian does not include the phrase *et vita* found in the Greek and Vetus Latina versions of the gospel.

215. See Rom 6:8; 2 Tim 2:11–12; and Rev 20:6. See Fahey, *Cyprian and the Bible,* 429 and 552, who sees no allusion to the first or last passages, but on 512 does record that the pseudo-Pauline passage is quoted in Cyprian, *Ad Fort.* 5 (CCL 3.193).

216. This is the first time Cyprian used *transgredior* in this pamphlet, as a synonym for *excedo.*

217. See the use of *exeo* in sections 7 and (at n. 185, with the different translation reflecting more the view of the imagined opponent) and 18.

218. See Seneca, *Ep.* 65.24, where he asked about the nature of death, as either end (*finis*) or process of change (*transitus*), as Gummere translates it for Loeb. See Steven Lowenstam, "Seneca's *Epistle Sixty-five,*" *MAAR* 43–44 (1998–99): 63–78. It is clear from what Cyprian says in the rest of this section that he understood *transitus* both as a movement from this world to the next and as a change into the more perfect image of Christ or the imperishable nature of 1 Cor 15:53 mentioned in section 8.

219. There is no negative connotation in the use of *transgressus.*

220. See Rom 8:29; 1 Cor 15:49; 2 Cor 3:18; and Eph 4:22–24. Fahey, *Cyprian and the Bible,* 432 and 466, does not see any allusions to two of these passages. While, on 463–64, he does note Cyprian's use of the 1 Cor passage, the reference is only to *Ad Quir.* 2.10 (CCL 3.43); 3.11 (CCL 3.101); and *De habi.* 23 (CCL 3F.318), and on 487, the use of Eph passage, the reference is only to *Ad Quir.* 3.11 (CCL 3.102); *De habi.* 23 (CCL 3F.318); and *Ep.* 11.7.2 (CCL 3B.64).

221. Phil 3:20–21. The passage is also used in Cyprian, *Ad Quir.* 3.11 (CCL 3.101–102) (where the verb is given as *transformavit,* although *transformabit* is found in some manuscripts); and Cyprian, *Ep.* 76.2.4 (CCL 3C.611) (where the

verb is given as *transformaverit*). In our passage the verb is given as *transformabit* (although some manuscripts have *transformavit*). See Fahey, *Cyprian and the Bible*, 497–98; and Murphy, "Cyprian's Use of Philippians," 53. I have followed G. W. Clarke, *The Letters of St. Cyprian of Carthage*, 4: *Letters 67–82*, ACW 47 (New York: Newman Press, 1989), 97, for the translation.

222. John 17:24. See also Cyprian, *Ad Quir.* 3.58 (CCL 3.146). One may note that Cyprian has abridged the end of the verse in both instances, in addition to a couple of other minor variations. See Fahey, *Cyprian and the Bible*, 400–401. See n. 41 above.

223. While *profectio* has both the sense of "departure" (going from) and "setting forth" (going to), I have attempted to highlight Cyprian's positive perspective on death: not leaving something behind but going to something better, as we see in section 7 also where the verb occurs as the Christian response to the summons of Christ.

224. Gen 5:24. See Fahey, *Cyprian and the Bible*, 60–61, who points out that the fact that Enoch escaped death makes this passage a little problematic for Cyprian to use to argue in favor of Christians maintaining a joyful attitude in the face of death. See n. 41 above.

225. See n. 7 above.

226. Wis 4:11 and 14. See Fahey, *Cyprian and the Bible*, 176. See n. 41 above.

227. Ps 83:2–3 (LXX). See Fahey, *Cyprian and the Bible*, 146–47. See n. 41 above. The use of these three scriptural passages together also found in Cyprian, *Ad Quir.* 3.58 (CCL 3.143–46), is no coincidence. The question is whether or not Cyprian was borrowing from his own work or that of another.

228. See n. 7 above.

229. See Cyprian, *Ep.* 34.2 (CCL 3B.168), for a similar expression.

230. See n. 260 of the translation of *Ad Deme.*

231. *Caritas.*

232. One may note that in Cyprian, *Ad Quir.* 3.11 (CCL 3.103); and Cyprian, *De domi.* 14 (CCL 3B.98), the text reads *ambitio saeculi* rather than *ambitio mundi.*

233. One may note that in *Ad Quir.* 3.11 (CCL 3.103), the text reads *concupiscentia saeculi* rather than *concupiscentia mundi.*

234. 1 John 2:15–17. See Cyprian, *Ad Quir.* 3.11 (CCL 3.103); Cyprian, *De habi.* 7 (CCL 3F.294); and Cyprian, *De domi.* 14 (CCL 3A.98–99). The last sentence also appears in *Ad Quir.* 3.19 (CCL 3.114). See Fahey, *Cyprian and the Bible*, 527–29. See n. 207 above for other passages used in this same section of *Ad Quir.* 1 John 2:6 is associated with these verses of the same Johannine letter in *Ad Quir.* and *De habi.* but not in *De mort.* Interestingly, 1 John 2:6 is used in Cyprian, *Ep.* 58.1.3 (CCL 3C.320–21), a letter closely associated with our pamphlet.

235. See n. 2 above.

236. See n. 24 above. The reappearance of *turbo* from section 2 is not only a reference back to the pandemic itself but a sure sign that by reminding his readers of the introductory sections of the pamphlet Cyprian had started to present his conclusion.

237. See n. 49 above.

238. The *peroratio* of the pamphlet begins here with Cyprian returning to mention how the pestilence puts extra pressure on Christians to behave. See Scourfield, "The *De mortalitate* of Cyprian," 18. As pointed out in nn. 70, 185, and 223 above, arguments could focus on the leaving behind of one place as much as on the going to of another place.

239. Strabo 5.3.7 informs us that Augustus imposed a limit of seventy feet on the height of tenement blocks in Rome to prevent collapsing. From *Epit. de Caes.* 13.13, we are told that Trajan reduced that to sixty feet. Cyprian must have been talking about an all-too-common occurrence for the urban poor that made this metaphor readily probative of his argument. The emphasis is still on the idea of escape from somewhere undesirable and dangerous.

240. *Turbida et procellosa tempestas*: In section 2 Cyprian had written *ad procellas et turbines.* See n. 24 above. In section 1 the adjective *turbidus* had been used. *Tempestas* had been used in section 12, so here with the two adjectives, the sense of violence does not have to be included in the translation of *tempestas. Fluctus* had been used in sections 1, 6, and 12. See n. 66 above. The waves on a dangerous sea would have reminded Cyprian's readers of the start of the pamphlet and been another indication of him reaching his conclusion, establishing that he had proved what he set out to prove.

241. Even though Cyprian had just provided examples of the effects of old age, his conclusion is not that the deadly pestilence is a sign of the end of the world due to its fatigue caused by old age but its end due to the fact that this is the time determined by God. One may notice that in *Ad Deme.*, given the difference in addressee, Cyprian would rely on the old age argument rather than on God's end times. See Murphy, "Death, Decay and Delight," 80.

242. See n. 2 above.

243. Pontius, *V. Cyp.* 11 (CSEL 3/1.ci), noted that exile and banishment are no punishment for Christians because the whole world is their home, and they are strangers in their own hometowns. The idea derives from Phil 3:20, a verse that had been quoted in section 22. See n. 221 above.

244. See n. 7 above.

245. In *Ep.* 58.10.1–2 (CCL 3C.333–34), Cyprian wrote of the joys experienced by the just of being with God in the next life. The contrast is with the punishment of the damned rather than with what the just endure in this life. The notion of a restoration to paradise is not in the letter either.

246. The translation tries to capture some of the alliteration in *Quis non peregre constitutes properet in patriam regredi?* In *Ad Fort.* 13 (CCL 3.214), based on Rom 8:18, also used in *Ep.* 58.10.2 (CCL 3C.334), Cyprian again stressed that the rewards of the next life outweigh the suffering of the present and that the

true believer strives for such rewards. The idea of rushing to this reward, as found in the pamphlet, is not found in the other two texts, despite Hannan, *Thasci Caecili Cypriani*, 96.

247. The notion of the favorable wind contrasts and connects nicely with the storms and swirling tempests of section 2, as would be appropriate in the concluding sentences. What Cyprian did note in *Ad Fort.* 13 (CCL 3.215) is not that our time in this world should not be extended but that the transition between this life and the next should be swift (*velocitas*) and unexpected (*repente*).

248. The idea of greeting the patriarchs (Abraham, Isaac, Jacob) and all the apostles, prophets, and martyrs is also to be found in Cyprian, *Ep.* 58.10.1 (CCL 3C.334).

249. One is reminded of Heb 12:1, a New Testament work Cyprian never cited explicitly, according to Fahey, *Cyprian and the Bible*, 41.

250. See n. 248 above for the same grouping of others, besides the patriarchs, who await the Christian in heaven. Hannan, *Thasci Caecili Cypriani*, 96, notes the similarities with the later *Te Deum*. The order is certainly the same (apostles, prophets, and martyrs), suggesting Cyprian as an antecedent. See Maurice Frost, "*Te Deum Laudamus*," *JTS* 28 (1927): 403–7; Maurice Frost, "Two Texts of the *Te Deum Laudamus*," *JTS* 39 (1938): 388–91; and Maurice Frost, "Adaptations of the *Te Deum Laudamus*," *JTS* 43 (1942): 68. On the crowns for martyrdom and good works, see Dunn, "The White Crown of Works," and n. 32 above.

251. One is reminded of *De habi.*, which Cyprian had composed already. See Dunn, "Infected Sheep and Diseased Cattle," 1–20.

252. See Matt 6:19–20. Hannan, *Thasci Caecili Cypriani*, 96, saw parallels with Cyprian, *De laps.* 2 (CCL 3.221–22). The difference, however, is that in our pamphlet the virgins and the merciful are there to greet the arriving Christian while in *De laps.* the virgins and others are the ones coming into heaven. One is reminded of *De oper.*, a work Cyprian had not yet written. See Dunn, "Cyprian's Care for the Poor," 363–68.

253. See n. 2 above.

254. See n. 32 above.

BIBLIOGRAPHY

EDITIONS AND TRANSLATIONS OF CYPRIAN

Bévenot, Maurice. *St. Cyprian: The Lapsed, The Unity of the Catholic Church.* ACW 25. New York: Newman Press, 1957.

———, ed. "Sancti Cypriani De ecclesiae catholicae unitate." In *Sancti Cypriani Episcopi Opera,* part 1. Edited by R. Weber and M. Bévenot. CCL 3, 243–68. Turnhout: Brepols, 1972.

———, ed. "Sancti Cypriani De Lapsis." In *Sancti Cypriani Episcopi Opera,* part 1, ed. R. Weber and M. Bévenot. CCL 3, 217–42. Turnhout: Brepols, 1972.

Brent, Allen. *St. Cyprian of Carthage. On the Church: Select Treatises.* Popular Patristics Series 32. Crestwood, NY: St Vladimir's Seminary Press, 2006.

Cerretini, Antonella. *Cipriano: Trattati.* CTP 175. Rome: Città Nuova, 2004.

Ciccolini, L., ed. "Sancti Cypriani De habitu virginum." In *Sancti Cypriani Episcopi Opera,* part 3/5. Edited by P. Mattei and L. Ciccolini. CCL 3F, 283–320. Turnhout: Brepols, 2016.

Clarke, G. W. *The Letters of St. Cyprian of Carthage,* 4 vols. ACW 43–44 and 46–47. New York: Newman Press, 1984–89.

Conway, M. G. E. *Thasci Caecili Cypriani: De bono patientiae.* CUAPS 92. Washington, DC: Catholic University of America Press, 1957.

Deferrari, Roy J. *Saint Cyprian: Treatises.* FC 36. Washington, DC: Catholic University of America Press, 1958.

Fredouille, Jean-Claude. ed. *Cyprien de Carthage. A Démétrien.* SC 467. Paris: Les Éditions du Cerf, 2003.

Gallicet, Ezio. *Cipriano. A Demetriano.* CP 4. Turin: Società Editrice Internazionale, 1976.

Hannan, Mary Louise. *Thasci Caecili Cypriani—De Mortalitate: A Commentary, with an Introduction and Translation.* CUAPS 36. Washington, DC: Catholic University of America Press, 1933.

Hartel, Wilhelm ed. *S. Thasci Caecili Cypriani Opera Omnia.* CSEL 3/1. Vienna: C. Geroldi, 1868.

Moreschini, C., ed. "Sancti Cypriani De bono patientiae." In *Sancti Cypriani Episcopi Opera,* part 2. Edited by M. Simonetti and C. Moreschini. CCL 3A, 115–33. Turnhout: Brepols, 1976.

———, ed. "Sancti Cypriani De dominica oratione." In *Sancti Cypriani Episcopi Opera,* part 2. Edited by M. Simonetti and C. Moreschini. CCL 3A, 87–113. Turnhout: Brepols, 1976.

Parker, John Henry. *The Treatises of S. Cæcilius Cyprian, Bishop of Carthage, and Martyr, with Notes and Indices.* Library of Fathers of the Holy Catholic Church Anterior to the Division of the East and West 3. London: J. G. & F. Rivington, 1839.

Ruggiero, Mario. *Cipriano, Paolino di Nola, Uranio: Poesia e teologia della morte.* 2nd edition. CTP 42. Rome: Città Nuova, 1997.

Simonetti, M., ed. "Sancti Cypriani Ad Demetrianum." In *Sancti Cypriani Episcopi Opera,* part 2. Edited by M. Simonetti and C. Moreschini. CCL 3A, 34–51. Turnhout: Brepols, 1976.

———. ed. "Sancti Cypriani De mortalitate." In *Sancti Cypriani Episcopi Opera,* part 2. Edited by M. Simonetti and C. Moreschini. CCL 3A, 73–86. Turnhout: Brepols, 1976.

———. ed. "Sancti Cypriani De opere et eleemosynis." In *Sancti Cypriani Episcopi Opera,* part 2. Edited by M. Simonetti and C. Moreschini. CCL 3A, 53–72. Turnhout: Brepols, 1976.

———. ed. "Sancti Cypriani De zelo et livore." In *Sancti Cypriani Episcopi Opera,* part 2. Edited by M. Simonetti and C. Moreschini. CCL 3A, 16–32. Turnhout: Brepols, 1976.

Stewart-Sykes, Alistair. *Tertullian, Cyprian and Origen: On the Lord's Prayer.* Popular Patristics Series. Crestwood, NY: St. Vladimir's Press, 2004.

Stramondo, Giuseppina. *Studi sul De mortalitate di Cipriano: Studi, testo e traduzione, index verborum omnium.* Catania: Università di Catania, 1964.

Wallis, Ernest. "Cyprian." In *The Ante-Nicene Fathers,* vol. 5: *Hippolytus, Cyprian, Caius, Novatian, Appendix.* Edited by Alexander Roberts and James Donaldson, rev. A. Cleveland Coxe, 263–596. Buffalo, NY: Christian Literature Co., 1886.

Weber, R. ed. "Sancti Cypriani Ad Fortunatum." In *Sancti Cypriani Episcopi Opera,* part 1. Edited by R. Weber and M. Bévenot. CCL 3, 181–216. Turnhout: Brepols, 1972.

———. ed. "Sancti Cypriani Ad Quirinum." In *Sancti Cypriani Episcopi Opera*, part 1. Edited by R. Weber and M. Bévenot. CCL 3, 1–179. Turnhout: Brepols, 1972.

OTHER ANCIENT SOURCES

Aelius Aristides. *Orationes*. Translated by Charles A. Behr. *P. Aelius Aristides: The Complete Works*, 2 vols. Leiden: Brill, 1981–86.

Aeschylus. *Prometheus vinctus*. Translated by Alan H. Sommerstein. *Aeschylus: Persians, Seven Against Thebes, Suppliants, Prometheus Bound*. Loeb Classical Library. Cambridge, MA: Harvard University Press, 2009.

Ammianus Marcellinus. *Rerum gestarum*. Translated by John C. Rolfe. *Ammianus Marcellinus: History*. Loeb Classical Library, 3 vols. Cambridge, MA: Harvard University Press, 1939–50.

Aristotle. *Rhetorica*. Translated by J. H. Freese. *Aristotle: Art of Rhetoric*. Loeb Classical Library. Cambridge, MA: Harvard University Press, 1926.

Arnobius. *Adversus nationes*. Edited by A. Reifferscheid. *Arnobii Adversus nationes Libri VII*. CSEL 4. Vienna: C. Gerold. 1875.

Augustine. *Sermo* 313C (Guelf. 26). Edited by German Morin. *Miscellanea Agostiniana. Testi e studi*, vol. 1: *Sancti Augustini Sermones post Maurinos reperti*, 529–31. Rome: Tipografia Poliglotta Vaticana, 1930. Translation in Edmund Hill. *The Works of Saint Augustine: A Translation for the 21st Century*, part 3: *Sermons*, vol. 9: *Sermons 306–340A*. Hyde Park, NY: New City Press, 1994.

Aurelius Victor. *De Caesaribus*. Translated by H. W. Bird. *Aurelius Victor: De Caesaribus*. Translated Texts for Historians 17. Liverpool: Liverpool University Press, 1994.

Caesar. *Bellum Gallicum*. Translated by H. J. Edwards. *Caesar: The Gallic War*. Loeb Classical Library. Cambridge, MA: Harvard University Press, 1917.

Cassius Dio. *Historia Romana*. Translated by E. Cary. *Dio Cassius: Roman History*. Loeb Classical Library, 9 vols. Cambridge, MA: Harvard University Press, 1914–27.

Cicero. *De divinatione*. Translated by W. A. Falconer. *Cicero: On Old Age, On Friendship, On Divination*. Loeb Classical Library. Cambridge, MA: Harvard University Press, 1923.

———. *De haruspicum responsis*. Translated by N. H. Watts. *Cicero: Pro Archia, Post reditum in Senatu, Post reditum ad Quirites, De domo suo, De haruspicum responsis, Pro Plancio.* Loeb Classical Library. Cambridge, MA: Harvard University Press, 1923.

———. *De inventione.* Translated by H. M. Hubbell. *Cicero: De inventione, De optimo genere oratorum, Topica.* Loeb Classical Library, Cambridge, MA: Harvard University Press, 1949.

———. *De natura deorum.* Translated by H. Rackham. *Cicero: On the Nature of the Gods, Academics.* Loeb Classical Library. Cambridge, MA: Harvard University Press, 1933.

———. *De senectute.* Translated by W. A. Falconer. *Cicero: On Old Age, On Friendship, On Divination.* Loeb Classical Library. Cambridge, MA: Harvard University Press, 1923.

———. *Epistulae ad Atticum.* Translated by D. R. Shackleton Bailey. *Cicero's Letters to Atticus.* Harmondsworth: Penguin Classics, 1978.

———. *Epistulae ad familiares.* Translated by D. R. Shackleton Bailey. *Cicero's Letters to His Friends,* 2 vols. Harmondsworth: Penguin Classics, 1978.

———. *In Catilinam.* Translated by C. Macdonald. *Cicero: In Catilinam 1–4, Pro Murena, Pro Sulla, Pro Flacco.* Loeb Classical Library. Cambridge, MA: Harvard University Press, 1976.

———. *In Vatinium.* Translated by R. Gardner. *Cicero: Pro Sestio, In Vatinium.* Loeb Classical Library. Cambridge, MA: Harvard University Press, 1958.

———. *In Verrem.* Translated by L. H. G. Greenwood. *Cicero: The Verrine Orations,* 2 vols. Loeb Classical Library. Cambridge, MA: Harvard University Press, 1928–35.

———. *Tusculanae disputationes.* Translated by J. E. King. *Cicero: Tusculan Disputations.* Loeb Classical Library. Cambridge, MA: Harvard University Press, 1927.

De rebaptismate. Edited by P. Mattei. "Pseudo Sancti Cypriani De rebaptismate." In *Sancti Cypriani Episcopi Opera,* part 3/5. Edited by P. Mattei and L. Ciccolini. CCL 3F, 547–79. Turnhout: Brepols, 2016.

Epitome de Caesaribus. Translated by T. M. Banchich (www.roman-emperors.org/epitome.htm).

Eusebius. *Historia ecclesiastica.* Translation by J. H. Lawlor. *Eusebius: Ecclesiastical History.* Loeb Classical Library, 2 vols. Cambridge, MA: Harvard University Press, 1930.

Eutropius. *Breviarium.* Translation by H. W. Bird. *Eutropius: Breviarium.* Translated Texts for Historians 14. Liverpool: Liverpool University Press, 1993.

Fronto. *Laudes fumi et pulveris.* Translated by C. R. Haines. *Marcus Cornelius Fronto.* Loeb Classical Library, 2 vols. Cambridge, MA: Harvard University Press, 1919–20.

Galen. *Methodus medendi.* Translated by Ian Johnston and G. H. R. Horsley. *Galen: Method of Medicine.* Loeb Classical Library. Cambridge, MA: Harvard University Press, 2011.

Gregory I. *Moralia in Iob.* Edited by M. Adriaen. *Gregorius Magnus. Moralia sive expositio in Iob,* CCL 143, 143A, and 143B, 3 vols. Turnhout: Brepols, 1979–85.

Historia Augusta. Translated by David Magie. *Historia Augusta.* Loeb Classical Library, 3 vols. Cambridge, MA: Harvard University Press, 1921–32.

Horace. *Carmen saeculare.* Translated by Niall Rudd. *Horace: Odes and Epodes.* Loeb Classical Library. Cambridge, MA: Harvard University Press, 2004.

———. *Epistulae.* Translated by H. Rushton Fairclough. *Horace: Satires, Epistles, The Art of Poetry.* Loeb Classical Library. Cambridge, MA: Harvard University Press, 1926.

———. *Epodi.* Translated by Niall Rudd. *Horace: Odes and Epodes.* Loeb Classical Library. Cambridge, MA: Harvard University Press, 2004.

Jerome, *Epistulae.* Edited by Isidor Hilberg, revised by M. Kamptner. *Eusebii Hieronymi Epistulae.* CSEL 54–56, 4 vols. Vienna: Österreichischen Akademie der Wissenschaften,1996.

Justinian. *Digesta.* Edited by Theodor Mommsen and Paul Krüger. *Corpus Iuris Civilis,* vol. 1: *Institutiones, Digesta.* 25th edition. Berlin: Weidmann, 1963.

Juvenal. *Saturae.* Translated by Susanna Morton Braund. *Juvenal and Perseus.* Loeb Classical Library. Cambridge, MA: Harvard University Press, 2004.

Lactantius. *De mortibus persecutorum.* Edited by Samuel Brandt and George Laubmann. *L. Caecilii Firmiani Lactantii opera omnia.* CSEL 27, 2 vols. Vienna: F. Tempsky, 1893–97.

———. *Divinae institutiones.* Edited by Samuel Brandt and George Laubmann. *L. Caecilii Firmiani Lactantii opera omnia.* CSEL 19. Vienna: F. Tempsky, 1890.

Lucretius. *De rerum natura.* Translated by W. H. D. Rouse and Martin F. Smith. *Lucretius: On the Nature of Things.* Loeb Classical Library. Cambridge, MA: Harvard University Press, 1924.

Martial. *Epigrammaton.* Translated by D. R. Shackleton Bailey. *Martial: Epigrams.* Loeb Classical Library, 3 vols. Cambridge, MA: Harvard University Press, 1993.

Minucius Felix. *Octavius.* Edited by Karl Halm. *M. Minucii Felicis Octavius et Iulii irmici Materni Lib. De errore profanarum religionum.* CSEL 2. Vienna: C. Geroldi, 1867. Translated by G. W. Clarke. *The Octavius of Marcus Minucius Felix.* ACW 39. New York: Newman Press, 1974.

Orosius. *Historia adversus paganos.* Edited by K. Zangemeister. *Pauli Orosii. Historiarum aduersum paganos libri VII accredit eiusdem Liber apologeticus.* CSEL 7. Vienna: C. Geroldi, 1882. Translated by A. T. Fear. *Orosius: Seven Books of History against the Pagans.* Translated Texts for Historians 54. Liverpool: Liverpool University Press, 2010.

Ovid. *Metamorphoses.* Translated by Frank Justus Miller. *Ovid: Metamorphoses.* Loeb Classical Library. 2 vols. Cambridge, MA: Harvard University Press, 1916.

———. *Tristia.* Translated by Arthur Leslie Wheeler. *Ovid: Tristia, Ex Ponto.* Loeb Classical Library. Cambridge, MA and London: Harvard University Press, 1939.

Plato. *Alcibiades.* Translated by W. R. M. Lamb. *Plato: Charmides, Alcibiades, Hipparchus, The Lovers, Theages, Minos, Epinomis.* Loeb Classical Library. Cambridge, MA: Harvard University Press, 1927.

———. *Apologia.* Translated by Harold North Fowler. *Plato: Euthyphro, Apology, Crito, Phaedo, Phaedrus.* Loeb Classical Library. Cambridge, MA: Harvard University Press, 1914.

———. *Charmides.* Translated by W. R. M. Lamb. *Plato: Charmides, Alcibiades, Hipparchus, The Lovers, Theages, Minos, Epinomis.* Loeb Classical Library. Cambridge, MA: Harvard University Press, 1927.

———. *Leges.* Translated by R. G. Bury. *Plato: Laws, Books 1–6.* Loeb Classical Library. Cambridge, MA: Harvard University Press, 1926.

———. *Phaedrus.* Translated by Harold North Fowler. *Plato: Euthyphro, Apology, Crito, Phaedo, Phaedrus.* Loeb Classical Library. Cambridge, MA: Harvard University Press, 1914.

———. *Philebus.* Translated by Harold North Fowler and W. R. M. Lamb. *Plato: Statesman, Philebus, Ion.* Loeb Classical Library. Cambridge, MA: Harvard University Press, 1925.

———. *Timaeus.* Translated by R. G. Bury. *Plato: Timaeus, Critias, Cleitophon, Menexenus, Epistles.* Loeb Classical Library. Cambridge, MA: Harvard University Press, 1929.

Pliny the Elder. *Naturalis historia.* Translated by H. Rackham and D. E. Eichholz. *Pliny: Natural History.* Loeb Classical Library, 10 vols. Cambridge, MA: Harvard University Press, 1938–62.

Pliny the Younger. *Epistulae.* Translated by Betty Radice. *Pliny: Letters.* Loeb Classical Library, 2 vols. Cambridge, MA: Harvard University Press, 1969.

Plutarch. *Vita Antonii.* Translated by Bernadotte Perrin. *Plutarch: Lives, Demetrius and Antony, Pyrrhus and Gaius Marius.* Loeb Classical Library. Cambridge, MA: Harvard University Press, 1920.

Pontius. *Vita Caecilii Cypriani.* Edited by Wilhelm Hartel. *S. Thasci Caecili Cypriani opera omnia.* CSEL 3/1, xc–cx. Vienna: C. Geroldi, 1868.

Quintilian, *Institutio oratoria.* Translated by H. E. Butler. *The Institutio Oratoria of Quintilian.* Loeb Classical Library, 4 vols. Cambridge, MA: Harvard University Press, 1920–22.

Rhetorica ad Herennium. Translated by H. Caplan. *[Cicero]: Ad Herennium.* Loeb Classical Library. Cambridge, MA: Harvard University Press, 1954.

Sallust. *Bellum Iugurthinum.* Translated by J. C. Rolfe, ed. John T. Ramsey. *Sallust: The War with Catiline, The War with Jugurtha.* Loeb Classical Library. Cambridge, MA: Harvard University Press, 2013.

———. *Epistulae ad Caesarem senem de re publica.* Translated by John T. Ramsey. *Sallust: Fragments of the Histories, Letters to Caesar.* Loeb Classical Library. Cambridge, MA: Harvard University Press, 2015.

Seneca the Younger. *De beneficiis.* Translated by J. W. Baore. *Seneca: Moral Essays,* vol. 3. Loeb Classical Library. Cambridge, MA: Harvard University Press, 1935.

———. *De brevitate vitae.* Translated by J. W. Basore. *Seneca: Moral Essays,* vol. 2. Loeb Classical Library. Cambridge, MA: Harvard University Press, 1932.

———. *De consolatione ad Helviam.* Translated by J. W. Basore. *Seneca: Moral Essays,* vol. 2. Loeb Classical Library. Cambridge, MA: Harvard University Press, 1932.

———. *De consolatione ad Marciam.* Translated by J. W. Basore. *Seneca: Moral Essays,* vol. 2. Loeb Classical Library. Cambridge, MA: Harvard University Press, 1932.

———. *De consolatione ad Polybium.* Translated by J. W. Basore. *Seneca: Moral Essays,* vol. 2. Loeb Classical Library. Cambridge, MA: Harvard University Press, 1932.

———. *De constantia sapientis.* Translated by J. W. Basore. *Seneca: Moral Essays,* vol. 1. Loeb Classical Library. Cambridge, MA: Harvard University Press, 1928.

———. *De ira.* Translated by J. W. Basore. *Seneca: Moral Essays,* vol. 1. Loeb Classical Library. Cambridge, MA: Harvard University Press, 1928.

———. *De otio.* Translated by J. W. Basore. *Seneca: Moral Essays,* vol. 2. Loeb Classical Library. Cambridge, MA: Harvard University Press, 1932.

———. *De providentia.* Translated by J. W. Basore. *Seneca: Moral Essays,* vol. 1. Loeb Classical Library. Cambridge, MA: Harvard University Press, 1928.

———. *De vita beata.* Translated by J. W. Basore. *Seneca: Moral Essays,* vol. 2. Loeb Classical Library. Cambridge, MA: Harvard University Press, 1932.

———. *Epistulae.* Translated by Richard M. Gummere. *Seneca: Epistles.* Loeb Classical Library, 3 vols. Cambridge, MA: Harvard University Press, 1917–25.

———. *Phaedra.* Translated by John G. Fitch. *Seneca: Tragedies,* vol. 1: *Hercules, Trojan Women, Medea, Phaedra.* Loeb Classical Library. Cambridge, MA: Harvard University Press, 2002.

Strabo. *Geographica.* Translated by Horace Leonard Jones. *Strabo: Geography.* Loeb Classical Library, 8 vols. Cambridge, MA: Harvard University Press, 1917–32.

Suetonius. *Claudius.* Translated by J. C. Rolfe. *Suetonius: Lives of the Caesars.* Loeb Classical Library, 2 vols. Cambridge, MA: Harvard University Press, 1914.

Tacitus. *Annales.* Translated by John Jackson. *Tacitus: Annals.* Loeb Classical Library, 3 vols. Cambridge, MA: Harvard University Press, 1931–37.

———. *Historiae.* Translated by Clifford H. Moore. *Tacitus: Histories,* 2 vols. Cambridge, MA: Harvard University Press, 1925–31.

Tertullian. *Ad nationes.* Edited by J. G. Ph. Borleffs. "Q. S. Fl. Tertulliani Ad Nationes." In *Quinti Septimi Florentis Tertulliani opera,* vol. 1. CCL 1, 9–75. Turnhout: Brepols, 1954.

———. *Ad Scapulam.* Edited by E. Dekkers. "Q. S. Fl. Tertulliani Ad Scapulam." In *Quinti Septimi Florentis Tertulliani opera,* vol. 2. CCL 2, 1125–32. Turnhout: Brepols, 1954.

———. *Adversus Iudaeos.* Edited by A. Kroymann. "[Q. S. Fl. Tertulliani] Adversus Iudaeos." In *Quinti Septimi Florentis Tertulliani opera,* vol. 2. CCL 2, 1338–96. Turnhout: Brepols, 1954.

———. *Adversus Marcionem.* Edited by A. Kroymann. "Q. S. Fl. Tertulliani Adversus Marcionem." In *Quinti Septimi Florentis Tertulliani opera,* vol. 1. CCL 1, 438–726. Turnhout: Brepols, 1954.

———. *Apologeticum.* Edited by E. Dekkers. "Q. S. Fl. Tertulliani Apologeticum." In *Quinti Septimi Florentis Tertulliani opera,* vol. 1. CCL 1, 77–171. Turnhout: Brepols, 1954.

———. *De cultu feminarum.* Edited by A. Kroymann. "Q. S. Fl. Tertulliani De cultu feminarum." In *Quinti Septimi Florentis Tertulliani opera,* vol. 1. CCL 1, 341–70. Turnhout: Brepols, 1954.

———. *De idololatria.* Edited by A. Reifferscheid and G. Wissowa. "Q. S. Fl. Tertulliani De idololatria." In *Quinti Septimi Florentis Tertulliani opera,* vol. 2. CCL 2, 1100–24. Turnhout: Brepols, 1954.

———. *De praescriptione haereticorum.* Edited by R. F. Refoulé. "Q. S. Fl. Tertulliani De praescriptione haereticorum." In *Quinti Septimi Florentis Tertulliani opera,* vol. 1, CCL 1, 186–224. Turnhout: Brepols, 1954.

———. *De resurrectione mortuorum.* Edited by J. G. Ph. Borleffs. "Q. S. Fl. Tertulliani De resurrectione mortuorum." In *Quinti Septimi Florentis Tertulliani opera,* vol. 2, CCL 2, 920–1012. Turnhout: Brepols, 1954.

Thucydides. *Historia.* Translated by C. F. Smith. *Thucydides: History of the Peloponnesian War.* Loeb Classical Library, 4 vols. Cambridge, MA: Harvard University Press, 1919–23.

Velleius Paterculus. *Historiae.* Translated by F. W. Shipley. *Velleius Paterculus: Compendium of Roman History.* Loeb Classical Library. Cambridge, MA: Harvard University Press, 1924.

Virgil. *Georgica.* Translated by H. Rushton Fairclough, revised by G. P. Goold. *Virgil: Eclogues, Georgics, Aeneid: Books 1–6.* Loeb Classical Library. Cambridge, MA: Harvard University Press, 1916.

Xenophon. *Memorabilia.* Translated by E. C. Marchant and O. J. Todd, revised by Jeffrey Henderson. *Xenophon: Memorabilia, Oeconomicus, Symposium, Apology.* Revised edition. Loeb Classical Library, Cambridge, MA: Harvard University Press, 2013.

Zosimus. *Historia nova.* Edited and translated by François Paschoud, *Zosime. Histoire nouvelle.* Collection des Universités de France. 3 vols. Paris: Les Belles Lettres, 2003. Translated by Ronald T. Ridley. *Zosimus: New History.* Byzantina Australiensia 2. Canberra: Australian Association for Byzantine Studies, 1982.

MODERN STUDIES

Aldrete, G. S. "Hammers, Axes, Bulls, and Blood: Some Practical Aspects of Roman Animal Sacrifice." *JRS* 104 (2014): 28–50.

Alexis-Baker, Andy. "*Ad Quirinum* Book Three and Cyprian's Catechumenate." *JECS* 17 (2009): 357–80.

Alföldy, Géza. "Der heilige Cyprian und die Krise des römischen Reiches." *Historia* 22 (1973): 479–501.

———. "The Crisis of the Third Century as Seen by Contemporaries." *GRBS* 15 (1974): 89–111.

Anderson, Graham. *The Second Sophistic: A Cultural Phenomenon in the Roman Empire.* London: Routledge, 1993.

Ando, Clifford. *Imperial Rome AD 193 to 284: The Critical Century.* Edinburgh History of Ancient Rome. Edinburgh: Edinburgh University Press, 2012.

———. *The Matter of the Gods: Religion and the Roman Empire.* The Transformation of the Classical Heritage 44. Berkeley: University of California Press, 2008.

Ansuategui, Antonio Duplá. "Incitement to Violence in Late Republican Political Oratory." In *Political Communication in the Roman World,* ed. Cristina Rosillo-López. Impact of Empire 27, 179–200. Leiden: Brill, 2017.

Antonelli, R., et al. "Petrographic Characterization and Provenance Determination of the Crystalline Marbles Used in the Roman City of *Banasa* (Morocco): New Data on the Import of Iberian Marble in Roman North Africa." *Archaeometry* 57 (2015): 405–25.

Balfour, I. L. S. "Tertullian's Description of the Heathen." In *SP,* vol. 17/2, ed. Elizabeth A. Livingstone. Papers presented at the Eighth International Conference on Patristic Studies, Oxford 1979, 785–89. Oxford: Pergamon, 1982.

Baltussen, Han. "Cicero's *consolatio ad se*: Character, Purpose and Impact of a Curious Treatise." In *Greek and Roman Consolations: Eight Studies of a Tradition and Its Afterlife*, ed. Han Baltussen, 67–92. Swansea: Classical Press of Wales, 2013.

———. "Personal Grief and Public Mourning in Plutarch's *Consolation to His Wife*." *AJP* 130 (2009): 67–98.

———. "Introduction." In *Greek and Roman Consolations: Eight Studies of a Tradition and Its Afterlife*, ed. Han Baltussen, xiii–xxv. Swansea: Classical Press of Wales, 2013.

Bandol, Radu. "Voluntas as liberum arbitrium at Saint Augustine and Three Meanings of the servum arbitrium at Martin Luther." *Philobiblon* 17 (2012): 402–20.

Barnes, Timothy David. *The Sources of the* Historia Augusta. Collection Latomus 155. Brussels: Latomus, 1978.

———. *Tertullian: A Historical and Literary Study*. Revised edition. Oxford: Clarendon Press, 1985.

Bartelink, Gerhard. "Le theme du monde vieilli." *Orpheus* 4 (1983): 342–54.

Beatrice, Pier Franco. "On the Meaning of 'Profane' in the Pagan-Christian Conflict of Late Antiquity: The Fathers, Firmicus Maternus and Porphyry before the Orphic 'Prorrhesis' (OF 245.1 Kern)." *Illinois Classical Studies* 30 (2005): 137–65.

Becker, Adam, and Annette Yoshiko Reed, eds. *The Ways That Never Parted: Jews and Christians in Late Antiquity and the Early Middle Ages*. Texts and Studies in Ancient Judaism. Tübingen: Mohr Siebeck, 2003.

Benedictow, Ole J. *Black Death 1346–1353: The Complete History*. Woodbridge: Boydell Press, 2004.

Benko, Stephen. *Pagan Rome and the Early Christians*. Bloomington: Indiana University Press, 1984.

Benson, Edward White. *Cyprian: His Life, His Times, His Work*. London: Macmillan, 1897.

Bévenot, Maurice. "Cyprian's Platform in the Rebaptism Controversy." *HJ* 19 (1978): 123–42.

Birley, A. R. "Caecilius Capella: Persecutor of Christians, Defender of Byzantium." *GRBS* 32 (1991): 81–98.

———. "Decius Reconsidered." In *Les empereurs illyriens. Acts du colloque de Strasbourg (11–13 octobre 1990)*. Edited by E. Frézouls and H. Jouffroy. Contributions et Travaux de l'Institut d'Histoire

Romaine, Université de Strasbourg 8, 57–80. Strasbourg: Civi Romaine, 1998.

———. *Marcus Aurelius: A Biography.* 2nd edition. London: B. T. Batsford, 1987.

———. "Persecutors and Martyrs in Tertullian's Africa." *IAB* 29 (1992): 37–68.

———. "Rewriting Second- and Third-century History in Late Antique Rome: the *Historia Augusta.*" *Classica* 19 (2006): 19–29.

Blackburn, Lee. "Razing Cain: Two North African Christians on the Forgiveness of Debts." *Leaven* 19 (2011): 86–90.

Blanchard-Lemée, Michèle, Mongi Ennaïfer, Hédi Slim, and Latifa Slim. *Mosaics of Roman Africa: Floor Mosaics from Tunisia.* Translated by Kenneth D. Whitehead. English edition. London: British Museum Press, 1996.

Blettner, Elizabeth. "One Made Many and Many Made One: The Role of Asyndeton in Aristotle's Rhetoric." *Ph & Rh* 16 (1983): 49–54.

Bloomfield, Morton W. *The Seven Deadly Sins: An Introduction to the History of a Religious Concept, with Special Reference to Medieval English Literature.* Lansing, MI: Michigan State University Press. 1952.

Bobertz, Charles A. "An Analysis of *Vita Cypriani* 3.6–10 and the Attribution of *Ad Quirinum* to Cyprian of Carthage." *VC* 46 (1992): 112–28.

———. "Cyprian of Carthage as Patron: A Social Historical Study of the Role of Bishop in the Ancient Christian Community of North Africa." PhD diss., Yale University, 1988.

———. "The Historical Context of Cyprian's *De Unitate.*" *JTS* n.s. 41 (1990): 107–11.

Boersma, Hans. "'Numbed with Grief': Gregory of Nyssa on Bereavement and Hope." *Journal of Spiritual Formation and Soul Care* 7 (2014): 46–59.

Bonner, Stanley F. *Roman Declamation in the Late Republic and Early Empire.* Liverpool: University of Liverpool Press, 1949.

———. *Education in Ancient Rome: From the Elder Cato to the Younger Pliny.* Berkeley: University of California Press, 1977.

Bosworth, A. B. "The Historical Context of Thucydides' Funeral Oration." *JHS* 120 (2000): 1–16.

Bradley, Keith. *Slavery and Society at Rome.* Cambridge: Cambridge University Press, 1994.

Brennan, Tad. *The Stoic Life: Emotions, Duties, and Fate.* Oxford: Oxford University Press, 2005.

Brent, Allen. *Cyprian and Roman Carthage.* Cambridge: Cambridge University Press, 2010.

———. *The Imperial Cult and the Development of Church Order: Concepts and Images of Authority in Paganism and Early Christianity before the Age of Cyprian.* Supplements to *Vigiliae Christianae* 45. Leiden: Brill, 1999.

Bright, D. E. "The Plague and the Structure of *De rerum natura.*" *Lat* 30 (1971): 607–32.

Bruce, Scott G., ed. *The Penguin Book of Hell.* London: Penguin Classics, 2018.

Bruggisser, Philippe. *Symmaque ou le rituel épistolaire de l'amitié littéraire. Recherches sur le premier livre de la correspondence.* Paradosis 35. Freiburg: Éditions universitaires, 1993.

Buell, Denise Kimber. *Why This New Race? Ethnic Reasoning in Early Christianity.* New York: Columbia University Press, 2005.

Burke, Peter. "Tradition and Experience: The Idea of Decline from Bruni to Gibbon." *Daedalus* 105/3 (Summer 1976): 137–52.

Burns, J. Patout. *Cyprian the Bishop.* Early Church Monographs. London: Routledge, 2002.

Bursche, Aleksander. "The Battle of Abritus, the Imperial Treasury and Aurei in Barbaricum." *Numismatic Chronicle* 173 (2013): 151–70.

Byrne, Joseph P. *The Black Death.* Greenwood Guides to Historic Events of the Medieval World. Westport, CT: Greenwood Press, 2004.

Cain, Andrew. "In Ambrosiaster's Shadow: A Critical Re-Evaluation of the Last Surviving Letter Exchange between Pope Damasus and Jerome." *REAug* 51 (2005): 257–77.

———. "Tertullian, Cyprian, and Lactantius in Jerome's *Commentary on Galatians.*" *REAug* 55 (2009): 23–51.

Cameron, Alan. *The Last Pagans of Rome.* Oxford: Oxford University Press, 2011.

Carrier, Richard. "The Prospect of a Christian Interpolation in Tacitus, *Annals* 15.44." *VC* 68 (2014): 264–83.

Castagna, Luigi. "Vecchiaia e morte del mondo in Lucrezio, Seneca e San Cipriano." *Aevum Antiquum* 13 (2000): 239–63.

Chapa, J. "Consolatory Patterns? 1 Thess 4:13–18." In *The Thessalonian Correspondence,* ed. R. F. Collins. Bibliotheca Ephemeridum

Theologicarum Lovaniensium 87, 220–28. Leuven: Peeters, 1990.

Chastagnol, André. *Histoire Auguste. Les empereurs romains des IIe et IIIe siècles.* Paris: Bouquins, 1994.

Clarke, G. W. "Dating the Death of the Emperor Decius." *Zeitschrift für Papyrologie und Epigraphik* 37 (1980): 114–16.

———. "The Secular Profession of St. Cyprian of Carthage." *Lat* 24 (1965): 633–38.

———. "Some Observations on the Persecution of Decius." *Antichthon* 3 (1969): 63–76.

———. "Two Measures in the Persecution of Decius? Two Recent Views." *Bulletin of the Institute of Classical Studies* 20 (1973): 118–23.

Clarke, M. L. *Rhetoric at Rome: A Historical Survey.* 3rd edition. Revised by D. H. Berry. London: Routledge, 1996.

Cokayne, Karen. *Experiencing Old Age in Ancient Rome.* Routledge Classical Monographs. London: Routledge, 2003.

Commagre, H. S., Jr. "Lucretius' Interpretation of the Plague." *HSCP* 62 (1957): 105–18.

Cunningham, Mary B., and Pauline Allen, eds. *Preacher and Audience: Studies in Early Christian and Byzantine Homiletics.* A New History of the Sermon 1. Leiden: Brill, 1998.

Daniel-Hughes, Carly. *The Salvation of the Flesh in Tertullian of Carthage: Dressing for the Resurrection.* New York: Palgrave Macmillan, 2011.

Daunton-Fear, Andrew. *Healing in the Early Church: The Church's Ministry of Healing and Exorcism from the First to the Fifth Century.* Eugene, OR: Wipf and Stock, 2009.

Davenport, Caillan and Christopher Mallan. "Dexippus' *Letter of Decius*: Context and Interpretation." *Museum Helveticum* 70 (2013): 57–73.

Dean, James M. *The World Grown Old in Later Medieval Literature.* Cambridge, MA: Medieval Academy of America, 1997.

DeVore, David J. "'The Only Event Mightier Than Everyone's Hope': Classical Historiography and Eusebius' Plague Narrative." *Histos* 14 (2020): 1–34.

De Villiers, G. R., and E. Germiquet. "*Religio* and *Superstitio* in Early Christianity and Graeco-Roman Society: Christian Perspectives on Paganism." *Acta Patristica et Byzantina* 9 (1998): 52–69.

de Wet, Chris L. "The Book of Tobit in Early Christianity: Greek and Latin Interpretations from the 2nd to the 5th Century CE." *HTS Theological Studies* 76 (2020): 1–13.

Dighton, Aerynn. "*Mutatio vestis*: Clothing and Political Protest in the Late Roman Republic." *Phoenix* 71 (2017): 345–69.

Dircks, J. H. "Pestilence Narratives in Classical Literature: A Study in Creative Imitation: I. Homer, Sophocles, Thucydides, and Lucretius." *American Journal of Dermatopathology* 22 (2000): 197–202.

Dodgeon, Michael H., and Samuel N. C. Lieu, eds. *The Roman Eastern Frontier and the Persian Wars (AD 226–363): A Documentary History*. London: Routledge, 1994.

Dominik, William J., ed. *Roman Eloquence: Rhetoric in Society and Literature*. London: Routledge, 1997.

Downing, F. Gerald. "Cosmic Eschatology in the First Century: Pagan, Jewish and Christian." *L'Antiquité Classique* 64 (1995): 99–109.

Drijvers, Jan Willem. "A Roman Image of the 'Barbarian' Sasanians." In *Romans, Barbarians, and the Transformation of the Roman World*, ed. Ralph W. Mathisen and Danuta Shanzer, 67–76. Farnham: Ashgate, 2011.

Dulles, Avery. *A History of Apologetics*. San Francisco: Ignatius Press, 2005.

Dunbabin, Katherine M. D. *Mosaics of the Greek and Roman World*. Cambridge: Cambridge University Press, 1999.

Duncan-Jones, P. R. "The Impact of the Antonine Plague." *JRA* 9 (1996): 108–36.

Dunn, Geoffrey D. "The Carthaginian Synod of 251: Cyprian's Model of Pastoral Ministry." In *I concili della cristianità occidentale secoli III–V*. XXX Incontro di studiosi dell'antichità Cristiana, Rome 3–5 May 2001, SEAug 78, 235–57. Rome: Institutum Patristicum Augustinianum, 2002.

———. "*Censuimus*: Cyprian and the Episcopal Synod of 253." *Lat* 63 (2004): 672–88.

———. "Cyprian and His *Collegae*: Patronage and the Episcopal Synod of 252." *JRH* 27 (2003): 1–13.

———. *Cyprian and the Bishops of Rome: Questions of Papal Primacy in the Early Church*. ECS 11. Strathfield, NSW: St. Pauls Publications, 2006.

———. "Cyprian and Women in a Time of Persecution." *JEH* 57 (2006): 205–25.

———. "Cyprian's Care for the Poor: The Evidence of *de Opere et Eleemosynis.*" In SP 42, ed. F. Young, M. Edwards, and P. Parvis. Papers presented to the Fourteenth International Conference on Patristic Studies, Oxford 2003, 363–68. Leuven: Peeters, 2006.

———. "Cyprian's Rival Bishops and Their Communities." *Aug* 45 (2005): 61–93.

———. "Ecclesiology in Early North African Christianity: The Parable of the Wheat and the Weeds." *Aug* 57 (2017): 371–401.

———. "'For it is improper to be addicted to the tedium of affliction': Christian Responses to Pandemic in Late Antiquity and the Early Middle Ages." *VP* 77 (2021): 247–84.

———. "Heresy and Schism According to Cyprian of Carthage." *JTS* n.s. 55 (2004): 551–74.

———. "Infected Sheep and Diseased Cattle, or the Pure and Holy Flock: Cyprian's Pastoral Care of Virgins." *JECS* 11 (2003): 1–20.

———. "*Nam quae foris exercentur nullum habent salutis effectum*: Cyprian and the Synod of September 256." In *Pagani e Cristiani alla ricerca della Salvezza (I–III sec.).* XXXIV Incontro di studiosi dell'antichità cristiana, Rome 5–7 May 2005, SEAug 96, 513–24. Rome: Institutum Patristicum Augustinianum, 2006.

———. "References to Mary in the Writings of Cyprian of Carthage." In *SP* 42, ed. F. Young, M. Edwards, and P. Parvis. Papers presented to the Fourteenth International Patristics Conference, Oxford 2003, 369–78. Leuven: Peeters, 2006.

———. "Rhetorical Structure in Tertullian's *Ad Scapulam.*" *VC* 56 (2002): 47–55.

———. *Tertullian.* The Early Church Fathers. London: Routledge, 2004.

———. *Tertullian's* Aduersus Iudaeos*: A Rhetorical Analysis.* North American Patristics Society Patristic Monograph Series 19. Washington, DC: Catholic University of America Press, 2008.

———. "Turn the Other Cheek: Patience and Non-retaliation in the Early Christian African Tradition." In *Cristianesimo e violenza: gli autori cristiani di fronte a testi biblici 'Scomodi.'* XLIV Incontro di studiosi dell'antichità cristiana, Rome 5–7 May 2016, SEAug 151, 323–340. Rome: Institutum Patristicum Augustinianum, 2018.

———. "The White Crown of Works: Cyprian's Early Pastoral Ministry of Almsgiving in Carthage." *CH* 73 (2004): 715–40.

———. "Widows and Other Women in the Pastoral Ministry of Cyprian of Carthage." *Aug* 45 (2005): 295–307.

Dunn, James D. G. *The Partings of the Ways between Christianity and Judaism and Their Significance for the Character of Christianity*. London: SCM Press, 2006.

Dupont, Anthony, Shari Boodts, Gert Partoens, and Johan Leemans, eds. *Preaching in the Patristic Era: Sermons, Preachers, and Audiences in the Latin West*. A New History of the Sermon 6. Leiden and Boston: Brill, 2018.

Duval, Yvette. *Les chrétientés d'Occident et leur évêque au IIIe siècle*. Plebs in ecclesia constituta (Cyprien, Ep. 63). CEASA 176. Paris: Institut d'Études Augustiniennes, 2005.

Edwards, Catharine. *The Politics of Immorality in Ancient Rome*. Cambridge: Cambridge University Press, 1993.

Edwards, Mark, Martin Goodman, Simon Price, and Christopher Rowland. "Introduction." In *Apologetics in the Roman Empire: Pagans, Jews, and Christians*, ed. Mark Edwards, Martin Goodman, Simon Price with Christopher Rowland, 1–13. Oxford: Oxford University Press, 1999.

Edwards, O. C., Jr. *A History of Preaching*. Nashville: Abingdon Press, 2004.

Edwell, Peter. *Rome and Persia at War: Imperial Competition and Contact 193–363 CE*. Abingdon: Routledge, 2021.

Emilie, Gertrude. "Cicero and the Roman Pietas." *CJ* 39 (1944): 536–42.

Erdkamp, Paul. *The Grain Market in the Roman Empire: A Social, Political and Economic Study*. Cambridge: Cambridge University Press, 2005.

Evans, R. F. "On the Problem of Church and Empire in Tertullian's *Apologeticum*." In *SP*, vol. 14/3, ed. Elizabeth A. Livingstone. Papers presented at the Sixth International Conference on Patristic Studies, Oxford 1971, 21–36. Berlin: Akademie-Verlag, 1976.

Fahey, Michael A. *Cyprian and the Bible: A Study in Third-Century Exegesis*. Tübingen: Eberhard-Karls-Universität, 1971.

Faraone, C. A., and F. S. Naiden, eds. *Greek and Roman Animal Sacrifice*. Cambridge: Cambridge University Press, 2012.

Favez, Charles. *La consolation latine chrétienne*. Paris: J. Vrin, 1937.

Felton, D. "Monstrosity or Disability? Ancient Accounts of Accelerated Ageing." *Folklore* 123 (2012): 355–61.

Ferguson, Everett. *Baptism in the Early Church: History, Theology, and Liturgy in the First Five Centuries.* Grand Rapids, MI: Eerdmans, 2009.

Fern, Mary Edmond. *The Latin Consolatio as a Literary Type.* St. Louis: St. Louis University, 1941.

Finley, M. I. "The Elderly in Classical Antiquity." *Greece & Rome* 28 (1981): 156–71.

Fischer, Joseph A. "Die Konzilien zu Karthago und Rom im Jahr 251." *AHC* 11 (1979): 263–86.

———. "Das Konzil zu Karthago im Mai 252." *AHC* 13 (1981): 1–11.

———. "Das Konzil im Frühjahr 253." *AHC* 13 (1981): 12–26.

———. "Das Konzil zu Karthago im Spätsommer 256." *AHC* 16 (1984): 1–39.

Fischer, Mosche. "Marble Imports and Local Counterparts: Luxury Business in Roman Palestine." *Topoi. Orient-Occident Supplément* 8 (2007): 249–69.

Fitzgerald, William. *Slavery and the Roman Literary Imagination.* Cambridge: Cambridge University Press, 2000.

Flemming, Rebecca. "Galen and the Plague." In *Galen's Treatise Περὶ Ἀλυπίας (*De indolentia*) in Context: A Tale of Resilience*, ed. Caroline Petit. Studies in Ancient Medicine 52, 219–44. Leiden and Boston: Brill, 2019.

Fogleman, Alex. "'Since Those Days All Things Have Progressed for the Bettr': Tradition, Progress, and Creation in Ambrose of Milan." *HTR* 113 (2020): 440–59.

Fortenbaugh, William F. "Quintilian 6.2.8–9: *Ethos* and *Pathos* and the Ancient Tradition." In *Peripatetic Rhetoric after Aristotle*, ed. William W. Fortenbaugh and David C. Mirhady. Rutgers University Studies in Classical Humanities 6, 183–91. New Brunswick, NJ: Transaction Publishers, 1994.

Frost, Maurice. "*Te Deum Laudamus.*" *JTS* 28 (1927): 403–7.

———. "Two Texts of the *Te Deum Laudmaus.*" *JTS* 39 (1938): 388–91.

———. "Adaptations of the *Te Deum Laudamus.*" *JTS* 43 (1942): 68.

Frýdek, Miroslav. "Terminology of Roman Criminal Law: *Crimen et delictum.*" *Journal on European History of Law* 1 (2010): 69–72.

Gallala, Wissem, et al. "A Multi-Analytical Approach for Determining the Provenance of the Marbles from Ruspina Roman Baths

(Monastir, Tunisia)." *Archaeological and Anthropoligical Sciences* 9 (2017): 1275–78.

Gallicet, Ezio. "L'Antico Testamento nell'*Ad Demetrianum* di Cipriano." *Aug* 22 (1982): 199–202.

Gardner, Hunter H. *Pestilence and the Body Politic in Latin Literature.* Oxford: Oxford University Press, 2019.

Garnsey, Peter. *Famine and Food-supply in the Graeco-Roman World: Responses to Risk and Crisis.* Cambridge: Cambridge University Press, 1988.

Gassman, Mattias. "Cyprian's Early Career in the Church of Carthage." *JEH* 70 (2019): 1–17.

Gatzemeier, Susanne. Ut ait Lucretius: *Die Lukrezrezeption in der lateinischen Prosa bis Laktanz.* Hypomnemnata 189. Göttingen: Vandenhoeck and Ruprecht, 2013.

Gildenhard, Ingo. Paideia Romana: *Cicero's Tusculan Disputations.* Cambridge Classical Journal Proceedings of the Classical Philological Society Supplementary Series 30. Cambridge: Cambridge Philological Society, 2007.

Goldman-Petri, Megan. "The Altar of P. Perelius Hedulus in Carthage and Social Aspects of Provincial Image-Making." In *The Social Dynamics of Roman Imperial Imagery*, ed. Amy Russell and Monica Hellström, 180–214. Cambridge: Cambridge University Press, 2020.

Gordon, Richard. "*Superstitio*, Superstition and Religious Repression in the Late Roman Republic and Principate (100 BCE–300 CE)." *Past & Present* 199 supp. 3 (2008): 72–94.

Gorostidi Pi, Diana. "'Too Young to Die': Grief and Mourning in Ancient Rome." *Thersites* 9 (2019): 71–88.

Gothóni, René. "*Religio* and *Superstitio* Reconsidered." *Archiv für Religionspsychologie* 21 (1994): 37–46.

Grant, Michael. *The Antonines: The Roman Empire in Transition.* London: Routledge, 1994.

Grant, Robert M. *Greek Apologists of the Second Century.* Philadelphia: Westminster Press, 1988.

Groisard, Jocelyn. "Catastrophe and Cyclical Time in Ancient Thought." *The Journal of Social Sciences and Humanities* 514 (2018): 183–98.

Gros, P. "Colline de Byrsa: les vestiges romains." In *Pour sauver Carthage. Exploration et conservation de la cité punique, romaine et byzantine*, ed. Abdelmajid Ennabli, 99–103. Paris and Tunis: UNESCO/INAA, 1992.

Gros, P., and J. Deneauve. "Hypothèses sur le centre monumental de la Carthage romaine, d'après les recherches récentes sur la colline de Byrsa, par MM. Pierre Gros et Jean Deneauve." *CRAI* 124 (1980): 299–332.

Gunderson, Erik. *The Cambridge Companion to Ancient Rhetoric*. Cambridge: Cambridge University Press, 2009.

Gutiérrez Garcia-M., Anna. "The Exploitation of Local Stone in Roman Times: The Case of North-Eastern Spain." *World Archaeology* 43 (2011): 318–41.

Hall, S. G. "Stephen I of Rome and the One Baptism." In *SP*, vol. 17/2, ed. Elizabeth A. Livingstone. Papers presented at the 8th International Conference on Patristic Studies, Oxford 1979, 796–98. Oxford: Pergamon Press, 1982.

Hallman, Joseph M. "The Mutability of God: Tertullian to Lactantius." *TS* 42 (1981): 374–86.

Haneih, Ahmed Mohammed Abu, Sadiq Abdelall, and Afif Hasan. "Sustainable Development of Stone and Marble Sector in Palestine." *Journal of Cleaner Production* 84 (2014): 581–88.

Harper, Kyle. *Slavery in the Late Roman World, AD 275–425*. Cambridge: Cambridge University Press, 2011.

———. "Pandemics and Passages to Late Antiquity: Rethinking the Plague of c. 249–279 Described by Cyprian." *JRA* 28 (2015): 223–60.

———. "Another Eye-witness to the Plague Described by Cyprian and Notes on the 'Persecution of Decius.'" *JRA* 29 (2016): 473–76.

———. *The Fate of Rome: Climate, Disease, and the End of an Empire*. 2nd edition. Princeton: Princeton University Press, 2017.

Harries, Jill. *Law and Crime in the Roman World*. Cambridge: Cambridge University Press, 2012.

Heck, Eberhard. *ΜΗ ΘΕΟΜΑΧΕΙΝ oder: Die Bestrafung des Gottesverächters. Untersuchungen zu Bekämpfung und Aneigung römischer religio bei Tertullian, Cyprian und Laktanz*. Studien zur klassischen Philologie 24. Frankfurt am Main: Peter Lang, 1987.

Herlihy, David. *The Black Death and the Transformation of the West*. Cambridge, MA: Harvard University Press, 1997.

Hilali, Arbia. "Rome and Agriculture in *Africa Proconsularis*: Land and Hydraulic Development." *RBPH* 91 (2013): 113–25.

Hillman, Aubrey L., et al. "Lead Pollution Resulting from Roman Gold Extraction in Northwestern Spain." *Holocene* 27 (2017): 1465–74.

Hirt, Alfred Michael. *Imperial Mines and Quarries in the Roman World: Organizational Aspects 27 BC–AD 235.* Oxford: Oxford University Press, 2010.

Hobson, Matthew S. *The North African Boom: Evaluating Economic Growth in the Roman Province of Africa Proconsularis (146 B.C.–A.D. 439).* Journal of Roman Archaeology Supplement Series 100. Portsmouth, RI: Journal of Roman Archaeology, 2015.

Hope, Valerie M., and Janet Huskinson, eds. *Memory and Mourning: Studies on Roman Death.* Oxford: Oxbow, 2011.

Hopkins, D. R. *The Greatest Killer: Smallpox in History.* Chicago: University of Chicago Press, 1988.

Horrox, Rosemary. *The Black Death.* Manchester: Manchester University Press, 1994.

Houghton, H. A. G. *The Latin New Testament: A Guide to Its Early History, Texts, and Manuscripts.* Oxford: Oxford University Press, 2016.

Houghton, H. A. G., C. M. Kreinecker, R. F. MacLachlan, and C. J. Smith. *The Principal Pauline Epistles: A Collation of Old Latin Witnesses.* New Testament Tools, Studies and Documents 59. Leiden and Boston: Brill, 2019.

Hoyer, Daniel. "Public Feasting, Elite Competition, and the Market Economy of Roman North Africa." *Journal of North African Studies* 18 (2013): 574–91.

Huebner, Sabine R. "The 'Plague of Cyprian': A Revised View of the Origin and Spread of a 3rd-c. CE Pandemic." *JRA* 34 (2021): 151–74.

Hutchinson, G. O. *Cicero's Correspondence: A Literary Study.* Oxford: Clarendon Press, 1998.

Inwood, Brad, ed. *The Cambridge Companion to the Stoics.* Cambridge: Cambridge University Press, 2003.

Ivanov, Teofil, and Stojan Stojanof. *ABRITUS: Its History and Archaeology.* Razgrd: Cultural and Historical Heritage Directorate, 1985.

Janssen, L.F. "'Superstitio' and the Persecution of the Christians." *VC* 33 (1979): 131–59.

Johnson, Maxwell E. *The Rites of Christian Initiation: The Evolution and Interpretation.* Collegeville, MN: Liturgical Press, 1999.

Jones, A. H. M. *The Later Roman Empire 284–602: A Social, Economic, and Administrative Survey*. Oxford: Blackwell, 1964.

Jones, Alexander. "Greco-Roman Astronomy and Astrology." In *The Cambridge History of Science*, ed. Alexander Jones, 374–401. Cambridge: Cambridge University Press, 2018.

Jones, Christopher P. "The Historicity of the Neronian Persecution: A Response to Brent Shaw." *NTS* 63 (2017): 146–52.

Joshel, Sandra R. *Slavery in the Roman World*. Cambridge: Cambridge University Press, 2010.

Kahlos, Maijastina. *Debate and Dialogue: Christian and Pagan Cultures c. 360–430*. Ashgate New Critical Thinking in Religion, Theology and Biblical Studies Series. Farnham: Ashgate, 2007.

Kay, Philip. *Rome's Economic Revolution*. Oxford: Oxford University Press, 2014.

Kearns, Amber Lynn. "A Plague in a Crisis: Differential Diagnosis of the Cyprian Plague and Its Effects on the Roman Empire in the Third Century CE." MA thesis, University of Arizona, 2018.

Kehoe, Dennis. "Agriculture in Roman North Africa." In *A Companion to Ancient Agriculture*, ed. David Hollander and Timothy Howe. Blackwell Companions to the Ancient World, 499–516. Chichester: Wiley Blackwell, 2020.

Kennedy, George A. *A New History of Classical Rhetoric*. Princeton, NJ: Princeton University Press, 1994.

———. *New Testament Interpretation through Rhetorical Criticism*. Chapel Hill: University of North Carolina Press, 1984.

Keresztes, Paul. "The Decian *libelli* and Contemporary Literature." *Lat* 34 (1975): 761–81.

———. "Nero, the Christians and the Jews in Tacitus and Clement of Rome." *Lat* 43 (1984): 404–13.

———. "Two Edicts of the Emperor Valerian." *VC* 29 (1975): 81–95.

Koch, Hugo. *Cyprianische Untersuchungen*. Arbeiten zur Kirchengeschichte 4. A. Marcus Bonn and E. Weber, 1926.

Konstan, David. "Problems in the History of Christian Friendship." *JECS* 4 (1996): 87–113.

Koplow, D. A. *Smallpox: The Fight to Eradicate a Global Scourge*. Berkeley: University of California Press, 2003.

Le Saint, William P. *Tertullian: Treatises on Penance. On Penitence and On Purity*. ACW 28. New York: Newman Press, 1959.

Levison, John R. "The Roman Character of Funerals in the Writings of Josephus." *JSJ* 33 (2002): 245–77.

Lewis, Jack P. "The Offering of Abel (Gen 4:4): A History of Interpretation." *JETS* 37 (1994): 481–96.

Liebeschuetz, Wolf. "Was There a Crisis of the Third Century?" In *Crises and the Roman Empire*, ed. Olivier Hekster, Gerda de Kleijn, and Daniëlle Slootjes, Proceedings of the Seventh Workshop of the International Network Impact of Empire, Nijmegen, June 20–24, 2006. Impact of Empire 7, 11–20. Leiden: Brill, 2007.

Little, Lester K. ed. *Plague and the End of Antiquity: The Pandemic of 541–750.* Cambridge: Cambridge University Press, 2007.

Lomiento, G. "Cipriano per la preparazione al martirio dei Tibaritani (Ep. 58)." *Annali della Facoltà di Magistero dell'Università di Bari* 3 (1962): 3–35.

Lowenstam, Steven. "Seneca's *Epistle Sixty-five*." *MAAR* 43–44 (1998–99): 63–78.

Luckensmeyer, David. *The Eschatology of First Thessalonians.* Novum Testamentum et Orbis Antiquus 71. Göttingen: Vandenhoeck and Ruprecht, 2009.

Luckensmeyer, David, and Neil Bronwen. "Reading First Thessalonians as a Consolatory Letter in Light of Seneca and Ancient Handbooks on Letter-Writing." *NTS* 62 (2015): 31–48.

Lunn-Rockliffe, Sophie. "Cyprian on the Senescence of the World." *Revue des Études Tardo-antiques* Supplement 5 (2018): 267–76.

MacDonald, Michael J., ed. *The Oxford Handbook of Rhetorical Studies.* Oxford: Oxford University Press, 2017.

McDonough, Scott. "Were the Sasanians Barbarians? Roman Writers on the 'Empire of the Persians.'" In *Romans, Barbarians, and the Transformation of the Roman World*, ed. Ralph W. Mathisen and Danuta Shanzer, 55–65. Farnham: Ashgate, 2011.

McGowan, Andrew. "Eating People: Accusations of Cannibalism against Christians in the Second Century." *JECS* 2 (1994): 413–42.

McGuckin, John A. "Does Lactantius Denigrate Cyprian?" *JTS* n.s. 39 (1988): 119–24.

McNeill, William H. *Plagues and Peoples.* Garden City, NY: Doubleday, 1976.

Mackin Jr., James A. "Schismogenesis and Community: Pericles' Funeral Oration." *QJS* 77 (1991): 251–56.

Magli, Giulio, Antonio César González-García, Juan Belmonte Aviles, and Elio Antonello, eds. *Archaeoastronomy in the Roman World.* Historical and Cultural Astronomy. Cham: Springer, 2019.

Malherbe, Abraham J. *Moral Exhortation, A Greco-Roman Sourcebook.* Library of Early Christianity 4. Philadelphia: Westminster Press, 1986.

Malsbary, Gerald. "Pietas and the Origins of Western Culture." *Logos* 4 (2001): 93–116.

Mattei, Paul. "'Extra ecclesiam nulla salus' et puissance du nom de Jésus. Tensions et fractures dans la théologie du *De rebaptismate.*" In *SP,* vol. 24, ed. Elizabeth A. Livingstone. Papers presented at the Eleventh International Conference on Patristic Studies, Oxford 1991, 300–305. Leuven: Peeters, 1993.

———. "Remarques sur la tradition textuelle (manuscrite et imprimée) du *De rebaptismate.*" In *SP,* vol. 36, ed. M. F. Wiles and E. J. Yarnold with P. M. Parvis. Papers presented at the Thirteenth International Conference on Patristic Studies, Oxford 1999, 35–45. Leuven: Peeters, 2001.

———. "Tradition et notions connexes dans la querelle baptismale. Le cas du Ps.-Cyprien, *De rebaptismate.*" In *La Tradizione: forme e modi.* XVIII Incontro di studiosi dell'antichità Cristiana, Rome 7–9 May 1989, SEAug 31, 325–39. Rome: Institutum Patristicum Augustinianum, 1990.

Meyer, Michel. *Philosophy and the Passions: Toward a History of Human Nature.* Translated by Robert F. Barsky. Philadelphia: Penn State University Press, 2000.

Middleton, J. Richard. *The Liberating Image: The* Imago Dei *in Genesis 1.* Grand Rapids, MI: Brazos Press, 2005.

Molcho, Michal. "Crocodile Breeding in the Crocodile Cults of the Graeco-Roman Fayum." *Journal of Egyptian Archaeology* 100 (2014): 181–93.

Monceaux, Paul. *Histoire littéraire de l'Afrique chrétienne depuis jusqu'à l'invasion arabe,* part 2: *St. Cyprien et son temps.* Paris: Ernest Leroux, 1902.

Morel, Jean-Paul. "Mission archéologique de Carthage-Byrsa." *Les Nouvelles de l'archéologie* 123 (2011): 39–43.

Moss, Candida R. *Ancient Christian Martyrdom: Diverse Practices, Theologies, and Traditions.* Anchor Yale Bible Reference Library. New Haven: Yale University Press, 2012.

Murphey, Rhoads. "The Decline of North Africa since the Roman Occupation: Climatic or Human?" *Annals of the Association of American Geographers* 41 (1951): 116–32.

Murphy, Edwina. "'As Far as My Poor Memory Suggested': Cyprian's Compilation of *Ad Quirinum*." *VC* 68 (2014): 533–50.

———. *The Bishop and the Apostle: Cyprian's Pastoral Exegesis of Paul.* Studies of the Bible and Its Reception 13. Berlin: De Gruyter, 2018.

———. "Cyprian, Paul, and Care for the Poor and Captive; Offering Sacrifices and Ransoming Temples." *ZAC* 20 (2016): 418–36.

———. "Cyprian's Use of Philippians: To Live Is Christ and to Die Is Gain." *Aug* 56 (2016): 35–56.

———. "Death, Decay and Delight in Cyprian of Carthage." *Scr* 15 (2019): 79–88.

———. "Divine Ordinances and Life-Giving Remedies: Galatians in the Writings of Cyprian of Carthage." *JTI* 8 (2014): 81–101.

———. "Imitating the Devil: Cyprian on Jealousy and Envy." *Scr* 14 (2018): 75–91.

———. "Sell Your Possessions: Cyprian, Luke, and Wealth." *Colloquium* 49 (2017): 11–23.

———. "Widows, Welfare and the Wayward: 1 Timothy 5 in Cyprian's *Ad Quirinum*." In *SP* 94, ed. Markus Vinzent. Papers presented at the Seventeenth International Conference on Patristic Studies, Oxford 2015, 67–74. Leuven: Peeters, 2017.

Noormann, Rolf. Ad salute consulere: *Die Paränese Cyprians im Kontext antiken und frühchristlichen Denkens.* Forschungen zur Kirchen- und Dogmengeschichte 99. Göttingen: Vandenhoeck and Ruprecht, 2009.

O'Brien, Mary Bridget. *Titles of Address in Christian Latin Epistolography to 543 A.D.* CUAPS 21. Washington, DC: Catholic University of America Press, 1930.

Oldstone, Michel B. A. *Viruses, Plagues, and History.* 2nd edition. Oxford: Oxford University Press, 2010.

Orbán, Á. P. *Les dénominations du monde chez les premiers auteurs chrétiens.* Graecitas Christianorum Primaeva 4. Nijmegen: Dekker and van de Vegt, 1970.

Ovadiah, Asher. "*Deisidaimonia, Superstitio and Religio*: Graeco-Roman, Jewish and Early Christian Concepts." *Liber Annuus* 64 (2014): 417–40.

Parkin, Tim G. *Demography and Roman Society*. Baltimore: Johns Hopkins University Press, 1992.

———. *Old Age in the Roman World: A Cultural and Social History*. Baltimore: Johns Hopkins University Press, 2003.

Parrish, David. *Season Mosaics of Roman North Africa*. Archaeologica 46. Rome: Giorgio Bretschneider, 1984.

———. "Two Mosaics from Roman Tunisia: An African Variation of the Season Theme." *American Journal of Archaeology* 83 (1979): 279–85.

Pascal, Carlo. "Lucrezio e Cipriano." *Rivista di Filologia e d'Istruzione Classica* 31 (1903): 555–57.

Petitmengin, Pierre. "Un monument controversé, le 'Saint Cyprien' de Baluze et Dom Maran (1726)." *RHT* 5 (1975): 97–136.

Porter, Stanley E., ed. *Handbook of Classical Rhetoric in the Hellenistic Period 330 B.C.–A.D. 400*. Leiden: Brill, 1997.

Potter, David S. *The Empire at Bay, AD 180–395*. Routledge History of the Ancient World. London and New York: Routledge, 2014. 2nd edition.

Prchlík, Ivan. "*Auctor nominis eius Christus*. Tacitus' Knowledge of the Origins of Christianity." *Acta Universitatis Carolinae Philologica* 2 (2017): 95–110.

Price, Simon. "Latin Christian Apologetics: Minucius Felix, Tertullian, and Cyprian." In *Apologetics in the Roman Empire: Pagans, Jews, and Christians*, ed. Mark Edwards, Martin Goodman, Simon Price, with Christopher Rowland, 105–29. Oxford: Oxford University Press, 1999.

Quacquarelli, Antonio. "S. Cipriano: 'La pestilenza' e la 'Lettera ai Tibariti' sulla preparazione al martirio." In *Morte e immortalità nella catechesi dei padri del III–IV secolo*. Convegno di studio e aggiornamento Facoltà di Lettere cristiane e classiche (Pontificium Institutum Altioris Latinitatis), Rome, 16–18 March 1984. Biblioteca di Scienze Religiose 66, 29–40. Rome: Libreria Ateneo Salesiano, 1985.

Quasten, Johannes. "'Vetus superstitio et nova religio.' The Problem of *Refrigerium* in the Ancient Church of North Africa." *HTR* 33 (1940): 253–66.

Raven, Susan. *Rome in Africa*. 3rd edition. London: Routledge, 1993.

Recla, Matthew. "*Homo profanes*: The Christian Martyr and the Violence of Meaning-Making." *Critical Research on Religion* 2 (2014): 147–64.

Reff, Daniel T. *Plagues, Priests, and Demons: Sacred Narratives and the Rise of Christianity in the Old World and the New.* Cambridge: Cambridge University Press, 2005.

Rickman, G. E. "The Grain Trade under the Roman Empire." *Memoirs of the American Academy in Rome* 36 (1980): 261–75.

Rives, J. B. "The Decree of Decius and the Religion of Empire." *JRS* 89 (1999): 135–54.

———. *Religion and Authority in Roman Carthage from Augustus to Constantine.* Oxford: Clarendon Press, 1995.

Rohrbacher, David. "The Sources of the *Historia Augusta* Re-examined." *Histos* 7 (2013): 146–80.

Rosa, Fernando. "Lucrezio e il senso della malattia nel *De rerum natura.*" *Medicina nei Secoli* 19 (2007): 763–81.

Rosen, William. *Justinian's Flea: The First Great Plague and the End of the Roman Empire.* London: Penguin, 2007.

Rüpke, Jörg. "*Religio and Religiones* in Roman Thinking." *Les Études Classiques* 75 (2007): 67–78.

———. *Religious Deviance in the Roman World: Superstition or Individuality?* Translated by David M. B. Richardson. Cambridge: Cambridge University Press, 2016.

Sage, Michael M. *Cyprian.* Patristic Monograph Series 1. Cambridge, MA: Philadelphia Patristic Foundation, 1975.

Sandbach, F. H. *The Stoics.* 2nd edition. Bristol: Bristol Press, 1989.

Sauer, Jochen. "*Consolatio ad Helviam.*" In *Brill's Companion to Seneca: Philosopher and Dramatist,* ed. Gregor Damschen and Andreas Heil, 171–73. Leiden: Brill, 2014.

———. "*Consolatio ad Mariam.*" In *Brill's Companion to Seneca: Philosopher and Dramatist,* ed. Gregor Damschen and Andreas Heil, 134–39. Leiden: Brill, 2014.

———. "*Consolatio ad Polybium.*" In *Brill's Companion to Seneca: Philosopher and Dramatist,* ed. Gregor Damschen and Andreas Heil, 167–69. Leiden: Brill, 2014.

Savon, Hervé. "Une Consolation imitée de Sénèque et de saint Cyprien (Pseudo-Jérôme, *epistula* 5, *ad amicum aegrotum*)." *RecAug* 14 (1979): 153–90.

Schiesaro, Alessandro. "Lucretius' Apocalyptic Imagination." *Materiali e discussion per l'analisi dei testi classici* 84 (2020): 27–93.

Schimmel, S. *The Seven Deadly Sins: Jewish, Christian and Classical Reflections on Human Psychology.* Oxford: Oxford University Press, 1997.

Schultz, Celia E. "Roman Sacrifice, Inside and Out." *JRS* 106 (2016): 58–76.

Scourfield, J. H. D. *Consoling Heliodorus: A Commentary on Jerome, Letter 60*, OCM. Oxford: Clarendon Press, 1993.

———. "The *De mortalitate* of Cyprian: Consolation and Context." *VC* 50 (1996): 12–41.

———. "Towards a Genre of Consolation." In *Greek and Roman Consolations: Eight Studies of a Tradition and its Afterlife*, ed. Han Baltussen, 1–36. Swansea: Classical Press of Wales, 2013.

Seagraves, Richard. *Pascentes cum disciplina: A Lexical Study of the Clergy in the Cyprianic Correspondence.* Paradosis 37. Fribourg: Editions Universitaires, 1993.

Selinger, Reinhard. *The Mid-Third Century Persecutions of Decius and Valerian.* 2nd edition. Frankfurt am Main: Peter Lang, 2004.

Sellars, John. *Stoicism.* Ancient Philosophies 1. Berkeley and Los Angeles: University of California Press, 2006.

Shaw, Brent D. *Environment and Society in Roman North Africa.* Variorum Collected Studies. Aldershot: Ashgate, 1995.

———. "The Myth of the Neronian Persecution." *JRS* 105 (2015): 73–100.

Shear, Julia L. "'Their Memories Will Never Grow Old': The Politics of Remembrance in the Athenian Funeral Orations." *CQ* 63 (2013): 511–36.

Sherman, Irwin W. *The Power of Plagues.* 2nd edition. Washington, DC: ASM Press, 2017.

Sicking, C. "The General Purport of Pericles' Funeral Oration and Last Speech." *Hermes* 123 (1995): 404–25.

Sider, Robert Dick. *Ancient Rhetoric and the Art of Tertullian.* London: Oxford University Press, 1971.

———. *Christian and Pagan in the Roman Empire: The Witness of Tertullian.* Selections from the Fathers of the Church 2. Washington, DC: Catholic University of America Press, 2001.

Sim, David C. "Death after Life or Life after Death?" *Scr* 11 (2015): 143–59.

Skibiński, Tomasz, and Maciej Książyk. "Postawa chrześcijan wobec Zarazy Cypriana w świetle źródel epoki." *VP* 78 (2021): 121–40.

Sorabji, Richard. *Perception, Conscience and Will in Ancient Philosophy.* Variorum Collected Studies. London: Routledge, 2013.

Spaeth, Barbette Stanley. "The Goddess Ceres in the Ara Pacis Augustae and the Carthage Relief." *American Journal of Archaeology* 98 (1994): 65–100.

Spineto, Natale. "L'escatologia nel mondo classico." *Annali di Storia dell'Esegesi* 16 (1999): 7–20.

Stark, Rodney. "Religious Competition and Roman Piety." *Interdisciplinary Journal of Research on Religion* 2 (2006) (www.religjournal.com/articles/article_view.php?id=18).

Stathakopoulos, Dionysios Ch. *Famine and Pestilence in the Late Roman and Early Byzantine Empire: A Systematic Survey of Subsistence Crises and Epidemics.* Birmingham Byzantine and Ottoman Monographs 9. London: Routledge, 2004.

Stowers, Stanley K. *Letter Writing in Greco-Roman Antiquity.* Library of Early Christianity 5. Philadelphia: Westminster Press, 1986.

Strange, Steven, ed. *Stoicism: Traditions and Transformations.* Cambridge: Cambridge University Press, 2004.

Swancutt, Diana M. "Paraenesis in Light of Protepsis: Troubling the Typical Dichotomy." In *Early Christian Paraenesis in Context*, ed. James Starr and Troels Engberg-Pedersen. Beihefte zur Zeitschrift für die neutestamentliche Wissenschaft und die Kunde der älteren Kirche 125, 113–56. Berlin: Walter de Gruyter, 2004.

Swift, Louis J. "Forensic Rhetoric in Tertullian's *Apologeticum.*" *Lat* 27 (1968): 864–77.

Syme, Ronald. *Emperors and Biography: Studies in the* Historia Augusta. Oxford: Clarendon Press, 1971.

Taylor, Miriam S. *Anti-Judaism and Early Christian Identity: A Critique of the Scholarly Consensus.* Studia Post-Biblica 46. Leiden: E. J. Brill, 1995.

Tellbe, Mikael, and Tommy Wasserman with Ludvig Nyman. *Healing and Exorcism in Second Temple Judaism and Early Christianity.* WUNT 2. Series 511. Tübingen: Mohr Siebeck, 2019.

Tilby, Angela. "From Evil Thoughts to Deadly Sins: Evagrius of Pontus's Psychology of Sin." In *Wilderness: Essays in Honour of Frances Young*, ed. R. S. Sugirtharajah, 143–52. London: T & T Clark, 2005.

———. *The Seven Deadly Sins: Their Origin in the Spiritual Teaching of Evagrius the Hermit.* London: SPCK, 2009.

Toner, Jerry. *Roman Guide to Slave Management: A Treatise by Nobleman Marcus Sidonius Falx.* New York: Abrams, 2016.

Treggiari, Susan. *Terentia, Tullia and Publilia: The Women of Cicero's Family*. London: Routledge, 2007.

Twelftree, Graham H. *In the Name of Jesus: Exorcism among Early Christians*. Grand Rapids, MI: Baker Academic, 2007.

Ulrich, Jörg, Anders-Christian Jacobsen, and Maijastina Kahlos, eds. *Continuity and Discontinuity in Early Christian Apologetics*. Early Christianity in the Context of Antiquity 5. Frankfurt am Main: Peter Lang, 2009.

Van der Lans, Birgit, and Jan N. Bremmer. "Tacitus and the Persecution of the Christians: An Invention of Tradition?" *Eirene* 53 (2017): 299–331.

Van Slyke, Daniel G. "The Human Agents of Exorcism in the Early Christian Period: All Christians, Any Christians, or a Select Few Christians?" *Antiphon* 16 (2012): 179–223.

Vlassopoulos, Kostas. *Historicising Ancient Slavery*. Edinburgh Studies in Ancient Slavery. Edinburgh: Edinburgh University Press, 2021.

Vos, Nienke. "A Universe of Meaning: Cyprian's Use of Scripture in Letter 58." In *Cyprian of Carthage: Studies in His Life, Language, and Thought*, ed. Henk Bekker, Paul van Geest, and Hans van Loon, LAHR 3, 65–93. Leuven: Peeters, 2010.

Watts, Edward. "Introduction: Freedom of Speech and Self-Censorship in the Roman Empire." *RBPH* 92 (2014): 157–66.

Wessel, Susan. "A Comparative Study of Anger in Antiquity and Christian Thought." *Journal of Ethics in Antiquity and Christianity* 2 (2020):40–49.

Wightman, Edith Mary. "The Plan of Roman Carthage: Practicalities and Politics." In *New Light on Ancient Carthage*, ed. John Griffiths Pedley, 29–46. Ann Arbor: University of Michigan Press, 1980.

Wilcox, Amanda. "Sympathetic Rivals: Consolation in Cicero's Letters." *AJP* 126 (2005): 237–55.

Wilhite, David E. *Ancient African Christianity: An Introduction to a Unique Context and Tradition*. London: Routledge, 2017.

Wilkinson, Richard. *The Complete Gods and Goddesses of Ancient Egypt*. London: Thames and Hudson, 2017.

Williams, Craig A. *Roman Homosexuality: Ideologies of Masculinity in Classical Antiquity*. Oxford: Oxford University Press, 1999.

Wolfram, Herwig. *History of the Goths.* Translated by Thomas J. Dunlap. English edition. Berkeley: University of California Press, 1988.

Young, Frances. *A History of Exorcism in Catholic Christianity.* Palgrave Historical Studies in Witchcraft and Magic. London: Palgrave Macmillan, 2016.

SCRIPTURE INDEX

AUTHOR INDEX

ANCIENT (INCLUDING ANONYMOUS WORKS)

MODERN

GENERAL INDEX